Careers in Sports Medicine & Training

Careers in Sports Medicine & Training

SALEM PRESS
A Division of EBSCO Information Services, Inc.
Ipswich, Massachusetts

GREY HOUSE PUBLISHING

Cover Image: Run off your heels. By Yuri_Acurs via iStock.

∞ The paper used in these volumes conforms to the American National Standard for Permanence of Paper for Printed Library Materials, Z39.48 1992 (R2009).

Publisher's Cataloging-In-Publication Data
(Prepared by The Donohue Group, Inc.)

Title: Careers in sports medicine & training.
Other Titles: Careers in sports medicine and training | Careers in--
Description: [First edition]. | Ipswich, Massachusetts : Salem Press, a division of EBSCO Information Services, Inc. ; [Amenia, New York] : Grey House Publishing, [2018] | Includes bibliographical references and index.
Identifiers: ISBN 9781682179239 (hardcover)
Subjects: LCSH: Sports medicine--Vocational guidance--United States. | Physical education and training--Vocational guidance--United States. | Athletic trainers--Vocational guidance--United States.
Classification: LCC RC1210 .C37 2018 | DDC 617.1027023--dc23

First Printing

PRINTED IN THE UNITED STATES OF AMERICA

CONTENTS

PUBLISHER'S NOTE

Careers in Sports Medicine & Training contains twenty-four alphabetically arranged chapters describing specific occupations for those with a desire to work in the fields of sports medicine and training: the various areas of medical specialization that athletes depend upon to stay fit and competitive; sports and athletic training and conditioning, including personal trainers, instructors, and coaches; and therapy, including sport psychology, diet and nutrition and health education. Merging scholarship with occupational development, this single comprehensive guidebook provides students passionate about finding a career in sports medicine and training with the necessary insight into the wide array of options open, from acupuncture to yoga. The book's twenty-four profiles offer guidance regarding what job seekers can expect in terms of training, advancement, earnings, job prospects, working conditions, relevant associations, and more. *Careers in Sports Medicine & Training* is specifically designed for a high school and undergraduate audience and is edited to align with secondary or high school curriculum standards.

Scope of Coverage

Understanding the wide scope of jobs for those interested in sports medicine and training is important for anyone preparing for a career that involves both traditional careers in medicine, therapy, and training like cardiologist, podiatrist, and surgeon; massage therapist, personal trainer; rehabilitation counselors; and acupuncturists and massage therapists. *Careers in Sports Medicine & Training* offer lengthy chapters on a broad range of occupations including jobs such as Cardiologist, Chiropractor, Exercise Physiologist, Health Coach, Neuropsychologist, and Sport Psychologist. This excellent reference presents possible career paths and occupations within high-growth and emerging fields in this industry.

Careers in Sports Medicine & Training is enhanced with numerous charts and tables, including projections from the US Bureau of Labor Statistics, and median annual salaries or wages for those occupations profiled. Each chapter also notes those skills that can be applied across broad occupation categories. Interesting enhancements, like **Fun Facts**, **Famous Firsts**, and dozens of photos, add depth to the discussion. Additional highlights in the book include **Conversation With**—a two-page interview with a professional working in a related job—that offer insight into specific areas of sports medicine and training, such as biomedical engineer, sports coach/ instructor, fitness trainer and educator, orthotist and prosthetist, and podiatrist. The respondents share their personal career paths, detail potential for career advancement, offer advice for students, and include a "try this" for those interested in embarking on a career in their profession.

Essay Length and Format

Each chapter ranges in length from 3,500 to 4,500 words and begins with a Snapshot of the occupation that includes career clusters, interests, earnings, and employment outlook. This is followed by these major categories:

- **Overview** includes detailed discussions on: Sphere of Work; Work Environment; Occupation Interest; A Day in the Life. Also included here is a Profile that outlines working conditions, educational needs, and physical abilities. You will also find the occupation's Holland Interest Score, which matches up character and personality traits with specific jobs.
- **Occupational Specialties** lists specific jobs that are related in some way, like Corrective Exercise Specialist, Sports Nutritionist, or Strength and Conditioning Coach. Duties and Responsibilities are also included.
- **Work Environment** details the physical, human, and technological environment of the occupation profiled.
- **Education, Training, and Advancement** outlines how to prepare for this field while in high school, and what college courses to take, including licenses and certifications needed. A section is devoted to the Adult Job Seeker, and there is a list of skills and abilities needed to succeed in the job profiled.
- **Earnings and Advancements** offers specific salary ranges, and includes a chart of metropolitan areas that have the highest concentration of the profession.
- **Employment and Outlook** discusses employment trends, and projects growth to 2026. This section also lists related occupations.
- **Selected Schools** list those prominent learning institutions that offer specific courses in the profiles occupations.
- **More Information** includes associations that the reader can contact for more information.

Special Features

Several features continue to distinguish this reference series from other career-oriented reference works. The back matter includes:

- Appendix A: Guide to Holland Code. This discusses John Holland's theory that people and work environments can be classified into six different groups: Realistic; Investigative; Artistic; Social; Enterprising; and Conventional. See if the job you want is right for you!
- Appendix B: General Bibliography. This is a collection of suggested readings, organized into major categories.
- Subject Index: Includes people, concepts, technologies, terms, principles, and all specific occupations discussed in the occupational profile chapters.

Acknowledgments

Thanks are due to Allison Blake, who took the lead in developing "Conversations With," with help from Vanessa Parks, and to the professionals who communicated their work experience through interview questionnaires. Their frank and honest responses provide immeasurable value to *Careers in Sports Medicine & Training*. The contributions of all are gratefully acknowledged.

INTRODUCTION TO CAREERS IN SPORTS MEDICINE & TRAINING

Introduction

Sports medicine and training encompasses a wide number of possible careers, from aides and therapists to surgeons and psychologists. Some people come to these occupations directly from the world of sports while others find their way into this field because of their passion for helping others to feel better and achieve their goals.

There have been several exciting changes in this field, including new degree programs that specialize on sports, fitness, body movement, and more. Many of these programs and career opportunities fall into the broad category of exercise science.

Exercise science degree careers can fall into any of the four main health-fitness sectors: sport, industry, health, and education.

- *Sport*: Working as a strength and conditioning coach working with individual athletes and teams. Using exercise science skills for program design, execution and monitoring.
- *Industry*: Working as an occupational health officer in staff development for companies and corporations.
- *Health*: Working for a hospital or clinic developing training and exercise programs for general health, injury rehabilitation, and disabilities.
- *Education*: Working for a college or university teaching exercise and sport science.

Education and Training

An undergraduate degree in this field also serves as a great foundation for advanced study in exercise science and other areas such as exercise physiology, medicine, cardiac rehabilitation, physical therapy, sports nutrition, sports medicine, biomechanics or other health related disciplines.

Exercise science degree programs in Canada and the United States are typically designed to provide the knowledge, skills, and abilities to become a competent professional in entry-level health and fitness careers by focusing on the study of physical activity and the associated acute and chronic physiological responses and adaptations resulting from it. Some programs may offer complimentary coursework in health/fitness business management principles to prepare for a role as a health and fitness manager, or as an entrepreneur. Many undergraduate exercise science degree programs involve internships or hands-on experience to learn more about using the equipment and techniques of sports medicine.

Careers with an Exercise Science Degree

What this degree is helpful however, is for providing a knowledge base and foundation that can be directly or indirectly applied to the following occupations and career fields:

Recreation and Leisure

- Activity Specialist
- Camp Director
- Recreation and Leisure Supervisor
- Recreation and Sports Director
- Recreation Therapist
- Community Program Director

Fitness

- Aerobics Instructor
- Fitness Coach
- Fitness Consultant
- Gym Manager
- Personal Trainer
- Spa Manager
- Sports Facility Manager

Sports Medicine

- Anatomist
- Cardiac Rehabilitation Specialist
- Chiropractor
- Ergonomist
- Osteopathic Physician
- Physiologist
- Physiotherapist
- Registered Nurse
- Sports Medicine Physician

Athletics

- Athletic Director
- Athletic Scout
- Athletic Therapist
- Sports Agent
- Sports Coach
- Strength and Conditioning Coach

Health and Wellness

- Dietitian
- Health Care Aide
- Health Care Consultant
- Health Educator
- Massage Therapist
- Sports Nutritionist
- Wellness Coordinator

Therapy

- Exercise Physiologist
- Kinesiologist
- Occupational Therapist
- Occupational Therapist Assistant
- Orthopedic Technician
- Physical Therapy Assistant

Education

- Physical Education Teacher
- University Professor
- Research Assistant

Sales and Business

- Entrepreneur
- Retail Sales Associate
- Sporting Goods Sales Rep

Types of Employers that Hire Exercise Science Graduates

With an interest, experience, and education in exercise science, you may find work with one of the following types of employers:

- Athletic Associations
- College and University Sport Associations
- Colleges and Universities
- Country Clubs
- Government Agencies
- Health and Fitness Clubs
- High Schools
- Hospitals
- Private and non-profit
- Professional Sports Teams and Leagues

- Rehabilitation Clinics
- Sport Marketing & Management Agencies
- Sporting Arenas and Stadiums
- Sporting Goods Companies
- Sports Medicine Clinics
- Self-employment (as a consultant, contractor or entrepreneur)

Earnings

The salary you could earn depends primarily on what career you pursue. For example, if you go on to become a sports medicine doctor, your earnings may be different, for better or for worse, from what you would earn if you choose to become the strength and conditioning coach for a college basketball team.

Other factors that determine how much you can earn include, but are not limited to, the following:

- Your level of education (such as if you went on to graduate studies)
- The industry in which you find work
- The type of job you have
- The size and type of your employer
- The region in which you work
- Other work experience you may have accrued
- Other skills you may have

Gaining Experience in Exercise

Pursuing an internship opportunity (also known as a field placement, practicum, or co-op opportunity) in a career field related to your exercise science degree is the best way to gain work experience for your future career while you're still in school.

Internships allow you to gain professional experience while earning school credit and also give employers the opportunity to gain valuable temporary team members. Another important benefit of internships is that they give you a chance to experience what actual day-to-day work in the field is like. This is the best way to truly figure out if a career in this field is well suited for you or not.

Advancement

An advanced degree (such as a professional, masters, or doctoral degree) enables you to develop highly specialized knowledge. This can open the doors to careers that aren't accessible with only an undergraduate degree, including many applied, research, consulting and teaching positions.

A bachelor of science degree in exercise science serves as excellent preparation for further study in various fields. If you are considering a career in a field related to exercise science, then you should strongly consider further study. This may be in the form of a graduate or professional degree in exercise science or other health related disciplines, such as:

- Athletic Therapy
- Biomechanics
- Cardiac Rehabilitation
- Chiropractic
- Kinesiology
- Medicine (and sports medicine)
- Nursing
- Occupational Therapy
- Physiology
- Physiotherapy
- Sports Nutrition
- Sports Psychology

Acupuncturist

OVERVIEW

Sphere of Work

Acupuncture and other types of Oriental medicine are ancient and empirical systems of medicine based on the concept of *qi* (pronounced "chee"), which is usually translated as energy. Practitioners identify a pattern of energetic imbalance within a patient and the seek to improve the energy balance by means of acupuncture needling, cupping, acupressure, exercises such a *tai ji quan* and *qi gong*, as well as Chinese herbal preparations. Patients considered from a holistic perspective that takes into account physical, mental, and emotional health. Practitioners work to assist their patients by working collaboratively with their patients to determine the best course of action. This type of treatment is almost completely free from side effects and can be a relatively inexpensive form of treatment. Its reputations as an effective, safe, and affordable option to other treatments has led to a growth in public awareness and increased demand for practitioners capable of offering these types of treatment.

A career as an acupuncturist can offer several important advantages. Of course, there is the reward of working in a field where you can help others overcome challenges, but you can also expect to earn a good salary and have the opportunity to create a flexible work schedules that benefit both the practitioner and the client.

Work Environment

Acupuncturists work in a variety of settings, including multi-disciplinary clinics with other health care professionals, hospitals, or in private practice.

Other career options include teaching, translating, publishing, research, or working with an herb or acupuncture supply company.

Acupuncture is one modality among several others in what is known as complementary and alternative medicine (CAM). Both the World Health Organization (WHO) and a 1997 National Institutes of Health (NIH) Consensus Statement have recognized acupuncture as effective in treating a wide variety of health conditions.

Earnings

There are approximately 30,000 AOM licensees in the United States. A recent estimate of the National Certification Commission for Acupuncture and Oriental Medicine (NCCAOM) indicates that the median annual income for AOM licensees is $52,000 and has been increasing. Some practitioners may earn in excess of this amount, with reported income in some instances exceeding $100,000. Variables affecting income may include the nature of your practice, geographic location, and personal factors such as your ability to relate well to patients, professional demeanor, and marketing savvy.

Famous First

The 5,000-year-old mummified body of Ötzi the Iceman was found with 15 groups of tattoos, and many were positioned at points where pain relief treatments similar to acupressure or acupuncture might have been applied. Ötzi's bones showed "age-conditioned or strain-induced degeneration" in the lumbar spine and wear-and-tear degeneration in the knee and ankle joints. This finding has been cited as evidence that practices similar to acupuncture may have been used in Europe 5 millennia ago, some 2,000 years before their earliest use in China.

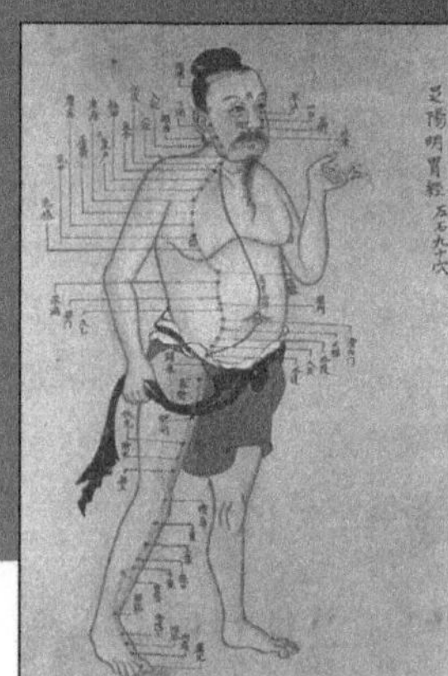

Education

While there are no requirements for any particular level of education, many acupuncturists do attend schools, while others opt to follow an "apprenticeship" approach to learning the skills and techniques required by acupuncture. However, most states require a license in order to practice as an acupuncturist; education is a key component in meeting the necessary standards. To satisfy the education requirements for licensure as an acupuncturist, you may be required to present evidence of the satisfactory completion of at least sixty semester hours at an accredited college or university, including nine semester hours in the biosciences. Biosciences are defined as biological sciences and do not include chemistry or physics.

You should also be able to show the satisfactory completion of an approved professional acupuncture program registered by the education department as licensure qualifying or accredited by the Accreditation Commission for Acupuncture and Oriental Medicine (ACAOM) or another accrediting agency, or the equivalent. Schools should offers their students either pre-accreditation (candidacy) or full accreditation status with the Accreditation Commission for Acupuncture and Oriental Medicine (ACAOM).

A program that is "equivalent" to one taught in a qualifying school should meet the following standard: The program must consist of a minimum of 4,050 hours of classroom instruction, supervised clinical experience, and out-of-classroom or out-of-clinic study assignments. As part of the 4,050 hours, the program must include:

- at least 200 classroom instructional hours in the biosciences including anatomy, physiology and pathology;
- at least 600 classroom instructional hours in acupuncture including acupuncture principles; acupuncture channel and point theory; acupuncture physiology; acupuncture pathology; acupuncture clinical examination and diagnosis; acupuncture techniques; acupuncture treatment principles; and sterilization and precautions; and
- at least 650 hours of supervised clinical acupuncture experience in general health problems to include acupuncture diagnosis; therapeutic treatment planning; acupuncture needling technique; moxibustion; electroacupuncture; pre- and post-treatment

instruction; contraindications and precautions; treatment of emergencies; when to refer to appropriate health professionals; and acupuncture hygiene.

The length of training at most schools is about three years for acupuncture and four years for Oriental medicine programs. The study of Oriental medicine includes both acupuncture and Chinese herbal medicine.

A professional acupuncture curriculum must consist of at least 47 semester credits (705 hours) in Oriental medical theory, diagnosis and treatment techniques in acupuncture and related studies; 22 semester credits (660 hours) in clinical training; 30 semester credits (450 hours) in biomedical clinical sciences; and 6 semester credits (90 hours) in counseling, communication, ethics, and practice management.

A professional Oriental medicine curriculum must consist of at least 47 semester credits (705 hours) in Oriental medical theory, diagnosis and treatment techniques in acupuncture and related studies; 30 semester credits (450 hours) in didactic Oriental herbal studies; 29 semester credits (870 hours) in integrated acupuncture and herbal clinical training; 34 semester credits (510 hours) in biomedical clinical sciences; and 6 semester credits (90 hours) in counseling, communication, ethics, and practice management.

Examination Requirements

You must successfully complete the National Certification Commission for Acupuncture and Oriental Medicine's (NCCAOM) Acupuncture with Point Location exam and Foundations of Oriental Medicine exam. For information regarding the examinations and course, including costs, dates of administration, and content, contact:

National Certification Commission for Acupuncture and Oriental Medicine
76 South Laura Street, Suite 1290
Jacksonville, FL 32202
Phone 904-598-1005
Fax 904-598-5001
E-mail info@nccaom.org
Web www.nccaom.org External Link Icon

Certification

Passage of NCCAOM's national certification examinations is strongly recommended for the following reasons: (1) passage of one or more of these examinations is generally required or accepted as a condition of licensure in most states that regulate the practice of AOM by statute; (2) AOM licensees who wish to practice in more than one state may enhance the interstate portability of their license; and (3) the examinations of NCCAOM are generally regarded as a reliable measure of entry-level competency within the AOM profession. Persons who pass the Commission's certification exams in Oriental Medicine, acupuncture, and Chinese herbology are awarded the designation "Diplomate" as follows: Dipl OM, Dipl Ac, and Dipl CH.

Licensure

Some 45 states and the District of Columbia currently provide for the licensure (or a comparable form of practice authorization) for AOM practitioners. The law of each state should be consulted for specific education, training, examination, and application requirements. In most states, one or more of NCCAOM's examination modules is required or accepted as a route of licensure. Graduation from an ACAOM accredited or candidate school is required to take NCCAOM's national certifying examinations. The website of NCCAOM (http://www.nccaom.org/regulatory-affairs/state-licensure-map) provides licensure information for states that recognize its national examinations.

In most states, practitioners are designated "Licensed Acupuncturists (LAc)," but in some states they may be designated "Acupuncture Physicians" or "Doctors of Oriental Medicine." These doctoral designations, however, are licensure titles conferred by the state and do not reflect earned academic degrees at the doctoral level.

Currently, interstate reciprocity within the AOM profession is not uniform and the law of each state determines the extent to which that state will recognize an AOM license conferred by another state. Persons who desire to practice in more than one state should contact the AOM licensing boards in states of interest to identify specific requirements. As passage of one or more of NCCAOM's national certifying examinations is generally required or accepted in most states that regulate the practice of AOM by statute (but not California), persons who wish to practice in more than one state would be well advised to pass one or more of NCCAOM's examinations to enhance the interstate portability of their license.

Practicing as an Acupuncturist

The law of each state determines what is permitted as part of actual practice. The practice of acupuncture is often defined as the stimulation of certain points on or near the surface of the human body by the inserting of needles to prevent or modify the perception of pain, to normalize physiological functions, or to treat certain diseases or dysfunctions of the body. A number of state statutes noting acupuncture as being useful in controlling and regulating the flow and balance of energy in the body or normalizing energetic physiological function. Other state statutes define acupuncture as traditional or modern Chinese or Oriental medical concepts or to modern techniques of diagnostic evaluation.

State laws may also authorize acupuncture licensees to use additional therapies such as moxibustion, cupping, dietary guidelines, Oriental or therapeutic massage, therapeutic exercise, electroacupuncture, acupressure, herbal therapy, injection and laser therapy, homeopathy, ion cord devices, ordering of western diagnostic tests, magnets, or qi gong. Some states may also permit acupuncturists to treat animals.

Fun Fact

Acupuncture needles are really thin, about as wide as just two hairs. But the original needles? They were made of stone, bamboo, and bone. Ouch!

Source: www.mayfloweracupuncture.com

Conversation With . . .
CHAD BONG, MS, L.OM L.MT, CSCS

Acupuncturist
Philadelphia Sports Acupuncture
Philadelphia, PA
Acupuncture, 9 years

1. What was your individual career path in terms of education/training, entry-level job, or other significant opportunity?

Originally I planned on becoming a strength and conditioning coach, so I did a master's in exercise science at Northern Michigan University. During my second year of graduate school, I went to massage school on the weekends. That's where I was introduced to acupuncture. After graduation, I started my first business, as an in-home personal trainer and massage therapist. It was very successful, but after watching my wife use acupuncture to recover from a broken back, I decided to move from Philadelphia to Colorado to go to Southwest Acupuncture School in Boulder. (Acupuncture school ranges from 3 to 4 years, depending on if you study Chinese herbal medicine as well.)

While I was in acupuncture school, I had the opportunity to study with one of the leaders in the field of sports acupuncture, Whitfield Reaves. After finishing his apprenticeship program, he asked me to help him write his book, "The Acupuncture Handbook of Sports Injuries and Pain." I also assisted him in teaching, to develop skills and learn from him.

After graduating, I moved back to Philadelphia and started Philadelphia Sports Acupuncture. Part of my business was working as an independent contractor with the University of Pennsylvania Student Health Department, providing acupuncture to patients.

I've now been working in the field for nine years. Besides running my practice, I'm the CEO and founder of the Sports Acupuncture Alliance, which is focused on creating a stronger community amongst acupuncturists who specialize in sports acupuncture. We put together an annual conference. I also teach at both the Won Institute in Philadelphia and Tri-state College of Acupuncture in New York, mostly classes focused on sports injuries.

And I host the Pinpoint Performance Podcast. That may be a good resource for students interested in the path of an acupuncturist who specializes in sports injuries, as I've interviewed many of the leaders in the field. I've asked all of them about the path they took to get where they are.

2. **What are the most important skills and/or qualities for someone in your profession?**

   The most important quality is to truly care about and have compassion for your patients. Another important skill is an understanding of how injuries are viewed in the medical community. Being able to communicate with doctors and physical therapists in their language has given me a huge advantage and is the reason I had the opportunity to work at the University of Pennsylvania.

   Developing your palpation skills and mastering needle techniques is extremely important. Mastering palpation skills is all about focused practice. I have students try to find 1- to 2-inch piece of thread under a stack of paper, then keep adding more paper. I like my students to be able to feel the thread under 50 sheets of paper. If you can do over 75, you're doing pretty good; over 100 is exceptional.

3. **What do you wish you had known going into this profession?**

   Understanding that you will likely have to run a business—as well as be an acupuncturist—is very important. Many people underestimate this challenge. One of the best ways to learn how to run a practice is to work for multiple successful practices, so that you can learn a variety of things that work and don't work. This could be a part-time job during college. You should also think about what you would consider a successful practice, so you can decide how to get there. What types of patients do you want to treat? Will you accept insurance? Do you want a small one-person practice or a large office with multiple practitioners and a front desk staff? Understanding the basics of accounting would be a great idea. At least learn how to use QuickBooks or similar software.

4. **Are there many job opportunities in your profession? In what specific areas?**

   The opportunity to be hired as an employee in acupuncture is growing as more insurance plans cover acupuncture. And as acupuncture becomes more accepted, sports teams and hospitals are hiring acupuncturists. But at this time, most acupuncturists still have to run their own businesses.

5. **How do you see your profession changing in the next five years as it relates to fitness and/or sports injuries, how will technology impact that change, and what skills will be required?**

   I think in the next five years acupuncture will be covered by more insurance companies, which will allow more hospitals to hire acupuncturists. We will continue to grow in the sports world, with more acupuncturists on staff with teams.

   I'm not sure how technology will change acupuncture in the next few years. The basis of the profession is very old, and I don't expect the acupuncture needle to change significantly. However, as technology for practice management changes, hopefully it will streamline the process of taking treatment notes and running a clinic.

6. What do you enjoy most about your job? What do you enjoy least about your job?

What I enjoy most is that I get to spend every day helping people get healthy or stay healthy and continue to work towards their fitness and athletic goals. What I like least is, by far, the paperwork.

7. Can you suggest a valuable "try this" for students considering a career in your profession?

Get some acupuncture treatments. It's important that you've had experience with acupuncture before choosing it as a career. I would also suggest interviewing or shadowing an acupuncturist who specializes in sports acupuncture.

MORE INFORMATION

The national practitioner association for AOM professionals in the U.S. is the American Association of Acupuncture and Oriental Medicine (AAAOM). For information about AAAOM, see www.aaaomonline.org. Most states also have a state professional association and some states have several professional associations. The American Society of Acupuncturists (ASA) supports states in their work to advance acupuncture, and provides resources to its members, the public, legislators, and regulators. See http://www.asacu.org.

Athletic Trainer

Snapshot

Career Cluster(s): Health Science
Interests: Physical fitness, health, exercise science, educating and communicating with others
Earnings (median in 2017): $46,630 per year
Employment & Outlook through 2026: 23% (Much faster than average growth expected)

OVERVIEW

Sphere of Work

Athletic trainers work to examine, prevent, and treat sports-related injuries and illnesses of all types of people, especially athletes. They also help people physically rehabilitate and develop strategies to prevent further injuries, and they recommend customized diets and exercises. Trainers are typically employed by professional and college sports programs or hospitals and clinics, but some work for health clubs and summer camps as well. Trainers play an important role as a link between athletes and their teams, physicians, coaches, and other key people in an organization.

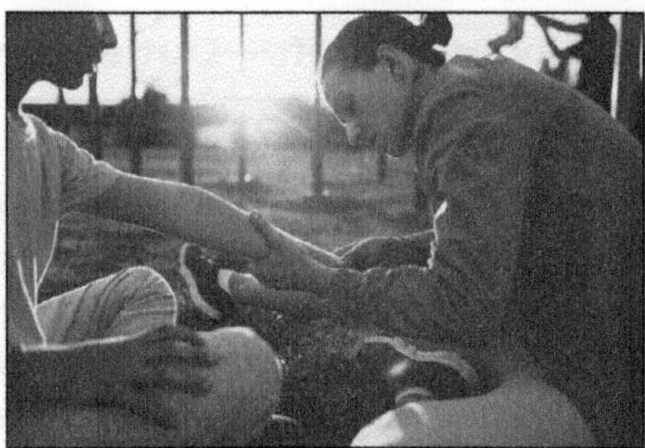

Work Environment

Athletic trainers' work environments vary based on the type of organization for which they work. Athletic trainers who work for a professional basketball team work primarily indoors, while a trainer who works for a football team spends a considerable amount of time outdoors. Those who work in hospitals or clinics typically work forty to fifty hours per week. Trainers traveling with professional or collegiate teams must also attend every practice and game, which means they may occasionally work up to twelve hours in a day. Because they are often the first responders in the event of an injury or illness on the field of play, athletic trainers may be exposed to blood and other bodily fluids in the course of their duties.

Profile

Interests: People, Things
Working Conditions: Work Outside, Work Both Inside and Outside
Physical Strength: Medium Work
Education Needs: Bachelor's Degree
Licensure/Certification: Required
Physical Abilities Not Required: Not Climb
Opportunities for Experience: Internship, Apprenticeship, Volunteer Work
Holland Interest Score*: SRE

* See Appendix A

Occupation Interest

Athletic trainers are able to combine a passion for physical fitness and health with the desire to help others from a wide range of backgrounds. They play an important role in the prevention of severe injuries, helping educate people about the dangers of concussions, dehydration, and other conditions and advising them how take the steps necessary to avoid muscle pulls and tears through proper stretches and exercises. Athletic trainers help people of all ages recover and rehabilitate following injuries.

A Day in the Life—Duties and Responsibilities

Athletic trainers assist in the prevention and treatment of and recovery from sports-related injuries and illnesses, not only for athletes, but for all kinds of people. Unlike personal trainers, athletic trainers do not focus on development of physical fitness but on the prevention and treatment of injuries. For this reason, athletic trainers are considered allied health professionals.

When injuries occur, athletic trainers provide first aid and basic care, such as massaging cramped muscles, wrapping fingers, ankles, and other body parts to protect them from further injury, using gauze and bandages to stop bleeding, and applying ice and heat packs to injured areas. Furthermore, athletic trainers assist in the injury recovery and rehabilitation process, designing special stretching exercises and corrective workouts to help athletes return to good health after an injury. Athletic trainers who work for professional or large collegiate sports teams travel extensively with a single team throughout the playing season. Trainers who work for smaller colleges and high schools may work with two or more other athletic programs.

Athletic trainers serve as a link between athletes, doctors, coaches, the team, and the athletes' families. Using their experience and knowledge of anatomy and physiology, trainers coordinate with doctors on the extent of a player's injuries and relay this information to the other parties involved. Additionally, athletic trainers order special equipment and supplies and maintain detailed information about the athletes they treat.

Duties and Responsibilities

- **Evaluating the physical condition of athletes**
- **Developing and prescribing exercise programs and diets with coaches and team physicians**
- **Advising athletes on the proper use of equipment and exercise**
- **Taping or wrapping limbs and/or muscles**
- **Prescribing protective and support equipment to allow athletes to continue competing**
- **Providing first aid and treating injuries**
- **Determining when players are fit to compete**

WORK ENVIRONMENT

Transferable Skills and Abilities

Communication Skills
- Speaking effectively
- Writing concisely

Interpersonal/Social Skills
- Being able to remain calm
- Being able to work independently
- Cooperating with others
- Perceiving others' feelings
- Working as a member of a team

Organization & Management Skills
- Handling challenging situations
- Organizing information or materials
- Paying attention to and handling details

Technical Skills
- Working with machines, tools or other objects
- Working with your hands

Unclassified Skills
- Being physically active
- Knowing the preventative and rehabilitative uses of sports equipment and exercise

Immediate Physical Environment

Athletic trainers work at sports arenas, stadiums, and university athletic centers, as well as hospitals and clinics, summer camps, dance companies, and high schools. These environments are usually busy, high-energy, and noisy. Workplace environments can also be intense because there is pressure to get star players back into a game quickly. When a player is injured, the trainer may be exposed to blood and other bodily fluids.

Human Environment

Athletic trainers interact with athletes and sports team personnel, including coaches, team managers, and athletic directors. They may also interact with other medical professionals in hospitals and clinics. They may also deal with athletes' families, equipment suppliers, stadium personnel, and/or school officials. During games there is usually an audience observing, so trainers should be comfortable around crowds.

Technological Environment

Athletic trainers use a variety of first aid and protective equipment, including mouth and face guards, air splints, therapeutic heat and cold compresses, and traction units. They must also utilize exercise equipment, including elliptical trainers and treadmills, as well as computer database, medical, and office management software.

EDUCATION, TRAINING, AND ADVANCEMENT

High School/Secondary

High school students should take physical education courses as well as first aid and nutrition classes. Study in anatomy, physiology, biology, psychology, and chemistry are also essential courses, as are math and physics. High school students should also be involved in extracurricular sports, to give them insight into how injuries can occur and be treated.

Suggested High School Subjects

- Applied Biology/Chemistry
- Applied Math
- Applied Physics
- Biology
- Chemistry
- English
- First Aid Training
- Foods & Nutrition
- Health Science Technology
- Nurse Assisting
- Physical Education
- Physics
- Physiology
- Psychology

Related Career Pathways/Majors

Health Science Cluster

- Therapeutic Services Pathway

Famous First

In 2011, Sue Falsone became Major League Baseball's first female head athletic trainer for the L.A. Dodgers. She graduated from Daemen College with a bachelor's degree in physical therapy, earned a master's degree in human movement science from the University of North Carolina, and achieved board certifications as a Clinical Specialist in Sports Physical Therapy, a Certified Athletic Trainer, and a Strength and Conditioning Specialist.

Postsecondary

Athletic trainers must obtain a bachelor's degree and complete both classroom and clinical training. Among the subjects recommended are sports medicine, health, human anatomy, nutrition, and biomechanics. Internships in the field are also a good idea. The majority of athletic trainers hold a master's degree in their field.

Related College Majors

- Health & Physical Education, General
- Medical Assistant Training
- Physical Therapy Assistant Training
- Sports Medicine & Athletic Training

Adult Job Seekers

Qualified athletic trainers should apply directly to the facilities or organizations that post openings. Many universities and colleges post jobs on their websites, as do hospitals and clinics. Trainers may also network with potential employers as well as peers by joining a trade association such as the National Athletic Trainers' Association.

Professional Certification and Licensure

Nearly every state requires that athletic trainers be certified or licensed. Applicants for certification usually must have a bachelor's or master's degree and must pass an examination. Athletic trainers who teach at high schools and similar institutions must also have teacher certification where required. Furthermore, first aid and CPR training are essential.

Additional Requirements

Athletic trainers should have strong communication skills and an ability to work with a variety of people who express differing opinions (such as coaches, team officials, and players). They should be able to handle complex tasks and stressful situations. Furthermore, athletic trainers must demonstrate excellent teaching skills, be physically fit, and motivate players to develop healthy habits.

Fun Fact

Imagine going to school to be an athletic trainer and ending up working in a plant that makes Doritos. That's exactly what Ami Adams does, working with 800 employees at a Frito-Lay factory in Connecticut.

Source: National Athletic Trainers' Association

EARNINGS AND ADVANCEMENT

The median annual wage for athletic trainers was $46,630 in May 2017. The lowest 10 percent earned less than $30,740, and the highest 10 percent earned more than $69,530.

In May 2017, the median annual wages for athletic trainers in the top industries in which they worked were as follows:

Educational services; state, local, and private	$49,460
Hospitals; state, local, and private	46,130
Fitness and recreational sports centers	44,150
Offices of physical, occupational and speech therapists, and audiologists	43,640

Most athletic trainers work full time. Athletic trainers who work with teams during sporting events may work evenings or weekends and travel often.

Athletic trainers may receive paid vacations, holidays, and sick days; life and health insurance; and retirement benefits. These are usually paid by the employer.

Median annual wages, May 2017

Other healthcare practitioners and technical occupations: $60,710

Athletic trainers: $46,630

Total, all occupations: $37,690

Note: All Occupations includes all occupations in the U.S. Economy. Source: U.S. Bureau of Labor Statistics, Occupational Employment Statistics

EMPLOYMENT AND OUTLOOK

Athletic trainers held about 27,800 jobs nationally in 2016. Employment of athletic trainers is projected to grow 23 percent from 2016 to 2026, much faster than the average for all occupations.

Demand for athletic trainers is expected to increase as people become more aware of the effects of sports-related injuries, and as the middle-aged and older population remains active. The effects of concussions are particularly severe and long lasting for child athletes. Although concussions are dangerous at any age, children's brains are still developing and are at risk for permanent complications. Some states require public secondary schools to employ athletic trainers as part of their sports programs. Because athletic trainers are usually onsite with athletes and are often the first responders when injuries occur, the demand for trainers in schools should continue to increase.

Sophisticated treatments in injury prevention and detection are projected to increase the demand for athletic trainers. Growth in an increasingly active middle-aged and older population will likely lead to an increased incidence of athletic-related injuries, such as sprains. Sports programs at all ages and for all experience levels will continue to create demand for athletic trainers.

Insurance and workers' compensation costs have become a concern for many employers and insurance companies, especially in areas where employees are often injured on the job. For example, military bases hire athletic trainers to help train and rehabilitate injured military personnel. These trainers also create programs aimed at keeping injury rates down. Depending on the state, some insurance companies recognize athletic trainers as healthcare providers and reimburse the cost of an athletic trainer's services.

Most athletic trainer jobs are related to sports, although many also work in non-sports settings. About one-third worked in public and private schools, primarily in universities, colleges and high schools. Around another one-third worked in health care, including jobs in hospitals, offices of physicians, and offices of other health practitioners. Some also worked in fitness and recreational sports centers.

Employment is expected to grow much faster than the average for all occupations through the year 2020, which means employment is projected to increase 29 percent or more. Job growth is primarily due to more people becoming aware of sports-related injuries at younger ages, especially concussions. The need for increased physical activity in the middle-aged and elderly populations will also contribute to the demand for athletic trainers.

Job prospects will be best for candidates with a bachelor's or master's degree from a program that is accredited by the Commission on Accreditation of Athletic Training Education (CAATE) and for those who have certification from the Board of Certification for the Athletic Trainer (BOC).

Percent change in employment, Projected 2016-26

Athletic trainers: 23%

Other healthcare practitioners and technical occupations: 12%

Total, all occupations: 7%

Note: All Occupations includes all occupations in the U.S. Economy. Source: U.S. Bureau of Labor Statistics, Employment Projections program

Related Occupations

- Emergency Medical Technician
- Fitness Trainer & Instructor
- Health & Fitness Center Manager
- Physical Therapist
- Sports Instructor & Coach

Conversation With . . . *GREG SMITH*

Retired Head Athletic Trainer
Washington Capitals
Pro Hockey Athletic Trainer, 24 years

1. What was your individual career path in terms of education/training, entry-level job, or other significant opportunity?

I always played sports growing up, but I had 46 operations to correct a birth defect. Until I was 16, I was basically on and off crutches. Back then, young people didn't get physical therapy; you just went back to what you wanted to do. I tried to figure out my own rehab, how to stay in shape, and keep my athletic ability up. By necessity, I got into competitive swimming and did that in high school and college.

I attended Salisbury State University and got a degree as an athletic trainer and physical education teacher with a concentration in special education. At the time, I was one of the only people in Maryland certified in adaptive physical education, which allowed me to specialize in special education physical education. I chose a rare elementary school with a pool, and it was awesome to work with the kids in the pool. I'd passed the National Athletic Trainer Association Exam, so I was also the trainer for a local high school.

I did that for two years, then got a master's in sports medicine from one of only two schools that offered the degree, California University of Pennsylvania.

I actually met the trainer for the Pittsburgh Penguins. At that time, the NHL had 24 teams and was going to expand to 31. I wanted to be part of that expansion. I didn't know hockey but I knew the body and knew the injuries. If I didn't know something, I worked hard to figure out the answer.

As a trainer, we're in charge of anything that happens medically on the field.

It's been exciting. I interned for the Washington Capitals, then worked for an American Hockey League team called the Baltimore Bandits for two years. I went on to the NHL's Anaheim Mighty Ducks for two years, then to the Washington Capitals for 18 years.

I chose hockey because of the speed and rate of injury. We play three to four games a week in this high-collision sport, skating on razor-sharp blades that can do some pretty good damage to tissue. I've had guys take a skate blade across the wrist.

I've hopped on the ice from the bench while the game was on due to the severity of injury. We once had to drag a guy to safety across the ice before he passed out from loss of blood, because at that point it was a life-threatening injury and we had to take care of it. The refs later apologized.

The season lasts eight months and we travel 4½ to 5 months of that. Even with a home game at 7 p.m., I'd leave home at 6 a.m. and get home at midnight. Last year, with my older son a senior in high school, I decided to retire because I had missed a lot of him growing up. I was fortunate because I had started a physical therapy company called Pivot Physical Therapy 16 years ago, so I had the financial ability to walk away. Now, I'm considering other options, including consulting.

2. What are the most important skills and/or qualities for someone in your profession?

In a health-related field, the biggest thing is compassion. Being hurt stinks and our job as trainers is to make it less so. Also, communication is important. At the end of the day, athletic trainers are salesmen because you sell your rehab protocol and what you want the athlete to do. You're dealing with a lot of competitive personalities. Sometimes you're in the heat of battle and you've got to tell your coach, "Your star player can't play the rest of the game." You have to take the heat and protect the athlete to make sure the athlete can compete safely.

You've got to have a level head and be cool under pressure—pressure from the athlete, coach, parent. You make split-second decisions.

Also, as an athletic trainer you've got to do constant continuing education to keep up. That's where a lot of people fall short. They don't understand that this is a high level of commitment.

3. What do you wish you had known going into this profession?

I wish I'd broadened my skills sooner, although I quickly figured out that I needed to. At this point, I'm also a massage therapist, a certified strength and conditioning coach, and hold an assistant physical therapist degree.

4. Are there many job opportunities in your profession? In what specific areas?

There's a big movement toward putting certified athletic trainers (ATs) in high schools, mainly because of heightened knowledge of concussion and concussion management. Maryland passed a law requiring certain protocols for a kid with a concussion that are best served by an AT. Going forward, more and more schools will mandate this and when the kids go to college they're going to want the same level of care. It's a ripple effect that we see in pro sports as well. There's going to be an increase in jobs.

5. How do you see your profession changing in the next five years as it relates to fitness and/or sports injuries? What role will technology play, and what skills will be required?

There's a big push for ATs right now for two reasons: the physical therapy position has changed from requiring a master's to a doctorate so the number of PTs is going down. Plus, we have an aging population that wants to stay active longer, so the need for physical therapy is going up. Right now there's a big push to allow insurance to pay, and if that happens it will open a whole new realm of opportunity at increased pay.

Artificial intelligence, or AI, is being used to figure out how to manage best practices and that will continue to change. We're seeing better diagnoses.

6. What do you enjoy most about your job? What do you enjoy least about your job?

I'm a very competitive person, and very few jobs allow you to be that close to such a competitive situation. The job's different every day. I got to see some really great places and travel the world, and I've had a great time.

Unfortunately, people count on you because there are very few people who can do your job. So, there are no days off.

7. Can you suggest a valuable "try this" for students considering a career in your profession?

We have a lot of high school athletic trainers, and that's a great opportunity to volunteer, hang around the training room, and test-drive your career before it becomes a full-time investment.

Conversation With . . .
KATIE WALSH FLANAGAN

Director of Sports Medicine
East Carolina University
Greenville, NC
Athletic Trainer, 35 years

1. What was your individual career path in terms of education/training, entry-level job, or other significant opportunity?

I went to Oregon State University, where I played field hockey and immediately got injured. The team doctor sent me to an athletic trainer who was able to help me continue playing. I thought that was the coolest thing ever, so I switched my major to athletic training.

I went to Illinois State for my master's and worked as an athletic trainer there and at Western Illinois University. I left the college setting for a few years to work with a professional indoor soccer team, Chicago Power. I was also working with the men's and women's U.S. National Soccer Teams and traveled all over the world with them. Then I went to Fresno State University in California, which is where I first started doing both athletic training and teaching. Due to budget cuts, a whole lot of us lost our jobs. So I went to the University of Southern California for a doctorate in Educational Leadership, then came to East Carolina University, where I've been practicing and teaching for the last 24 years. Currently, I'm the director of the sports medicine program for undergraduate students. I talk to about 500 students a year who want to get into this major; we accept 25.

2. What are the most important skills and/or qualities for someone in your profession?

Patience and dedication. When an athlete gets injured, to them, it's catastrophic; their career is over, their life is over. It takes a tremendous amount of patience to bring that athlete back. Over and over, the athletic trainer has to explain in laymen's terms to the coach, to the parent, to the grandparent, to the spouse, what happened, and where you are going.

And dedication because when an athlete tears their ACL, their lifeline is you. They're no longer with the team and they're no longer the "it" person. It takes a lot of dedication to keep that athlete focused and moving forward, getting stronger.

Athletic trainers (ATs) are often the first ones to show up at a game. I get to football six hours before kickoff and we're the last ones there. Almost every holiday, you have some sort of athletic event. Think of Thanksgiving and football. It's not a 9-to-5, I-want-to-go-home thing.

3. What do you wish you had known going into this profession?

Nothing. But what I want other people to know is that it's really a calling. Every student I meet wants to work in the NFL and wants to be in the spotlight. Go into it for the right reason—to be a health care provider. When that high school kid who slam dunks the ball comes running back and gives you the first high five, that's awesome.

4. Are there many job opportunities in your profession? In what specific areas?

The Bureau of Labor Statistics has said that from 2016 to 2026, athletic training will increase 22.8 percent. The majority of jobs are in high schools and colleges, but athletic trainers have a skillset that can put them pretty much anywhere. Athletics trainers work with Cirque de Soleil and they work for Frito-Lay. We work in clinics and retirement homes, hospitals, surgical centers, with the military, on Broadway, on Dancing with the Stars, on movie sets. Physical therapists traditionally work in a clinic and see patients based on insurance. ATs are typically hired by a team or a college or a company that has big factories, like Ford Motor Company, The Boeing Company or Frito-Lay. If you're working on the manufacturing line and strain your motor cuff, you just go to the third floor, see the athletic trainer, and go back to work. Frito-Lay and other big companies have softball and kickboxing and basketball leagues. Rather than take time off to go to the physician, the AT can take care of your strains and sprains.

5. How do you see your profession changing in the next five years as it relates to fitness and/or sports injuries, how will technology impact that change, and what skills will be required?

There are a group of people who call themselves "trainers." The trainer is someone who does not necessarily have an education or certification or license. They teach you how to lift weights and that sort of thing.

Athletic trainers are working really hard to make sure people refer to us as an athletic trainer or AT. We are a medical model. We're licensed and nationally certified. We can start IVs and give injections. People think all we do is tape ankles, but on the field, I can put an airway in through a football or hockey mask. I can determine pretty quickly if a person is unconscious due to a blood sugar issue, a concussion, or heat stroke.

I see more and more ATs getting involved in physician practices and clinics. That's going to be much more commonplace than the guy with a bucket running out to the football player.

6. **What do you enjoy most about your job? What do you enjoy least about your job?**

The people. Something will happen every day that is just quirky or funny, or maybe gut-wrenching. And you make a difference every day. Even if someone is sidelined for the rest of their career, you make an impact on how they move forward. My entire career has been working with 17- to 23-year-olds. It's energetic.

What I least enjoy is the required record keeping. It takes time. That's frustrating when it's the end of the day and you would like to go home.

7. **Can you suggest a valuable "try this" for students considering a career in your profession?**

Shadow an athletic trainer. Many high schools have them. In our program, we make students shadow for 75 hours before they apply, so that they really know what it's like. You have to stand out there when players are on the field and you've got to stay focused. You've got to be on. So if you're out there and you're kind of whiny that it's hot or rainy or cold, this may not be for you.

MORE INFORMATION

American College of Sports Medicine
P.O. Box 1440
Indianapolis, IN 46206-1440
317.637.9200
www.acsm.org

Board of Certification for the Athletic Trainer
1415 Harney Street, Suite 200
Omaha, NE 68102
877.262.3926
www.bocatc.org/index.php

Eastern Athletic Trainers' Association
The Lawrenceville School
Lawrenceville, NJ 08648
609.895.2105
www.goeata.org/

National Athletic Trainers Association
2952 Stemmons Freeway
Dallas, TX 75247
214.637.6282
ebd@nata.org
www.nata.org

Professional Football Athletic Trainers Society
contact@pfats.com
www.pfats.com/Home.aspx

Michael Auerbach/Editor

Biomedical Engineer

Snapshot

Career Cluster(s): Agriculture, Food & Natural Resources, Health Science, Manufacturing, Science, Technology, Engineering & Mathematics
Interests: Science, engineering, mathematics, solving problems
Earnings (median in 2017): $88,040 per year; $42.33 per hour
Employment & Outlook through 2026: 7% (As fast as average growth expected)

OVERVIEW

Sphere of Work

Biomedical engineering is very broad, combining engineering techniques with human biology to develop medically relevant technologies. Research in the field centers on prosthetic limbs, joint replacement devices, rehabilitation and assistive technologies, medical imaging, and genetic, tissue, and cellular engineering. The field is constantly spreading into new areas. Most of this expansion is linked to the needs of an aging population and the increased demand for medical devices and equipment designed by biomedical engineers.

Biomedical engineers often cross over into multidisciplinary skill sets and collaborate with mechanical engineers, physicists, biologists, and clinicians.

Work Environment

Working with scientists in and out of the lab is especially important for biomedical engineers. Communication skills are critical for collaboration with specialists across disciplines. Engineers, researchers, and clinicians use different approaches and technical languages, and ongoing communication facilitates day-to-day and project-specific communication.

It is also important for biomedical engineers to be mindful of a holistic, patient-focused approach, beyond the machines or technology at hand, and toward the patient who will benefit from the work.

Profile

Interests: Data, Things
Working Conditions: Work Inside
Physical Strength: Light Work
Education Needs: Bachelor's Degree, Master's Degree, Doctoral Degree
Licensure/Certification: Required
Physical Abilities Not Required: Not Climb, Not Kneel
Opportunities for Experience: Internship, Military Service
Holland Interest Score*: IRE

* See Appendix A

Occupation Interest

Biomedical engineering covers a diverse body of scientific knowledge and skills, and attracts graduates and professionals who have strong foundations in the sciences, engineering, or mathematics. Biomedical engineers are pragmatic, problem-solving people who are also enthusiastic about working in different scientific arenas.

Many universities also offer specific undergraduate and postgraduate programs in biomedical engineering, but engineers enter the field from a true variety of science disciplines.

A Day in the Life—Duties and Responsibilities

Biomedical engineers, like all engineers, are problem solvers. The medical application of their work is focused on making people's lives better, and requires a strong desire to collaborate.

A biomedical engineer's day can vary widely, depending on the area of specialty. Meetings and classes relating to medical safety issues may be held, and schedules outlined. Design and testing usually dominate daily work.

Some engineers may interact directly with surgeons who are looking for better technologies to improve surgery. The engineers will set about brainstorming design ideas that are safe and effective. Engineers in this area may also observe surgeries to better understand the limits and difficulties of a surgical procedure that requires design help.

Sometimes, the work centers on reworking manufacturing flaws in a design, and the engineer will work with a manufacturing specialist onsite or by phone to correct the problem. Other biomedical engineers might work one-on-one with patients using a rehabilitative device, such as a prosthetic limb, in order to improve the design and deliver higher performance or comfort. This will occur daily for those engineers in specific patient-centered practice, or on those occasions when clinical trials begin to test a new device with patients.

In an academic setting, biomedical engineers work with students at the undergraduate, graduate, doctoral, and post-doctoral level. Biomedical engineers might also work with entrepreneurs and manufacturers interested in building and marketing devices and technologies the engineer has created.

Duties and Responsibilities

- **Conducting research concerning behavioral, biological, psychological, or life systems**
- **Designing and developing new medical instruments and techniques, such as artificial organs, cardiac pacemakers, or ultrasonic imaging devices**
- **Recommending equipment design changes**
- **Studying engineering aspects of biomedical systems of humans**
- **Assisting medical personnel in observing or treating physical ailments or deformities**

OCCUPATION SPECIALTIES

Biomedical Equipment Technicians

Biomedical equipment technicians install, repair, and maintain medical equipment and instruments used in the health-care delivery field. They inspect and install medical and related technical equipment in medical and research facilities for use by physicians, nurses, scientists, or engineers involved in researching or treating physical ailments.

WORK ENVIRONMENT

Transferable Skills and Abilities

Communication Skills
- Speaking effectively
- Writing concisely

Organization & Management Skills
- Coordinating tasks
- Making decisions
- Managing people/groups
- Paying attention to and handling details

Research & Planning Skills
- Creating ideas
- Using logical reasoning

Technical Skills
- Performing scientific, mathematical and technical work
- Working with your hands

Immediate Physical Environment

Laboratory and office settings predominate. Research and design work relating to biomedical engineering may involve contact with human or animal tissue, and biomedical safety practices will be observed.

Plant Environment

Biomedical engineers can work in a variety of settings, from laboratories and hospitals, to corporate offices and university campuses.

Human Environment

Biomedical engineering requires strong collaboration skills. Depending on the field of biomedical engineering, professionals in this field interact with students and colleagues in fields across the scientific spectrum, as well as with technicians, managers, directors, patients, and in some cases, business specialists.

Technological Environment

Biomedical engineers use technologies that range from telephone, e-mail, and web conferencing, to computer design software, to increasingly complex and highly calibrated diagnostic tools and machinery.

EDUCATION, TRAINING, AND ADVANCEMENT

High School/Secondary

High school students can best prepare for a career in biomedical engineering with courses in algebra, calculus, geometry, trigonometry, biology, chemistry, physics, and computers. Advanced placement (AP) classes in these subjects are especially recommended. Drafting and art classes can also serve as precursors for future design work. Communication and problem-solving skills are vital for success in this occupation, so English and writing courses are also important.

Creating projects for science fairs and science clubs gives students the opportunity to design, invent, and learn from others prior to graduation. Summer programs and internships reinforce the fundamentals, and introduce students to the field and its impact on the world. Many universities in the United States and abroad offer science or technology camps to high school students.

Suggested High School Subjects

- Algebra
- Applied Biology/Chemistry

- Applied Communication
- Applied Math
- Applied Physics
- Biology
- Blueprint Reading
- Chemistry
- College Preparatory
- Composition
- Computer Science
- English
- Geometry
- Mathematics
- Science
- Trigonometry

Related Career Pathways/Majors

Agriculture, Food & Natural Resources Cluster

- Food Products & Processing Systems Pathway
- Natural Resources Systems Pathway

Health Science Cluster

- Biotechnology Research & Development Pathway
- Health Informatics Pathway
- Support Services Pathway

Manufacturing Cluster

- Health, Safety & Environmental Assurance Pathway

Science, Technology, Engineering & Mathematics Cluster

- Engineering & Technology Pathway

Postsecondary

This occupation has evolved from a variety of medical and technical disciplines, but is primarily based in engineering. Most biomedical engineers have an undergraduate degree and PhD in engineering, mathematics, or a related field.

Over 120 colleges and universities in the United States offer bioengineering or biomedical engineering programs. Typical coursework or research includes instruction in the fundamentals of biofluid mechanics, engineering electrophysiology, diagnostic imaging physics, neuroengineering, and drug design, development, and delivery. In addition to core courses, students can take electives related to their ultimate career goals.

University programs offer co-op study and internships. These programs offer concrete opportunities to work while gaining both academic credit and professional experience before graduation. They also represent concrete sources for industry contacts.

PhD internships and other research positions provide graduate students and graduates opportunities to work on engineering projects in an academic setting.

College and university students from bachelor's candidates to PhD levels are highly encouraged to make use of their academic career centers, and to actively approach professors as advisors and mentors with questions and ideas relating to these and other career and study opportunities.

Biomedical engineers in academia move from instructor to assistant professor, professor, and department chair by demonstrating consistency, excellence, and innovation in research, teaching, and departmental collaboration. Full professors almost always possess a doctoral degree.

Related College Majors

- Bioengineering/Biomedical Engineering
- Biomedical Engineering-Related Technology
- Engineering Mechanics
- Engineering Physics
- Engineering Science
- Engineering, General

Adult Job Seekers

Economic conditions and personal and family responsibilities can require professionals to take time away from active engineering work. A return to employment requires transition time. Updated resume credentials in education and research facilitate the transition period, and can take the form of continuing education, fellowships, scholarships, grants, or employment at a different level than previously held. Professional associations are often good sources for transition contacts and opportunities. For example, the Association for Women in Science (AWIS) has several fellowships for women returning to science.

Networking and interviewing are critical. Pursuing employment with a multidisciplinary approach can also broaden opportunities.

Professional Certification and Licensure

Engineers are encouraged to acquire certification or licensing according to national, state, and district regulations. Specialists whose work affects the health or safety of the public must hold this credential.

Additional Requirements

A strong commitment to study and learning are the hallmarks of aspiring biomedical engineers. Because they are experts in a highly specialized field, they have pursued long years of education in math and science. The recurring advice engineers give newcomers is to be proactive, ask questions, know the science, and stick with it.

EARNINGS AND ADVANCEMENT

Earnings depend on the type, size, and location of the employer and the employee's education, experience, capabilities and responsibilities.

The median annual wage for biomedical engineers was $88,040 in May 2017. The lowest 10 percent earned less than $52,070, and the highest 10 percent earned more than $142,610.

In May 2017, the median annual wages for biomedical engineers in the top industries in which they worked were as follows:

Research and development in the physical, engineering, and life sciences	$95,980
Navigational, measuring, electromedical, and control instruments manufacturing	94,480
Medical equipment and supplies manufacturing	88,190
Healthcare and social assistance	74,210
Colleges, universities, and professional schools; state, local, and private	61,990

Biomedical engineers usually work full time on a normal schedule. However, as with employees in almost any engineering occupation, biomedical engineers occasionally may have to work additional hours to meet the needs of patients, managers, colleagues, and clients. About 1 in 5 biomedical engineers worked more than 40 hours per week in 2016.

Median annual wages, May 2017

Engineers: $92,220

Biomedical engineers: $88,040

Total, all occupations: $37,690

Note: All Occupations includes all occupations in the U.S. Economy. Source: U.S. Bureau of Labor Statistics, Occupational Employment Statistics

EMPLOYMENT AND OUTLOOK

There were approximately 21,300 biomedical engineers employed nationally in 2016. Employment of biomedical engineers is projected to grow 7 percent from 2016 to 2026, about as fast as the average for all occupations. Biomedical engineers likely will see employment growth because of increasing possibilities brought by new technologies and increasing applications to medical equipment and devices. Smartphone technology and three-dimensional printing are examples of technology being applied to biomedical advances.

As the aging baby-boom generation lives longer and stays active, the demand for biomedical devices and procedures, such as hip and knee replacements, is expected to increase. In addition, as the public continues to become more aware of medical advances, increasing numbers of people will seek biomedical solutions to their health problems from their physicians.

Percent change in employment, Projected 2016-26

Engineers: 8%

Total, all occupations: 7%

Biomedical engineers: 7%

Note: All Occupations includes all occupations in the U.S. Economy. Source: U.S. Bureau of Labor Statistics, Employment Projections program

Related Occupations

Occupation	Job Duties	Entry-Level Education	2017 Median Pay
Agricultural Engineers	Agricultural engineers attempt to solve agricultural problems concerning power supplies, the efficiency of machinery, the use of structures and facilities, pollution and environmental issues, and the storage and processing of agricultural products.	Bachelor's degree	$74,780
Architectural and Engineering Managers	Architectural and engineering managers plan, direct, and coordinate activities in architectural and engineering companies.	Bachelor's degree	$137,720
Biochemists and Biophysicists	Biochemists and biophysicists study the chemical and physical principles of living things and of biological processes, such as cell development, growth, heredity, and disease.	Doctoral or professional degree	$91,190

(Continues on page 39)

Occupation	Job Duties	Entry-Level Education	2017 Median Pay
Chemical Engineers	Chemical engineers apply the principles of chemistry, biology, physics, and math to solve problems that involve the production or use of chemicals, fuel, drugs, food, and many other products. They design processes and equipment for large-scale manufacturing, plan and test production methods and byproducts treatment, and direct facility operations.	Bachelor's degree	$102,160
Electrical and Electronics Engineers	Electrical engineers design, develop, test, and supervise the manufacturing of electrical equipment, such as electric motors, radar and navigation systems, communications systems, and power generation equipment. Electronics engineers design and develop electronic equipment, including broadcast and communications systems, such as portable music players and Global Positioning System (GPS) devices.	Bachelor's degree	$97,970
Materials Engineers	Materials engineers develop, process, and test materials used to create a wide range of products, from computer chips and aircraft wings to golf clubs and biomedical devices. They study the properties and structures of metals, ceramics, plastics, composites, nanomaterials (extremely small substances), and other substances in order to create new materials that meet certain mechanical, electrical, and chemical requirements.	Bachelor's degree	$94,610
Mechanical Engineers	Mechanical engineers design, develop, build, and test mechanical and thermal sensors and devices, including tools, engines, and machines.	Bachelor's degree	$85,880

(Continues on page 40)

Occupation	Job Duties	Entry-Level Education	2017 Median Pay
Physicians and Surgeons	Physicians and surgeons diagnose and treat injuries or illnesses. Physicians examine patients; take medical histories; prescribe medications; and order, perform, and interpret diagnostic tests. They counsel patients on diet, hygiene, and preventive healthcare. Surgeons operate on patients to treat injuries, such as broken bones; diseases, such as cancerous tumors; and deformities, such as cleft palates.	Doctoral or professional degree	This wage is equal to or greater than $208,000 per year.
Sales Engineers	Sales engineers sell complex scientific and technological products or services to businesses. They must have extensive knowledge of the products' parts and functions and must understand the scientific processes that make these products work.	Bachelor's degree	$98,720

MORE INFORMATION

Association for Women in Science
1442 Duke Street
Alexandria, VA 22314
703.372.4380
awis@awis.org
www.awis.org
M Hildred Blewett Scholarship for "early career physicists"
www.awis.org/displaycommon.cfm?an=1&subarticlenbr=69
Satter Award, for graduate students
www.awis.org/displaycommon.cfm?an=1&subarticlenbr=67

Biomedical Engineering Society
8401 Corporate Drive, Suite 1125
Landover, MD 20785-2224
301.459.1999
info@bmes.org
www.bmes.org

National Action Council for Minorities in Engineering
440 Hamilton Avenue, Suite 302
White Plains, NY 10601-1813
914.539.4010
info@nacme.org
www.nacme.org

National Society of Black Engineers
205 Daingerfield Road
Alexandria, VA 22314
703.549.2207
info@nsbe.org
www.nsbe.org

Society of Hispanic Professional Engineers
13181 Crossroads Parkway North
Suite 450
City of Industry, CA 91746-3497
323.725.3970
shpenational@shpe.org
www.shpe.org

Society of Women Engineers
203 N. La Salle Street, Suite 1675
Chicago, IL 60601
877.793.4636
hq@swe.org
www.swe.org

Technology Student Association
1914 Association Drive
Reston, VA 20191-1540
703.860.9000
general@tsaweb.org
www.tsaweb.org

Try Engineering
445 Hoes Lane
Piscataway, NJ 08854-4141
tryengineering.org

Women in Biomedical Careers
National Institutes of Health
9000 Rockville Pike
Bethesda, MD 20892
womeninscience@nih.gov
womeninscience.nih.gov/women_scientist/kuoc.asp

Bill Rickards/Editor

Cardiologist

Snapshot

Career Cluster(s): Health Science
Interests: Research, surgery, science, helping others improve their health, communicating with others
Earnings (median in 2017): equal to or greater than $208,000 per year or $100.00 per hour
Employment & Outlook through 2026: 13% (Faster than average growth expected)

OVERVIEW

Sphere of Work

Cardiologists are medical doctors, internists, specializing in the diagnosis, treatment, and prevention of diseases of the heart and cardiovascular system. There are several areas of specialization, but most cardiologists fall into the following classifications: non-surgical, invasive, and interventional. Further specialization in pediatric cardiology, nuclear cardiology, or electrophysiology and other fields is also possible. Other cardiologists focus on conducting research and teaching cardiology at medical schools.

Non-surgical cardiologists provide medical advice on how patients can maintain heart health, and they perform non-invasive tests to determine whether patients have a heart condition. These tests include electrocardiograms and stress tests, and are performed in a medical office. Invasive cardiologists do much of the same work as non-surgical cardiologists, but they have the added ability and training to perform catheterizations, a procedure that helps the physician understand blood flow to the heart and determine the heart's ability to pump.

An interventional cardiologist has the skill and training to perform more invasive procedures, such as angioplasty, used to open blocked arteries and insert stents, in a clinical setting. These clinical procedures involve more risk and are most often performed at a hospital.

Work Environment

Cardiologists generally work in medical environments, such as hospitals and medical offices. These environments can be very busy. Hospitals, in particular, are extremely active, with frequent, daily interaction between the cardiologist and nurses, other doctors, medical technicians, and patients. Medical facilities and hospitals are sterile environments, and physicians and staff follow daily procedures to ensure that each patient is protected from germs and other health hazards.

To conduct patient consultations for on-going treatment and non-invasive work, cardiologists use medical offices with examination rooms where they can meet privately with patients. Medical offices keep a limited supply of related medical technology on the premises, which is used for non-invasive or non-surgical patient testing. When the cardiologist must use more invasive techniques to treat a patient, he or she might consult with a fellow cardiologist (trained to perform a specific procedure) or other medical personnel, such as nurses and medical technicians, to treat the patient in a clinical setting.

Cardiologists often work erratic, long hours. Their work day is further extended when the doctor is assigned to provide "on-call" services, which include answering patient calls after hours and, when necessary, going to the hospital to treat patients who need urgent care.

Profile

Interests: Data, People, Things
Working Conditions: Work Inside
Physical Strength: Light Work
Education Needs: Doctoral Degree
Licensure/Certification: Required
Physical Abilities Not Required: Not Climb
Opportunities for Experience: Military Service, Volunteer Work
Holland Interest Score*: ISR

* See Appendix A

Occupation Interest

Because heart disease is one of the most common public health issues, cardiologists work in a busy environment where their services are in high demand. Cardiology is also a growing field, where new discoveries and research lead to frequent changes in best practices. Cardiologists enjoy the benefits of working with state of the art technology, which is constantly being refined and upgraded. Cardiologists earn significant salaries, but are also subject to significant malpractice insurance costs.

A Day in the Life—Duties and Responsibilities

The daily responsibilities of a cardiologist vary based on his or her specialty. For example, a non-invasive cardiologist works primarily in the office of his or her medical practice, seeing as many as 30 patients a day. He or she will conduct tests, recommend medication, and/or dietary changes and exercise. When more invasive procedures are warranted, the non-surgical cardiologist may refer patients to other cardiologists. Invasive, non-interventional cardiologists perform these tasks as well, but they perform catheterizations in a catheterization laboratory or "*cath lab*," which also provides medical imaging equipment used during the procedure.

Interventional cardiologists perform the above duties and are further qualified to perform angioplasty (a procedure in which a balloon is used to enlarge arteries and clear arterial blockages as well as insert stents) and other procedures. Interventional cardiologists tend to work longer hours in the hospital than non-interventional specialists.

Other cardiologists choose to obtain additional training to work specifically with certain types of patients, for example, children. Many also receive training in the field of electrophysiology (the bioelectrical impulses that make the heart beat); this training qualifies them to implant pacemakers and to perform other procedures to correct irregular heartbeats.

Some cardiologists perform research in addition to practicing cardiology and teaching medical students. These doctors usually work in research laboratories, medical libraries, and universities, studying samples and conducting studies to learn more about cardiac and cardiovascular problems and treatments. They write frequent medical articles and share the results of their studies with peers at conferences and meetings.

Duties and Responsibilities

- **Examining patients**
- **Ordering or performing various tests and procedures**
- **Prescribing and administering medications and treatments**
- **Diagnosing diseases and conditions of the heart and circulatory system**
- **Teaching patients about preventative medicine**

WORK ENVIRONMENT

Immediate Physical Environment

Cardiologists spend a great deal of time working in medical offices. Non-invasive procedures and patient follow-ups take place in medical offices. The hospital environment is more complex and frenetic, with a great deal of social interaction and a higher caseload assigned to each doctor.

Human Environment

Cardiologists are in constant contact with patients during the course of their work, providing consultations, performing procedures, and studying patients for the purpose of medical research. Cardiologists also work closely with colleagues, nurses, physician assistants, medical technologists, hospital administrators, and other medical

Transferable Skills and Abilities

Communication Skills

- Speaking effectively
- Writing concisely
- Listening attentively
- Reading well
- Expressing thoughts and ideas

Interpersonal/Social Skills

- Being able to remain calm
- Being able to work independently
- Cooperating with others
- Providing support to others
- Working as a member of a team
- Being patient
- Having good judgment
- Being objective
- Being persistent

Organization & Management Skills

- Paying attention to and handling details
- Performing duties which change frequently
- Managing time
- Demonstrating leadership

Research & Planning Skills

- Developing evaluation strategies
- Using logical reasoning
- Identifying problems
- Identifying resources
- Analyzing information
- Solving problems

Technical Skills

- Performing scientific, mathematical and technical work

Work Environment Skills

- Working in a medical setting

professionals. Empathy, patience, and effective communication skills enhance patient interaction and treatment.

Technological Environment

Cardiologists must understand the application of a wide range of medical equipment, including electrocardiograms, diagnostic equipment, and surgical supplies. They rely on smart phones, computer systems, and related databases, all of which enable them to efficiently communicate with peers, conduct research, order medications, and organize patient records. The field of cardiology is dynamic, and technologies are constantly being improved and developed to enable doctors to perform with more precision.

EDUCATION, TRAINING, AND ADVANCEMENT

High School/Secondary

High school students interested in cardiology should take a wide range of mathematics and science courses, such as algebra, biology, chemistry, trigonometry, physiology, geometry, and psychology. Because doctors must be effective communicators, students can benefit from English and other humanities courses.

Suggested High School Subjects

- Algebra
- Biology
- Chemistry
- College Preparatory
- English
- Geometry
- Health Science Technology
- Humanities
- Mathematics
- Physics
- Physiology
- Psychology
- Science
- Sociology
- Statistics
- Trigonometry

Related Career Pathways/Majors

Health Science Cluster

- Therapeutic Services Pathway

Famous First

The first surgery on the heart itself was performed by Axel Cappelen on 4 September 1895 at Rikshospitalet in Kristiania, now Oslo. Cappelen repaired a bleeding coronary artery in a 24-year-old man who had been stabbed and was in deep shock upon arrival. The patient awoke and seemed fine for 24 hours, but became ill with a fever and died three days after the surgery.

Postsecondary

Future cardiologists should earn a bachelor's degree in science with a focus on pre-medical studies. They must attend medical school for another four years to receive a medical doctorate, followed by several more years of years of internships and residency. Upon completion of the residency, they are expected to obtain a cardiology fellowship, which lasts an additional two to five years.

Related College Majors

- Anatomy
- Human & Animal Physiology
- Medicine (M.D.)
- Osteopathic Medicine
- Pre-Medicine Studies

Adult Job Seekers

Adults seeking a career in cardiology must follow the same academic and clinical training path as any other, beginning with a bachelor's degree, medical school, internship, and residency.

Professional Certification and Licensure

Like other medical doctors, cardiologists are required to have a medical doctorate from an accredited medical school. They are also expected to obtain a professional medical license from the state in which they seek to practice, and to pass the United States Medical Licensing Examination upon graduation from medical school.

Additional Requirements

Cardiologists should have a strong interest in helping others, promoting good health practices, and restoring the health of patients. Strong communication skills and proven research capabilities are a necessity. Because cardiologists often treat patients with life-threatening illnesses, they should take particular care to develop communication skills that enable them to interact with patients in a sensitive yet concise manner. They should enjoy learning, because it is vital for them to keep up with current procedures and studies. Last but not least, they must be highly motivated individuals in order to successfully complete the years of specialized training that their field requires.

Fun Fact

Your heart's blood vessels are 60,000 miles long and circle the world twice. During an average person's lifespan, the heart pumps 1 million barrels of blood through them.

Source: menshealth.com

EARNINGS AND ADVANCEMENT

Wages for physicians and surgeons are among the highest of all occupations, with a median wage equal to or greater than $208,000 per year. Median wages showing the differences in pay between types of physicians and surgeons are not available, but mean (average) annual wages for physicians and surgeons in May 2017 were as follows:

Occupation	Wage
Anesthesiologists	$265,990
Surgeons	251,890
Obstetricians and gynecologists	235,240
Psychiatrists	216,090
Physicians and surgeons, all other	211,390
Family and general practitioners	208,560
Internists, general	198,370
Pediatricians, general	187,540

Many physicians and surgeons work long, irregular, and overnight hours. Physicians and surgeons may travel between their offices and hospitals to care for their patients. While on call, a physician may need to address a patient's concerns over the phone or make an emergency visit to a hospital or nursing home.

Neurologists may receive paid vacations, holidays, and sick days; life and health insurance; and retirement benefits. Self-employed neurologists must arrange for their own health insurance and retirement programs. Some employers provide for paid educational leave.

Median annual wages, May 2017

Physicians and surgeons: This wage is equal to or greater than $208,000 per year.

Health diagnosing and treating practitioners: $79,480

Total, all occupations: $37,690

Note: All Occupations includes all occupations in the U.S. Economy. Source: U.S. Bureau of Labor Statistics, Occupational Employment Statistics

EMPLOYMENT AND OUTLOOK

Overall employment of physicians and surgeons is projected to grow 13 percent from 2016 to 2026, faster than the average for all occupations.

The growing and aging population is expected to drive overall growth in the demand for physician services. As the older population grows and rates of chronic illnesses increase, consumers will seek high levels of care that use the latest technologies, diagnostic tests, and therapies.

Demand for physicians and surgeons is expected to increase despite factors that can temper growth. New technologies, such as improved information technologies or remote monitoring, are expected to allow physicians to treat more patients in the same amount of time. If adopted, new technologies can reduce the number of physicians who would be needed to complete the same tasks. In addition, physician assistants and nurse practitioner can do many of the routine duties of physicians and may be used to reduce costs at hospitals and doctor's offices.

Demand for physicians' services is sensitive to changes in healthcare reimbursement policies. Consumers may seek fewer physician services if changes to health coverage result in higher out-of-pocket costs for them.

Job prospects are expected to be very good because almost all graduates of domestic medical schools are matched to residencies (their first jobs as physicians) immediately after graduating.

Prospects should be especially good for physicians who are willing to practice in rural and low-income areas, because these areas tend to have difficulty attracting physicians. Job prospects also should be good for physicians in specialties dealing with health issues that mainly affect aging baby boomers. For example, physicians specializing in cardiology and radiology will be needed because the risks for heart disease and cancer increase as people age.

Percent change in employment, Projected 2016-26

Health diagnosing and treating practitioners: 16%

Physicians and surgeons: 13%

Total, all occupations: 7%

Note: All Occupations includes all occupations in the U.S. Economy. Source: U.S. Bureau of Labor Statistics, Employment Projections program

Related Occupations

- Allergist & Immunologist
- Anesthesiologist
- Neurologist
- Ophthalmalogist
- Pediatrician
- Physician
- Podiatrist
- Radiologist
- Surgeon

Related Military Occupations

- Physician & Surgeon

Conversation With . . .
JOHN HIGGINS, M.D.

Sports Cardiologist and Exercise Physiologist
McGovern Medical School
The University of Texas Health Science Center
Houston (UTHealth)
Sports Cardiologist, 10 years

Growing up in Australia, we had a little dachshund named Snoopy and my brothers, sister, and I loved playing with her. When I was about 6, she got sick and died and I vowed to myself I would become a veterinarian and save all future Snoopies.

Then, when I was 9, I was over at a friend's house on a hot sunny day. They had big glass doors on the back of their house. They had just been cleaned and were so spotless that I thought they were open. We were sprinting outside—"The first one outside gets to play on the bike!"—and I crashed through the big panes of glass. I lacerated about two inches of skin on my right knee.

The local family physician told me I would have to be stitched up. I had a negative view of doctors and was anxious. To distract me while he was suturing, he let me listen to my heart with his stethoscope. I was completely fascinated, and he explained this was an amazing pump. A life force.

Later I took biology and had one of those incredible teachers that reaches you. We learned about genetics and different systems of the body. At the same time, my brother's friend had just started medical school and would often come around. One thing led to another, and I never lost that passion.

* * * *

In Australia, we had to be in the top percentile to get into med school, so I cut back on sports and focused on my studies. I earned my Bachelor of Medicine and Bachelor of Science in an integrated program at Herston Medical School and the University of Queensland in Australia. My Doctor of Medicine is also from the University of Queensland. Later, during a professional transition, I earned a Master's of Philosophy in Epidemiology from the University of Cambridge in England. And 11 years after that, I earned my MBA from the George Washington University in Washington, D.C.

* * * *

Now I am Chief of Cardiology at LBJ General Hospital in Houston, and, in my role as a sports cardiologist, I work with the Houston Rockets and Rice University's sports teams. I'm also a professor of medicine and conduct research. About 75 percent of my time is clinical and about 15 percent is teaching—at the med school; lecturing about health and wellness at companies; and doing work with the media. I do a lot of outreach with the American Heart Association. My top research interests are sudden cardiac death in young athletes, energy drinks, endurance sports, and smartphone apps for health and wellness.

* * * *

I was always interested in the heart and liked cardiology because you could actually see things. Some areas of medicine depend on lab work. But with the heart, you have EKGs, echocardiograms (Echo)—you can see the structure and make a difference. I'm a big runner, so I got into the sports side of it. I like the idea that exercise can help patients no matter what medical problem they have. I got into that aspect of the work and became associated with the American College of Sports Medicine and did certifications, became a fellow, and got involved in boards and committees.

I'm part of a team that annually screens Rice athletes for conditions associated with sudden cardiac death using history, physical, EKG and Echo. I've developed screening guidelines to find underlying cardiovascular causes. And a colleague and I usually screen several Houston Rockets athletes with Stress Echocardiography, which allows them to be declared fit to play that season.

* * * *

My interest in energy drinks is focused on whether they are safe. The energy beverage market has grown dramatically since 1997, and many people are looking for an edge as they compete. A paper I did that reviewed existing research found that patients with hypertension should not consume energy beverages. We concluded that ingesting these beverages before an event or during training can result in restlessness and irritability; can increase blood pressure; and may result in dehydration. The long-term effects of these drinks have not been established. Coaches and athletic departments should take the initiative in addressing the issue of these drinks with their student athletes and educate them about the effects and risks.

I've also studied the benefits of fitness apps, which appear to help people reach their health and fitness goals.

* * * *

To be a good physician, you've got to be healthy yourself. Exercise is important to perform well under the stressful moments you have in medicine. It gives you the physical stamina, mental discipline, and flexibility to do well. You have to take time to recharge and take care of yourself.

* * * *

If you want to be a good doctor, you've got to be a great detective. I tell my residents—quoting Sherlock Holmes—that "Once you eliminate the impossible, whatever remains, no matter how improbable, must be the truth." Maybe there's something the patient hasn't told you. Sometimes you have to think out of the box. If something doesn't add up, dig deeper. Be a master listener. You've got to use all your senses and your heart and mind. Non-verbal cues will often give you missing information.

* * * *

We've got a lot of players in the health care system. They're all important, but as the physician, the buck stops with you. You've got to love the work. If you don't have that, work in something else you love.

You are treating the whole patient, so you've got to think of them as a person, not just as a diagnosis. As the late Maya Angelou said: "I've learned that people will forget what you said, people will forget what you did, but people will never forget how you made them feel." Always leave your patient with hope, and no matter who they are, treat them with dignity and respect.

MORE INFORMATION

American College of Cardiology
2400 N Street, NW
Washington, DC 20037
202.375.6000
resource@acc.org
www.acc.org

American College of Physicians
190 North Independence Mall W.
Philadelphia, PA 19106-1572
800.523.1546
www.acponline.org

American Heart Association
7272 Greenville Avenue
Dallas, TX 75231
800.242.8721
www.heart.org

American Medical Association
515 N. State Street
Chicago, IL 60654
800.621.8335
www.ama-assn.org

Centers for Disease Control and Prevention (CDC)
1600 Clifton Rd
Atlanta, GA 30333
www.cdc.gov

Michael Auerbach/Editor

Chiropractor

Snapshot

Career Cluster(s): Health Science
Interests: Science, working with your hands, desire to improve others' health, communicating with others
Earnings (median in 2017): $68,640 per year; $33.00 per hour
Employment & Outlook through 2026: 12% (Faster than average growth expected)

OVERVIEW

Sphere of Work

A chiropractor is a medical practitioner who mainly employs alternative, noninvasive health care methods to treat problems related to the human muscular, nervous, and skeletal systems, as well as to improve the overall health of the patient. Chiropractic medicine is founded on the idea that spinal misalignment and compression adversely affect the nervous system, limiting the immune system's ability to fight off disease and chronic conditions. A chiropractor uses techniques such as manual adjustment of the patient's spine and body parts in order to correct or treat health problems.

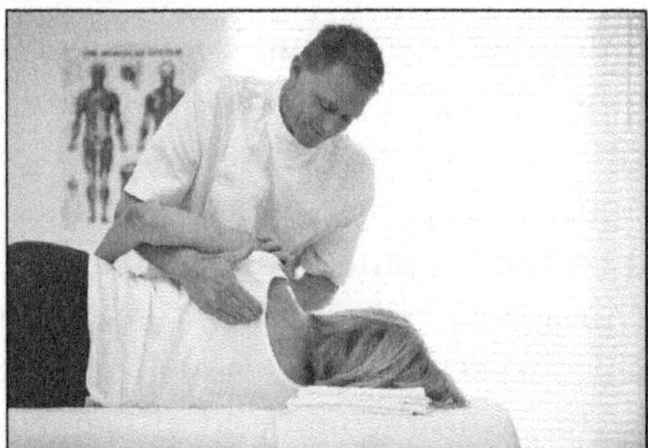

Work Environment

Like many other physicians, chiropractors normally work in private practices, often alone or with a small number of employees. In some cases, several chiropractors join together to establish a group practice within a larger hospital or clinic. Chiropractors usually work forty hours or more per week. Because most chiropractors are self-employed, they can maintain a flexible schedule, seeing patients during evenings and weekends, being "on-call," or making house calls. They stand for long periods and use their hands and arms extensively.

Profile

Interests: Data, People, Things
Working Conditions: Work Inside
Physical Strength: Medium Work
Education Needs: Doctoral Degree
Licensure/Certification: Required
Physical Abilities Not Required: Not Climb, Not Kneel
Opportunities for Experience: Part Time Work
Holland Interest Score*: ISR

* See Appendix A

Occupation Interest

Those interested in pursuing a career in chiropractic must have an affinity for effective, holistic treatment of bodily diseases. In essence, a chiropractor must understand and appreciate the merits of traditional Western medicine while applying the tenets of alternative medicine. The aspiring chiropractor should be physically strong and dexterous, as a chiropractor repeatedly performs bodily adjustments in his or her efforts to produce successful results.

A Day in the Life—Duties and Responsibilities

A chiropractor spends the majority of his or her day meeting, diagnosing, and treating patients. Like other doctors, chiropractors evaluate the state of a patient's health through physical examinations and interviews. They regularly order laboratory tests, x-rays, and other imaging procedures to determine whether a patient's problems can be adequately treated through chiropractic methods. They suggest appropriate treatment programs and usually manipulate and adjust a patient's spine using their hands and fingers. Most importantly, chiropractors study a patient's neuromusculoskeletal system using chiropractic diagnoses. Chiropractors also study a patient's medical history and recommend alternative treatments, which may include exercise regimes, a change of diet, herbal or vitamin supplements, massage, electric currents, acupuncture, or therapies involving light, water, or heat. Chiropractors may refer patients to other medical professionals if those patients require medical care beyond what chiropractic treatment can offer. Unlike other doctors, chiropractors cannot prescribe medication or perform any surgical procedure.

Some chiropractors specialize in a specific area of chiropractic, including orthopedics, pediatrics, internal disorders, or sports injuries. These specialists see patients with problems related to their specific area of expertise.

Self-employed chiropractors must also take on various administrative and management responsibilities, such as scheduling, bookkeeping, purchasing equipment, hiring staff, and communicating with insurance companies and other vendors. All chiropractors must document patient case histories and treatment plans.

Duties and Responsibilities

- **Analyzing a patient's condition through questioning, observation, examination, x-ray and laboratory services**
- **Advising the patient regarding the course of treatment to be followed, including counseling the patient about such matters as nutrition, exercise and stress management**
- **Performing a series of spinal adjustments from the base of the skull to the tip of the spine by hand and finger manipulation**
- **Treating patients using such measures as exercise, water, light, massage and heat therapy**
- **Referring patients requiring drugs or surgery to other health care specialists**
- **Maintaining accurate case history records of all patients**

WORK ENVIRONMENT

Transferable Skills and Abilities

Communication Skills

- Speaking effectively
- Writing concisely

Interpersonal/Social Skills

- Cooperating with others
- Working as a member of a team

Organization & Management Skills

- Following instructions
- Making decisions
- Paying attention to and handling details

Research & Planning Skills

- Developing evaluation strategies
- Using logical reasoning

Technical Skills

- Performing scientific, mathematical and technical work

Immediate Physical Environment

The majority of chiropractic care is performed in comfortable, clean, bright private office settings. Chiropractors who work in a hospital or clinic are exposed to a more bustling, noisy environment than those who work in private practices.

Human Environment

Chiropractors see multiple patients on a daily basis, and, like other physicians, they must be friendly, accommodating, and reassuring. They normally work with a small administrative staff, other chiropractors, acupuncturists, and/or massage therapists.

Technological Environment

Chiropractors use a wide variety of medical equipment to diagnose and treat patients. They commonly work with stethoscopes, x-ray and ultrasound machines, otoscopes, percussion hammers, traction units, electrocardiograph machines, and nerve interference detection instruments, among other devices. Familiarity with medical, scheduling, accounting, and database software is also important.

EDUCATION, TRAINING, AND ADVANCEMENT

High School/Secondary

High school students who are interested in becoming chiropractors should focus their academic studies in the sciences, anatomy, health, and communications. They should also supplement their foundational coursework with classes in mathematics, physiology, nutrition, and physical education. At home or in the local library, students can research and learn about alternative healing and holistic practices. They can also seek part-time assistant positions at local chiropractor clinics to gain familiarity with the profession.

Suggested High School Subjects

- Algebra
- Applied Math
- Applied Physics
- Biology
- Chemistry
- College Preparatory
- English
- Health Science Technology
- Physical Science
- Physics
- Physiology
- Psychology
- Trigonometry

Related Career Pathways/Majors

Health Science Cluster

- Therapeutic Services Pathway

Famous First

In 1895, Daniel David Palmer of Iowa performed the first chiropractic adjustment on Harvey Lillard. Lillard, who was partially deaf, was working in Palmers office without wearing a shirt. Palmer could see that Lillard had a vertebra out of position. Lillard told Palmer that ever since he moved the wrong way, and heard a 'pop' in his back, his hearing was affect. Palmer performed an adjustment and the following day, Lillard told Palmer, "I can hear that racket on the streets."

Postsecondary

In order to receive a doctor of chiropractic (DC) degree, prospective chiropractors must complete a four-year chiropractic program accredited by the Council on Chiropractic Education (CCE). To be admitted to a chiropractic program, candidates must have at least two or three years of undergraduate education. Many applicants have earned a bachelor's of science degree. Most undergraduates looking to enter chiropractic programs study biology, physics, and chemistry. Chiropractic programs offer students classroom, clinical, and laboratory experience in the sciences, spinal adjustment and manipulation, and physical and laboratory diagnosis.

Those interested in specializing in a particular chiropractic area pursue postdoctoral training in their field of interest. Chiropractic specialties include rehabilitation, pediatrics, and neurology, among others. To be granted "diplomate" status in a particular subfield, chiropractors must successfully pass specialty examinations offered by chiropractic specialty boards.

Related College Majors

- Anatomy
- Chiropractic (D.C., D.C.M.)
- Human & Animal Physiology

Adult Job Seekers

Chiropractors typically form strong networking connections with faculty members and colleagues during the course of their formal education. Many chiropractic programs offer work-study opportunities that allow students to gain practical experience in the field. Membership in a professional chiropractic association such as the American Chiropractic Association (ACA) can also provide networking, job-finding, and professional development opportunities.

After they receive their degree, some chiropractors join a multidiscipline practice where they work alongside physical therapists, massage therapists, acupuncturists, medical doctors, or other medical professionals. This kind of arrangement can provide new chiropractors with an existing patient base when they are starting out in the field. Many chiropractors later establish a solo practice.

Professional Certification and Licensure

All chiropractors must acquire a state license in order to perform chiropractic medicine and may only practice within the state in which they are licensed. Chiropractors must meet all requirements mandated by the state licensing board. Every state licensing board requires prospective chiropractors to have completed a minimum of two years of undergraduate coursework and hold a doctor of chiropractic degree in order to qualify for licensure. To be licensed, chiropractors must pass the National Board of Chiropractic Examiners examination, which consists of written and practical sections. Some states may administer additional or supplemental examinations. Licensed chiropractors must participate in continuing education programs each year to maintain their licensure.

Additional Requirements

Chiropractors, like other healthcare professionals, must possess strong problem-solving skills and desire to help improve the lives of their patients. They must also be empathic, understanding, and supportive of people who are suffering from serious ailments. Unlike other medical treatments, chiropractic treatment coverage varies greatly among health insurance carriers; therefore, chiropractors should be aware of and sensitive to their patients' financial constraints. Since many years of education are required to become a chiropractor, prospective chiropractors should be passionate about learning and committed to their goal.

Fun Fact

Your neck looks very different from a giraffe's, but both people and giraffes—and all mammals—have seven cervical vertebrae. This gives giraffes the flexibility to reach down for food and water; it gives people the ability to turn their necks.

Source: The Joint Corps

EARNINGS AND ADVANCEMENT

The median annual wage for chiropractors was $68,640 in May 2017. The median wage is the wage at which half the workers in an occupation earned more than that amount and half earned less. The lowest 10 percent earned less than $34,550, and the highest 10 percent earned more than $144,730.

In May 2017, the median annual wages for chiropractors in the top industries in which they worked were as follows:

Offices of physicians	$78,710
Offices of chiropractors	67,710

Earnings vary with the chiropractor's number of years in practice, geographic region of practice, and hours worked. Chiropractors tend to earn more as they build a client base and become owners of, or partners in, a practice.

Although most chiropractors worked full time, about 1 in 4 worked part time in 2016. Chiropractors may work in the evenings or on weekends to accommodate patients. Some chiropractors travel to patients' homes to give treatment. Self-employed chiropractors set their own hours.

Chiropractors may receive paid vacations, holidays, and sick days; life and health insurance; and retirement benefits. These are usually paid by the employer. Self-employed chiropractors must provide their own benefits.

Median annual wages, May 2017

Health diagnosing and treating practitioners: $79,480

Chiropractors: $68,640

Total, all occupations: $37,690

Note: All Occupations includes all occupations in the U.S. Economy. Source: U.S. Bureau of Labor Statistics, Occupational Employment Statistics

EMPLOYMENT AND OUTLOOK

There were approximately 47,400 chiropractors employed nationally in 2016. Most chiropractors are in solo practice, although some are in group practice or work for other chiropractors. A small number teach, conduct research at chiropractic institutions, or work in hospitals and clinics.

Employment of chiropractors is projected to grow 12 percent from 2016 to 2026, faster than the average for all occupations. People across all age groups are increasingly becoming interested in integrative or complementary healthcare as a way to treat pain and improve overall wellness. Chiropractic care is appealing to patients because chiropractors use nonsurgical methods of treatment and do not prescribe drugs.

Chiropractic treatment of the back, neck, limbs, and involved joints has become more accepted as a result of research and changing attitudes about additional approaches to healthcare. As a result, chiropractors are increasingly working with other healthcare workers, such as physicians and physical therapists, through referrals and complementary care.

The aging of the large baby-boom generation will lead to new opportunities for chiropractors because older adults are more likely than younger people to have neuromusculoskeletal and joint problems. Members of the aging population will likely continue to seek treatment for these conditions as they lead longer, more active lives.

Demand for chiropractic treatment is related to the ability of patients to pay, either directly or through health insurance. Although most insurance plans now cover chiropractic services, the extent of such coverage varies among plans.

Percent change in employment, Projected 2016-26

Health diagnosing and treating practitioners: 16%

Chiropractors: 12%

Total, all occupations: 7%

Note: All Occupations includes all occupations in the U.S. Economy. Source: U.S. Bureau of Labor Statistics, Employment Projections program

Related Occupations

- Physical Therapist
- Physician

Conversation With . . .
MOHAMMAD JAHADI

Doctor of Chiropractic
Owner, Chirofit Wellness Center
Cedar Park, TX
Chiropractor, 12 years

1. What was your individual career path in terms of education/training, entry-level job, or other significant opportunity?

I was a psych major at the University of Houston, but I was frustrated with what seemed to be the approach of medicating or overmedicating patients and not getting to the root of problems. I had worked as a personal trainer in high school and started a corporate wellness company when I was in college, so I decided to minor in kinesiology. With my background in personal training and psychology, I was fascinated by the mind/body connection. I wondered why it was that some days I went to the gym and could push out 110 percent, but other days, I was barely able to work out.

Before graduating, I was debating between a career in sports psychology or physical therapy and sought advice from a professor. He handed me a book for a chiropractic school that said, "Chiropractic, the art of healing without drugs and surgery." It resonated with me.

That year a new chiropractic school opened, Palmer College of Chiropractic Florida. Palmer was the founder of chiropractic. I was a member of the third graduating class. Along with other sports-minded students and a professor, I helped start the sports chiropractic club. We learned about sports injuries and techniques dealing with shoulders, limbs, elbows, and knees. Some in chiropractic would say chiropractic is manipulation of the spine and not the extremities. Later, I pursued an additional degree as a Certified Chiropractic Extremity Practitioner, dealing with sports injuries and limb injuries such as carpal tunnel and plantar fasciitis.

Through the club, I connected with a new National Indoor Football League team, the Daytona Beach Hogs. The coach brought me on as a student chiropractor and strength and conditioning coach. I really observed the athletes and realized I could watch a player move for about three to five minutes and pinpoint limitations, muscle tension, things that were slowing them down. The athletes were just loving it. The team became Daytona Beach Thunder. I worked with them and Daytona Beach Rugby for a couple of years and gained a lot from it.

Meanwhile, my wife got a job in a chiropractic office and learned the business side, which was a fantastic idea. When we moved back to Texas, we opened Chirofit Wellness Center, the largest such facility in the Austin area at the time. We brought a staff of massage therapists, personal trainer, rehab specialist, and registered dietician/nutritionist together under one roof to collaborate on patient care. I also work as team doctor for the Austin Wranglers Arena Football, Cedar Park Punishes Minor League Football, and Cedar Park High School Athletics.

2. What are the most important skills and/or qualities for someone in your profession?

You need to have passion for your patients; put your clients before money; and be passionate about what you're doing as a chiropractor, because there are a lot of naysayers in the medical world.

3. What do you wish you had known going into this profession?

I wish I had known about the battles that chiropractors face. We are constantly under attack by medical associations—not by individual doctors. The American and Texas Medical Associations continuously try to reduce our scope. It's not an agenda of better health care; it's an agenda of market share for medical doctors.

Also, students going into the field should understand that it will take a couple of years to get comfortable with your techniques and diagnostic abilities. We don't have a forced residency, but all of us worked for peanuts for a couple of years to really hone our skills.

4. Are there many job opportunities in your profession? In what specific areas?

We're seeing more and more athletes shifting to the sports chiropractic model. Many professional sports teams—NFL, NHL, NBA—and Olympic teams have a sports chiropractor on their sidelines. College and high school teams are starting to follow suit.

5. How do you see your profession changing in the next five years as it relates to fitness and/or sports injuries, how will technology impact that change, and what skills will be required?

I hope that our profession takes its place as a leader in fitness and sports medicine.

The medical model likes to work on you once something is broken or has gone wrong and they can fix it. Chiropractors can fix things as well, but we work to prevent injuries. I draw an analogy to NASCAR drivers. They don't wait until the engine blows before stopping by the pit crew. They're constantly stopping by to make sure their vehicle is at 100 percent. Athletes come to see me so that every time they get on the field, they can put it all out there and not worry about a hamstring slowing them down or a muscle cramp or a problematic shoulder.

6. **What do you enjoy most about your job? What do you enjoy least about your job?**

   I love being able to help patients who haven't been able to get help before. Patients often tell me, "I've already seen a medical doctor, I've seen an orthopedist, and I haven't been able to get this problem resolved." As doctors of chiropractic, we aim to treat the root cause of the problem.

   I wish I had more freedom in my schedule. I have chronic pain patients who need frequent care. Often I feel guilty if I go out of town for more than a week and can't be there to assist them or have to hand them off to someone else for treatments.

7. **Can you suggest a valuable "try this" for students considering a career in your profession?**

   Shadowing a chiropractor for a few months will give you a good understanding of the profession. Also, try to volunteer as an assistant for a local chiropractor.

MORE INFORMATION

American Chiropractic Association
Member Information Center
1701 Clarendon Boulevard
Arlington, VA 22209
703.276.8800
memberinfo@acatoday.org
www.acatoday.com

Congress of Chiropractic State Associations
12531 East Meadow Drive
Wichita, KS 67206
316.613.3386
www.cocsa.org

Council on Chiropractic Education
8049 N. 85th Way
Scottsdale, AZ 85258-4321
480.443.8877
cce@cce-usa.org
www.cce-usa.org

Council on Chiropractic Guidelines and Practice Parameters
P.O. Box 2542
Lexington, SC 29071
803.356.6809
www.ccgpp.org

Federation of Chiropractic Licensing Boards
5401 W. 10th Street, Suite 101
Greeley, CO 80634-4400
970.356.3500
info@fclb.org
www.fclb.org

International Chiropractors Association
6400 Arlington Boulevard, Suite 800
Falls Church, VA 22042
800.423.4690
chiro@chiropractic.org
www.chiropractic.org

National Board of Chiropractic Examiners
901 54th Avenue
Greeley, CO 80634
800.964.6223
www.nbce.org

World Chiropractic Alliance
2683 Via de La Valle, Suite G 629
Del Mar, CA 92014
800.347.1011
www.worldchiropracticalliance.org

Briana Nadeau/Editor

Dietitian & Nutritionist

Snapshot

Career Cluster(s): Agriculture, Food & Natural Resources, Health Science, Human Services, Science, Technology, Engineering & Mathematics
Interests: Science, mathematics, food, educating others, performing research, solving problems
Earnings (median in 2017): $59,410 per year; $28.56 per hour
Employment & Outlook through 2026: 15% (Much faster than average growth expected)

OVERVIEW

Sphere of Work

Dietitians and nutritionists are experts in the use of food and nutrition to promote health and manage disease. They advise people on what to eat in order to lead a healthy lifestyle or achieve a specific health-related goal. Dietitians and nutritionists are responsible for assessing patients' nutritional needs and planning healthy food regimens that help prevent and treat medical conditions. They manage institutional food programs, oversee meal preparation, recommend dietary modifications, and provide education to individuals and groups of all ages. Increased interest in public nutrition means there is a growing demand

for dietitians and nutritionists who analyze food products and report information on nutritional content and vitamin supplements, among other issues of concern, to the public. The primary difference between a dietitian and a nutritionist is education: a dietitian must have academic credentials and clinical experience, while a nutritionist typically does not.

Work Environment

Dietitians and nutritionists work in medical clinics, nursing homes, sports centers, hospitals, correctional facilities, schools, and corporations such as food manufacturing companies. Many travel to see patients who need at-home care. Some dietitians and nutritionists are consultants. This profession offers flexible hours in a variety of work settings, including kitchens, laboratories, and bright, organized offices. Kitchens can often be hot, crowded, fast-paced environments.

Profile

Interests: Data, People
Working Conditions: Work Inside
Physical Strength: Light Work
Education Needs: Bachelor's Degree, Master's Degree
Licensure/Certification: Required
Physical Abilities Not Required: Not Climb, Not Handle, Not Kneel
Opportunities for Experience: Military Service, Volunteer Work, Part Time Work
Holland Interest Score*: ISR, SEI, SIE

* See Appendix A

Occupation Interest

Individuals who wish to be dietitians and nutritionists should find satisfaction in working with people, educating patients, and making a positive impact on the nutritional status of individuals and communities. Those who excel in science and math may be well suited to the work. Dietitians and nutritionists tend to be patient, well organized, and detail oriented. They can listen attentively, express themselves clearly and articulately, analyze data to solve problems, and make sound decisions. Other valuable qualities include teamwork, initiative, and compassion for others.

A Day in the Life—Duties and Responsibilities

During a typical workday, dietitians and nutritionists visit patients, assess patients' or clients' nutritional needs, design and coordinate nutrition programs, evaluate and report results, and confer with other health professionals to balance patients' food needs with their medical needs. Dietitians and nutritionists encourage patient compliance with nutrition plans by teaching them how foods interact with specific medications or clinical treatments. In schools, hospitals, and other institutional settings, they may also meet with the clinical manager and dietetic technician for updates, provide medical nutrition therapy, or oversee food preparation. Those who are employed as consultants often suggest specific diet modifications for their clients.

Dietitians and nutritionists frequently work in a public health capacity by regulating food serving sizes, giving presentations on nutrition, or teaching the aging population how to shop for food. They may prepare and distribute a variety of educational materials on subjects related to health and nutrition. Many are involved in conducting nutrition research and enacting public policies that relate to food processing, consumer information about food, and national dietary guidelines and recommendations.

Many dietitians and nutritionists provide customized information for specific individuals. For example, a dietitian or nutritionist might teach a client with diabetes how to plan meals to balance the client's blood sugar. Others work with groups of people who have similar needs. For example, a dietitian or nutritionist might plan a diet with healthy fat and limited sugar to help clients who are at risk for heart disease. They may work with other healthcare professionals to coordinate patient care.

Dietitians and nutritionists who are self-employed may meet with patients, or they may work as consultants for a variety of organizations. They may need to spend time on marketing and other business-related tasks, such as scheduling appointments, keeping records, and preparing educational programs or informational materials for clients.

Duties and Responsibilities

- **Selecting, training and directing food-service workers**
- **Providing diet counseling services**
- **Coordinating dietary services with those of other departments**
- **Acting as a consultant to management**
- **Preparing records and reports**
- **Promoting sound eating habits through education and research**
- **Supervising the planning, preparation and service of meals**

OCCUPATION SPECIALTIES

Although many dietitians and nutritionists do similar tasks, there are several specialties within the occupations. The following are examples of types of dietitians and nutritionists:

Clinical dietitians and clinical nutritionists

Clinical dietitians and clinical nutritionists provide medical nutrition therapy. They work in hospitals, long-term care facilities, clinics, private practice, and other institutions. They create customized nutritional programs based on the health needs of patients or residents and counsel patients on how to improve their health through nutrition. Clinical dietitians and clinical nutritionists may further specialize, such as by working only with patients with specific conditions such as kidney disease, diabetes, or digestive disorders.

Community dietitians and community nutritionists

Community dietitians and community nutritionists develop programs and counsel the public on topics related to food, health, and nutrition. They often work with specific groups of people, such as adolescents or the elderly. They work in public health clinics, government and nonprofit agencies, health maintenance organizations (HMOs), and other settings.

Management dietitians

Management dietitians plan food programs. They work in food service settings such as cafeterias, hospitals, prisons, and schools. They may be responsible for buying food and for carrying out other business-related tasks, such as budgeting. Management dietitians may oversee kitchen staff or other dietitians.

WORK ENVIRONMENT

Transferable Skills and Abilities

Communication Skills
- Speaking effectively
- Writing concisely

Interpersonal/Social Skills
- Cooperating with others
- Providing support to others
- Working as a member of a team

Organization & Management Skills
- Coordinating tasks
- Managing people/groups
- Performing duties which change frequently

Research & Planning Skills
- Analyzing information
- Solving problems
- Using logical reasoning

Technical Skills
- Performing scientific, mathematical and technical work

Immediate Physical Environment

Dietitians and nutritionists tend to work in facilities that are clean, bright, and well ventilated. In offices, they sit at desks for extended periods. In kitchens and laboratories, they may be required to stand for a significant part of the day.

Human Environment

Dietitians and nutritionists interact with patients and their families, and with fellow staff members such as doctors, nurses, and dietetic technicians.

Technological Environment

Dietitians and nutritionists take measurements using scales, calorimeters, glucose meters, skinfold calipers, and bioelectric impedance machines. Financial and medical software, databases, and office suites help them track patient information such as weight, diet, medications, protein supplements, and lab results.

EDUCATION, TRAINING, AND ADVANCEMENT

High School/Secondary

High school students interested in becoming dietitians and nutritionists should focus on math, science, and communication courses. In addition, students should prepare themselves by participating in relevant extracurricular activities. To learn what dietitians and nutritionists do each day, interested students may find it useful to seek an internship. High school career counselors often have lists of internship opportunities. Aspiring dietitians and nutritionists should apply to college or university programs.

Suggested High School Subjects

- Applied Biology/Chemistry
- Applied Communication
- Applied Math
- Biology
- Chemistry
- College Preparatory
- Computer Science
- English
- Family & Consumer Sciences
- Food Service & Management
- Foods & Nutrition
- Health Science Technology
- Mathematics
- Physiology
- Science
- Sociology

Related Career Pathways/Majors

Agriculture, Food & Natural Resources Cluster

- Food Products & Processing Systems Pathway

Health Science Cluster

- Diagnostic Services Pathway
- Therapeutic Services Pathway

Human Services Cluster
- Counseling & Mental Health Services Pathway

Science, Technology, Engineering & Mathematics Cluster
- Science & Mathematics Pathway

Famous First

Hippocrates was a Greek physician, famous for the Hippocratic oath, historically taken by new doctors, exhorting them to "do no harm," and to teach the secrets of medicine to the next generation. He is also famous for another important saying, recorded sometime around 400 BCE: "Let thy food be thy medicine and thy medicine be thy food."

Postsecondary

A college degree provides the best opportunities for employment or advancement. College and university students looking to enter the field should study biology, food sciences, math, chemistry, medicine, physiology, administration and institution management, education, psychology, and counseling, in pursuit of an undergraduate degree in dietetics, nutrition, food service, or a related discipline. Students may gain experience and build connections through internships and co-ops that integrate clinical work with university-level coursework. Many dietitians and nutritionists choose to pursue a graduate degree after completing their undergraduate studies.

Related College Majors
- Dietetics/Human Nutritional Services
- Foods & Nutrition Science
- Foods & Nutrition Studies, General
- Human & Animal Physiology

Adult Job Seekers

Adults with a bachelor's or master's degree will have better job opportunities in this field. By joining professional associations such as the American Dietetic Association, adult job seekers can benefit from ongoing networking, professional development services, food and nutrition information, and mentorships to establish career and educational options. These professional organizations generally maintain job lists and advertise open dietitian and nutritionist positions.

Professional Certification and Licensure

For dietitians and nutritionists, licensure, certification, and registration requirements vary by state; therefore, candidates need to determine what the requirements are in the state or states where they want to work. Some states require that all practitioners of dietetics and nutrition be licensed, a process which entails doing specific coursework, passing an exam, and completing a supervised internship. Where certification is mandatory, those without it can still practice but cannot use certain titles.

The Commission on Dietetic Registration provides voluntary certification that is completely distinct from state licensure or certification. Registered dietitians (RDs) must fulfill education and work experience requirements in order to qualify for the certifying exam.

Additional Requirements

Dietitians and nutritionists must be resourceful and always willing to research the latest information, as the state of medical knowledge is frequently changing. Specializing in a particular body system or age group may be helpful for advancement in this field.

EARNINGS AND ADVANCEMENT

Earnings depend on the geographic location and size of the employer and the community and the employee's education, specialty area, and number of years in practice. Median annual earnings of dietitians and nutritionists were $59,410 in May 2017. The lowest ten percent earned less than $36,910, and the highest ten percent earned more than $83,070.

Dietitians and nutritionists may receive paid vacations, holidays, and sick days; life and health insurance; and retirement benefits. These are usually paid by the employer.

Many dietitians and nutritionists worked full time in 2016, although about 1 out of 4 worked part time. They may work evenings and weekends to meet with clients who are unavailable at other times.

Median annual wages, May 2017

Health diagnosing and treating practitioners: $79,480

Dietitians and nutritionists: $59,410

Total, all occupations: $37,690

Note: All Occupations includes all occupations in the U.S. Economy. Source: U.S. Bureau of Labor Statistics, Occupational Employment Statistics

EMPLOYMENT AND OUTLOOK

Dietitians and nutritionists held about 68,000 jobs in 2016. The largest employers of dietitians and nutritionists were as follows:

Hospitals; state, local, and private	30%
Government	14
Outpatient care centers	10
Nursing and residential care facilities	9
Self-employed workers	6

More than half of all jobs were in hospitals, nursing care facilities, outpatient care centers, or offices of physicians.

Employment of dietitians and nutritionists is projected to grow 15 percent from 2016 to 2026, much faster than the average for all occupations. In recent years, interest in the role of food and nutrition in promoting health and wellness has increased, particularly as a part of preventative healthcare in medical settings.

According to the Centers for Disease Control, more than one-third of U.S. adults are obese. Many diseases, such as diabetes and heart disease, are associated with obesity. The importance of diet in preventing and treating illnesses is now well known. More dietitians and nutritionists will be needed to provide care for people with these conditions.

Moreover, as the baby-boom generation grows older and looks for ways to stay healthy, there will be more demand for dietetic and nutrition services. In addition, there will be demand for dietitians and nutritionists in grocery stores to help consumers make healthy food choices.

Percent change in employment, Projected 2016-26

Health diagnosing and treating practitioners: 16%

Dietitians and nutritionists: 15%

Total, all occupations: 7%

Note: All Occupations includes all occupations in the U.S. Economy. Source: U.S. Bureau of Labor Statistics, Employment Projections program

Related Occupations

- Cook/Chef
- Food Service Manager
- Medical Scientist

Related Military Occupations

- Dietitian
- Food Service Manager

Conversation With . . .
JESSICA WAGNER

Nutritionist/Health Coach, 6 years

1. What was your individual career path in terms of education, entry-level job, or other significant opportunity?

Eight years prior to my nutrition and health counseling education, I had obtained a Bachelor's degree in East Asian Studies from Wittenberg University. There's a huge connection between how to live a healthy lifestyle and the philosophy of East Asian Studies. Then I worked for 10 years in international education, advising and counseling individuals, and learned that one-on-one counseling is my thing. During this time, I also realized I was not healthy in the workplace and other people weren't either. We weren't getting the basics, like fresh air and sunlight every day, in our cubicles. We were eating cafeteria food, or too busy to cook dinner. I got very sick, and wanted to cure myself naturally. So I received a post-bachelor's certificate in Health Counseling through The Center for Educational Outreach and Innovation at Teacher's College Columbia University and The Institute for Integrative Nutrition (IIN) in New York City. For nine months, I traveled there once a month for intensive study all day Saturday and Sunday and, quite often, Monday. Upon graduation, I was prepared to open my own health and nutritional counseling practice. A year later, I completed the Integrative Nutrition Immersion Graduate Program.

2. Are there many job opportunities in your profession? In what specific areas?

The most valuable opportunity in this profession is to open your own practice. I have created my own niche. I do workshops, I've done group programs, and I do one-on-one counseling, which is where I think my talent is. I offer one-on-one relationships to clients who need serious help. They can email or text me between sessions. I'm holding them by the hand and I think that's really needed. In addition to operating a business, there are opportunities in doctors' offices, yoga studios, gyms, chiropractic or other wellness practices. Corporations regularly look for health and nutrition coaches to provide workshops and counseling to employees.

3. What do you wish you had known going into this profession?

Only hands-on experience could prepare me to work effectively with people. Each person, depending on their personality and fears, will respond differently to your guidance. Most people are afraid to break old habits and will try to hold onto unhealthy patterns. With sensitivity, care, and respect, you can learn how to guide even the most fearful people. Nutritional knowledge alone doesn't make you a good health and nutrition coach. You need to be a good listener and a patient teacher.

4. How do you see your profession changing in the next five years?

I see this profession becoming much more mainstream. The public interest in conventional medicine is shifting to holistic-based approaches and preventative services. Doctors simply don't have the time to counsel their clients on how to make healthy lifestyle changes. I see every doctor's office having a health and nutrition coach. I also see health insurance coverage for this kind of preventive wellness service.

5. What role will technology play in those changes, and what skills will be required?

Technology is already playing a large role in this field. Many health and nutrition coaches provide counseling services over the phone and Internet, as I do. In addition, webinars are provided regularly for groups of clients. Being so easily accessible means clients are more apt to hire me.

6. Do you have any general advice or additional professional insights to share with someone interested in your profession?

If you want the flexibility of creating your own work hours and having an important impact on the lives of people, no other career that I know of can provide that in quite the same way that this profession does. Transforming the health and happiness of people is truly the best job anyone could have.

7. Can you suggest a valuable "try this" for students considering a career in your profession?

Call an admission's counselor at a school that offers training in this field and ask to sit in on a class. If you feel inspired, take it a step further by reading a good book recommended by the professor. If you still feel inspired, try out a healthy nutritional lifestyle for a good year or so, following the recommendations in the book. During this time, practice talking to people about your experiences. Offer tips to people looking for answers. Practice having simple conversations with individuals and being a mentor and advocate for their health.

[Note: This interview was conducted in 2014.]

MORE INFORMATION

Academy of Nutrition & Dietetics
120 South Riverside Plaza
Suite 2000
Chicago, IL 60606
800.877.1600
Website
www.eatright.org

Offers scholarships for studies in nutrition or dietetics:
www.eatright.org/CADE/content.aspx?id=7934
Commission on Dietetic Registration, credentialing agency for the ADA:
www.cdrnet.org

American Association for Nutritional Consultants
400 Oakhill Drive
Winona Lake, IN 46590
888.828.2262
www.aanc.net

American Society for Nutritional Sciences
9650 Rockville Pike, Suite 4500
Bethesda,MD 20814
301.634.7050
sec@nutrition.org
www.nutrition.org

Association for Healthcare Foodservice
455 S. 4th Street, Suite 650
Louisville, KY 40202
888.528.9552
info@healthcarefoodservice.org
www.healthcarefoodservice.org

Dietary Managers Association
406 Surrey Woods Drive
St. Charles, IL 60174
800.323.1908
info@dmaonline.org
www.dmaonline.org

International Association for Worksite Health Promotion
401 West Michigan Street
Indianapolis, IN 46202
317.637.9200
iawhp@acsm.org
www.acsm-iawhp.org

Susan Williams/Editor

Exercise Physiologist

Snapshot

Career Cluster(s): Education & Training; Health Sciences; Human Service; Science, Technology, Engineering & Mathematics
Interests: Customer and Personal Service, Biology, English Language, Education and Training, Medicine and Dentistry
Earnings (median in 2017): $49,090 per year; $23.60 per hour
Employment & Outlook through 2026: 13% (Faster than average)

OVERVIEW

Sphere of Work

Exercise physiologists analyze a patient's medical history to determine the best possible exercise and fitness regimen.

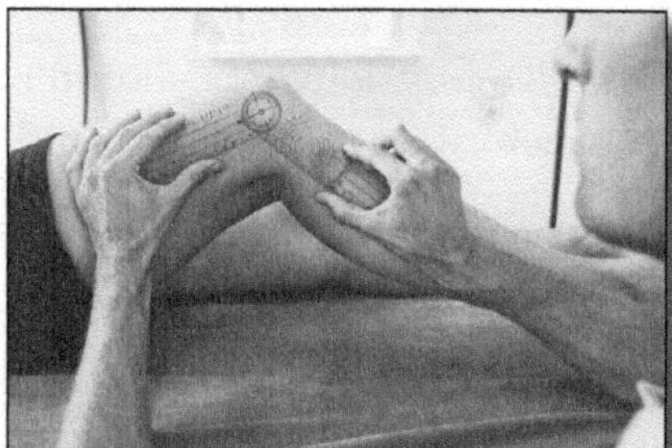

Exercise physiologists develop fitness and exercise programs that help patients recover from chronic diseases and improve cardiovascular function, body composition, and flexibility.

Profile

Working Conditions: Work indoors
Physical Strength: Performing physical activities that require considerable use of your arms and legs and moving your whole body, such as climbing, lifting, balancing, walking, stooping, and handling of materials
Education Needs: Bachelor's degree, Master's degree
Licensure/Certification: Required in most states
Opportunities for Experience: Internships, Military Service
Holland Interest Score*: SIR

* See Appendix A

Occupation Interest

People interested in a career as an exercise physiologist typically enjoy working with, communicating with, and teaching people. These occupations often involve helping or providing service to others. They must also be adept at starting up and carrying out projects. These occupations can involve leading people and making many decisions. Sometimes they require risk taking and often deal with business.

A Day in the Life—Duties and Responsibilities

Exercise physiologists work to improve overall patient health. Many of their patients suffer from health problems such as cardiovascular disease or pulmonary (lung) disease. Exercise physiologists provide health education and exercise plans to improve key health indicators.

Some physiologists work closely with primary care physicians, who may prescribe exercise regimens for their patients and refer them to exercise physiologists. The physiologists then work with patients to develop individualized treatment plans that will help the patients meet their health and fitness goals.

Exercise physiologists should not be confused with fitness trainers and instructors (including personal trainers) or athletic trainers.

Duties and Responsibilities

- **Analyze a patient's medical history to assess their risk during exercise and to determine the best possible exercise and fitness regimen for the patient**
- **Perform fitness and stress tests with medical equipment and analyze the resulting patient data**
- **Measure blood pressure, oxygen usage, heart rhythm, and other key patient health indicators**
- **Develop exercise programs to improve patients' health**

WORK ENVIRONMENT

Physical Environment

Laboratory and office settings predominate. Research and design work relating to biomedical engineering may involve contact with human or animal tissue, and biomedical safety practices will be observed.

Human Environment

This occupation often involves coordinating, training, supervising, or managing the activities of others to accomplish goals. Very advanced communication and organizational skills are required. Exercise physiologist professionals interact with students and colleagues in fields across the scientific spectrum, as well as with technicians, managers, directors, patients, and in some cases, business specialists.

Technological Environment

Exercise physiologists use a variety of tools and technologies including software for data base user interface and queries, graphics or photo imaging, medical, spreadsheet web page creation and editing, social media. They use electronic mail, telephones, digital video disk players or recorders, liquid crystal display projectors, notebook or laptop computers, personal digital assistant PDAs or organizers, and photocopiers.

Relevant Skills and Abilities

- **Compassion.** Because exercise physiologists work with patients who may be in considerable pain or discomfort, they must be sympathetic while working with patients.
- **Decision-making skills.** Exercise physiologists must make informed clinical decisions because those decisions could affect the health or livelihood of patients.
- **Detail oriented.** Exercise physiologists must record detailed, accurate information about their patients' conditions and about any progress the patients make. For example, they must ensure that patients are completing the appropriate stress tests or practicing the correct fitness regimen.
- **Interpersonal skills.** Exercise physiologists must have strong interpersonal skills and manage difficult situations. They must communicate clearly with others, including physicians, patients, and patients' families.
- **Active Listening.** Giving full attention to what other people are saying, taking time to understand the points being made, asking questions as appropriate, and not interrupting at inappropriate times.
- **Critical Thinking.** Using logic and reasoning to identify the strengths and weaknesses of alternative solutions, conclusions, or approaches to problems.
- **Reading Comprehension**. Understanding written sentences and paragraphs in work related documents.
- **Speaking.** Talking to others to convey information effectively.
- **Instructing.** Teaching others how to do something.
- **Service Orientation.** Actively looking for ways to help people.
- **Writing.** Communicating effectively in writing as appropriate for the needs of the audience.
- **Judgment and Decision Making.** Considering the relative costs and benefits of potential actions to choose the most appropriate one.
- **Monitoring.** Monitoring/Assessing performance of yourself, other individuals, or organizations to make improvements or take corrective action.
- **Social Perceptiveness.** Being aware of others' reactions and understanding why they react as they do.
- **Complex Problem Solving.** Identifying complex problems and reviewing related information to develop and evaluate options and implement solutions.
- **Active Learning.** Understanding the implications of new information for both current and future problem-solving and decision-making.
- **Persuasion.** Persuading others to change their minds or behavior.
- **Management of Personnel Resources.** Motivating, developing, and directing people as they work, identifying the best people for the job.

- **Systems Analysis.** Determining how a system should work and how changes in conditions, operations, and the environment will affect outcomes.
- **Systems Evaluation.** Identifying measures or indicators of system performance and the actions needed to improve or correct performance, relative to the goals of the system.
- **Time Management.** Managing one's own time and the time of others.

EDUCATION, TRAINING, AND ADVANCEMENT

High School/Secondary

Extensive skill, knowledge, and experience are needed for these occupations. Many require more than five years of experience. For example, surgeons must complete four years of college and an additional five to seven years of specialized medical training to be able to do their job. Employees may need some on-the-job training, but most of these occupations assume that the person will already have the required skills, knowledge, work-related experience, and/or training.

Famous First

Claudius Galenus (c. ~130–200 AD), was the first to use experiments to probe the functions of the body. He proposed that the "humoral imbalances" proposed by Hippocrates are related to specific organs and that they can affect the entire body. This idea permitted doctors to make more precise diagnoses. In addition to the four "humours" (black bile, phlegm, blood and yellow bile), Galen paired certain temperaments with the humours (sanguine and blood; phlegmatic and phlegm; yellow bile and choleric; and black bile and melancholy). His understanding of physiology held sway for nearly sixteen centuries.

College/Postsecondary

Exercise physiologists typically need at least a bachelor's degree in exercise physiology, exercise science, kinesiology, or a related field. Master's degree programs also are available. Programs include courses in science and health-related subjects, such as biology, anatomy, statistics, kinesiology, and nutrition, as well as clinical work. In 2017, there were about 60 programs in exercise physiology, exercise science, and kinesiology accredited by the Commission on Accreditation of Allied Health Education Programs (CAAHEP).

Coursework for this major generally includes classes in exercise science, biology, anatomy, physical education, nutrition, exercise techniques, and injury prevention. Additionally, students may be required to take classes to strengthen their teaching and interpersonal skills.

Adult Job Seekers

Adults seeking employment as an exercise physiologist should have, at minimum, a bachelor's degree in an area related to health, wellness, and community policy. They will benefit from joining professional organizations to help with networking and job searches.

Professional Certification and Licensure

Louisiana is the only state that requires exercise physiologists to be licensed, although some states have pending legislation to create licensure requirements.

Employers typically require exercise physiologists to have Basic Life Support (BLS) certification or Advanced Life Support (ACLS) certification, both of which include training in cardiopulmonary resuscitation (CPR).

The American Society of Exercise Physiologists (ASEP) offers the Exercise Physiologist Certified (EPC) certification, which physiologists can use to demonstrate their qualifications. To be eligible for certification, candidates must pass the ASEP exam and hold ASEP membership. In addition, candidates must have either a bachelor's degree in exercise physiology or a bachelor's degree in a related field, and they must have completed specific coursework requirements. To maintain certification, candidates must complete continuing education courses every 5 years.

The American College of Sports Medicine (ACSM) also offers certifications for exercise physiologists: the Certified Exercise Physiologist (EP-C) and the Certified Clinical Exercise Physiologist (CEP) credentials for candidates with a bachelor's degree, as well as the Registered Clinical Exercise Physiologist (RCEP) for candidates with a master's or higher degree. All three ACSM credentials require CPR certification and passing an exam. Candidates for the CEP and the RCEP also must have at least 400 and 600 hours of supervised clinical experience, respectively. All three ACSM certifications require candidates to complete continuing education courses every 3 years, and keep their CPR certification up to date.

Fun Fact

According to the American Physiological Society, every minute that you walk extends your life by 1½ to 2 minutes on average. Talk about the walk of life.

Source: www.physiologyinfo.org

EARNINGS AND ADVANCEMENT

The median annual wage for exercise physiologists was $49,090 in May 2017. The median wage is the wage at which half the workers in an occupation earned more than that amount and half earned less. The lowest 10 percent earned less than $34,250, and the highest 10 percent earned more than $78,410.

In May 2017, the median annual wages for exercise physiologists in the top industries in which they worked were as follows:

Government	$71,600
Hospitals; state, local, and private	48,660
Offices of physicians	48,220
Offices of physical, occupational and speech therapists, and audiologists	41,460

Median annual wages, May 2017

Health diagnosing and treating practitioners: $79,480

Exercise physiologists: $49,090

Total, all occupations: $37,690

Note: All Occupations includes all occupations in the U.S. Economy. Source: U.S. Bureau of Labor Statistics, Occupational Employment Statistics

EMPLOYMENT AND OUTLOOK

Exercise physiologists held about 15,100 jobs in 2016. The largest employers of exercise physiologists were as follows:

Employment of exercise physiologists is projected to grow 13 percent from 2016 to 2026, faster than the average for all occupations. Demand may rise as hospitals emphasize exercise and preventive care to help patients recover from cardiovascular and pulmonary diseases and improve their overall health.

Self-employed workers	53%
Hospitals; state, local, and private	26
Offices of physical, occupational and speech therapists, and audiologists	4
Offices of physicians	3
Government	3

Most exercise physiologists work full time.

Employment Trend, Projected 2016-26

Health diagnosing and treating practitioners: 16%

Exercise physiologists: 13%

Total, all occupations: 7%

Note: All Occupations includes all occupations in the U.S. Economy. Source: U.S. Bureau of Labor Statistics, Employment Projections program

Related Occupations

This table shows a list of occupations with job duties that are similar to those of exercise physiologists.

Occupation	Job Duties	Entry-Level Education	2017 Median Pay
Athletic Trainers	Athletic trainers specialize in preventing, diagnosing, and treating muscle and bone injuries and illnesses.	Bachelor's degree	$46,630
Nuclear Medicine Technologists	Nuclear medicine technologists prepare radioactive drugs and administer them to patients for imaging or therapeutic purposes.	Associate degree	$75,660
Occupational Therapists	Occupational therapists treat injured, ill, or disabled patients through the therapeutic use of everyday activities. They help these patients develop, recover, improve, as well as maintain the skills needed for daily living and working.	Master's degree	$83,200
Physical Therapists	Physical therapists, sometimes called PTs, help injured or ill people improve their movement and manage their pain. These therapists are often an important part of the rehabilitation, treatment, and prevention of patients with chronic conditions, illnesses, or injuries.	Doctoral or professional degree	$86,850
Recreational Therapists	Recreational therapists plan, direct, and coordinate recreation-based treatment programs for people with disabilities, injuries, or illnesses. These therapists use a variety of modalities, including arts and crafts; drama, music, and dance; sports and games; aquatics; and community outings to help maintain or improve a patient's physical, social, and emotional well-being.	Bachelor's degree	$47,680

(Continues on page 95)

Occupation	Job Duties	Entry-Level Education	2017 Median Pay
Respiratory Therapists	Respiratory therapists care for patients who have trouble breathing—for example, from a chronic respiratory disease, such as asthma or emphysema. Their patients range from premature infants with undeveloped lungs to elderly patients who have diseased lungs. They also provide emergency care to patients suffering from heart attacks, drowning, or shock.	Associate degree	$59,710
Chiropractors	Chiropractors treat patients with health problems of the neuromusculoskeletal system, which includes nerves, bones, muscles, ligaments, and tendons. They use spinal adjustments and manipulation, as well as other clinical interventions, to manage patients' health concerns, such as back and neck pain.	Doctoral or professional degree	$68,640
Fitness Trainers and Instructors	Fitness trainers and instructors lead, instruct, and motivate individuals or groups in exercise activities, including cardiovascular exercises (exercises for the heart and blood circulation), strength training, and stretching. They work with people of all ages and skill levels.	High school diploma or equivalent	$39,210

Conversation With . . .
STEVEN JONES

Clinical Exercise Services Manager
InnovAge
Denver, CO
Exercise Physiology, 10 years

1. What was your individual career path in terms of education/training, entry-level job, or other significant opportunity?

I began my career by obtaining the American College of Sports Medicine (ACSM) personal trainer certification, which gave me the opportunity to work as an exercise specialist with a medical group. That experience brought my passion for health and fitness to the forefront, so I decided to return to school to acquire my Bachelor of Science in exercise physiology. Soon after, I became an ACSM Clinical Exercise Physiologist and began working for InnovAge as a rehab aide. The majority of the people I worked with suffered from a myriad of chronic illnesses such as type 2 diabetes, hypertension, and chronic obstructive pulmonary disorder. Eventually, I identified a need for a clinical exercise program to help improve their quality of life. About two years after starting at InnovAge, I developed a clinical exercise services department, which I now manage. InnovAge is a healthcare company that helps seniors age in place with a Program of All-inclusive Care for the Elderly (PACE), an alternative to nursing homes. I also became an Exercise is Medicine Level III provider, which is a joint program of the ACSM and American Medical Association that aims to make physical activity assessment and promotion standard in clinical care. I also became a member of the Clinical Exercise Physiology Association (CEPA) Executive Committee.

2. What are the most important skills and/or qualities for someone in your profession?

People skills are a necessity in the exercise profession. You have to be a great communicator, which includes listening, empathizing, motivating, and encouraging. Furthermore, being self-motivated and conscientious about one's own health is important to encourage others to follow your exercise recommendations and seek behavior changes themselves. You're leading by example.

3. What do you wish you had known going into this profession?

It took me eight years to find exercise physiology. If I had realized how fulfilling this career would be, I would have changed paths sooner. To walk side by side with another individual on a life-changing journey and see them realize their achievements through their own hard work is truly an amazing experience. It makes this profession extremely satisfying.

4. Are there many job opportunities in your profession? In what specific areas?

Many opportunities, and specialties, exist in exercise physiology. Some of the job opportunities include positions in fitness and sport-specific training, clinical exercise physiology, rehabilitation, and group instruction. The field is so broad you can identify your niche and apply your skills and passion.

5. How do you see your profession changing in the next five years as it relates to fitness and/or sports injuries? What role will technology play, and what skills will be required?

There is an ever-increasing emphasis on the role of exercise to prevent chronic illnesses that are burdening our health care system. My hope is that insurance companies and health care systems will adopt or support exercise programs that have been proven through research to be necessary for good health. Adoption of these clinically-based exercise programs could have staggeringly positive effects on the population as a whole.

From personal fitness watches and apps to heart rate monitoring programs, exercise technology now enables precision in prescribing and implementing more effective exercise plans.

6. What do you enjoy most about your job? What do you enjoy least about your job?

My work allows me to make deep connections with individuals through exercise. I'm able to build meaningful relationships and not only teach, but also learn from those I train, especially older adults.

My least favorite part of the job is combating all the erroneous information about exercise and health on the internet that is not scientifically based. Everywhere you turn, there seems to be information that's not based on scientific principles or methods, which can lead to negative health outcomes.

7. Can you suggest a valuable "try this" for students considering a career in your profession?

Because the exercise science field is so diverse, I suggest shadowing in its numerous disciplines to find your niche. We all have unique skills and backgrounds. Research your interests in the exercise field and seek out as many learning opportunities as you can.

MORE INFORMATION

For more information about exercise physiologists and certifications, visit:

American Association of Cardiovascular and Pulmonary Rehabilitation (AACVPR)
330 N. Wabash Avenue
Suite 2000
Chicago, IL 60611
Phone: 312/321-5146
Fax: 312/673-6924
https://www.aacvpr.org/

American College of Sports Medicine (ACSM)
401 West Michigan Street
Indianapolis, IN 46202-3233
Phone: (317) 637-9200
Fax: (317) 634-7817
http://www.acsm.org/

American Council on Exercise (ACE)
4851 Paramount Drive
San Diego, California 92123
Phone: (888) 825-3636
https://www.acefitness.org

American Society of Exercise Physiologists
https://www.asep.org/

Clinical Exercise Physiology Association
401 W. Michigan St
Indianapolis, MI 46202
United States of America Click 'Google Maps' for a map and directions to the club
Phone: (317) 637-9200, ext. 147
https://www.acsm-cepa.org

Committee on Accreditation for the Exercise Sciences
http://www.coaes.org/

IDEA Health and Fitness Association
https://www.ideafit.com/

Innovage
8950 E. Lowry Boulevard
Denver, CO 80230
844-704-9613 TTY: 711
www.MyInnovAge.com

National Strength and Conditioning Association
1885 Bob Johnson Dr
Colorado Springs, CO 80906
Phone: (719) 632-6722
https://www.nsca.com/

Fitness Trainer & Instructor

Snapshot

Career Cluster(s): Education & Training, Hospitality & Tourism, Human Services
Interests: Exercise, being active, motivating others
Earnings (median in 2017): $39,210 per year; $18.85 per hour
Employment & Outlook through 2026: 10% (Faster than average growth expected)

OVERVIEW

Sphere of Work

Fitness trainers and instructors design, organize, and lead exercise and sports programs that allow individuals to improve their health through cardiovascular activity, strength training, and stretching exercises. They usually offer private lessons as well as group instruction. They teach the fundamentals of fitness by presenting clients with various techniques, helping them set individually tailored fitness goals, and motivating them physically and mentally to reach those goals. Fitness trainers and instructors often focus on one or more areas of fitness, such as aerobics, weight lifting, yoga, or Pilates.

Work Environment

Fitness trainers and instructors work in a variety of settings, from health clubs and exercise studios to resorts and universities. Some travel to clients' homes to provide regular instruction, while others organize fitness programs for large businesses. The majority of fitness trainers and instructors work indoors in cool climates; however, some offer instruction in pleasant outdoor environments. Most fitness trainers and instructors work full time with irregular hours, as they must cater to the schedules of their clients. They often work early in the morning, at night, on weekends, and during holidays. Fitness trainers and instructors spend most of their time standing, walking, and participating in physical activities.

Profile

Interests: People, Things
Working Conditions: Work Inside, Work Outside, Work Both Inside and Outside
Physical Strength: Medium Work
Education Needs: Bachelor's Degree
Licensure/Certification: Recommended
Physical Abilities Not Required: Not Climb
Opportunities for Experience: Internship, Volunteer Work
Holland Interest Score*: ESR

* See Appendix A

Occupation Interest

Those looking to become fitness trainers and instructors must be in excellent physical condition and have natural athletic ability. They should have a passion for instructing and motivating individuals. Sometimes clients are reluctant or unwilling to participate in specified activities, so fitness trainers and instructors should be firm, persuasive, and encouraging. Creativity and patience are also valuable traits. Fitness trainers and instructors must have strong customer service skills in order to find and maintain their clientele.

A Day in the Life—Duties and Responsibilities

Fitness trainers and instructors spend most of their day working with clients to achieve and build upon specified fitness goals. They begin by evaluating the physical strengths and weaknesses of each individual and providing corrective feedback for improvement. Fitness trainers and instructors design appropriate exercise programs based on the skill level, strength, and endurance of each client. They keep detailed records of clients' progress and advancement, noting accomplishments as well as areas that need improvement. Many fitness trainers and instructors have a background in nutrition and often advise clients on suitable diets, weight control techniques, and lifestyle modifications. They are responsible for informing clients of safety procedures and regulations related to sports and aerobic activities, as well as the proper use of exercise machines and other equipment.

When instructing large groups of people, fitness trainers and instructors plan lessons and routines, select music, and create innovative exercise programs. They must keep lessons and classes exciting, challenging, and safe for all participants. Classes may include cardiovascular exercises, such as aerobics or dance; strength training, such as lifting weights; or both. Instructors choose music that is appropriate for their exercise class and create a routine or a set of moves for participants to follow. Some may teach prechoreographed routines that were originally created by fitness companies or other organizations.

Because the skill levels of participants vary greatly, fitness trainers and instructors must offer alternative fitness regimens to accommodate all individuals within the group. They usually demonstrate a particular exercise method or sequence, observe participants in action, and correct any mistakes in order to prevent injury. Fitness trainers and instructors must also treat minor injuries, administer first aid, and refer clients to specialty physicians as needed.

Personal fitness trainers design and carry out workout routines specific to the needs of their clients. They may work with individual clients or teach group classes. In larger facilities, personal trainers often sell their training sessions to gym members. They start by evaluating their clients' current fitness level, personal goals, and skills. Then, they develop personalized training programs for their clients to follow, and they monitor the clients' progress.

Fitness trainers and instructors in smaller facilities often do a variety of tasks in addition to their fitness duties, such as tending the front desk, signing up new members, giving tours of the facility, or supervising the weight-training and cardiovascular equipment areas. Fitness trainers and instructors also may promote their facilities and instruction by various means, such as through social media, by writing newsletters or blog articles, or by creating posters and flyers.

Duties and Responsibilities

- **Demonstrate or explain how to perform various exercises and routines to minimize injuries and improve fitness**
- **Watch clients do exercises to ensure that they are using the correct techniques**
- **Provide alternative exercises during workouts or classes for different levels of fitness and skill**
- **Monitor clients' progress and adapt programs as needed**
- **Explain and enforce safety rules and regulations on sports, recreational activities, and the use of exercise equipment**
- **Give clients information or resources about nutrition, weight control, and lifestyle issues**
- **Give emergency first aid if needed**

OCCUPATION SPECIALTIES

Exercise Physiologists

Exercise physiologists develop, implement, and coordinate exercise programs that promote physical fitness. They may test individual's heart activity, measure body fat and perform blood tests to determine fitness and performance levels.

Personal Fitness Trainers

Personal fitness trainers work with an individual client or a small group. They may train in a gym or in clients' homes. Personal fitness trainers assess the client's level of physical fitness and help them set and reach their fitness goals.

Group Fitness Instructors

Group fitness instructors organize and lead group exercise classes, which can include aerobic exercises, stretching, or muscle conditioning. Some classes are set to music. In these classes, instructors may select the music and choreograph an exercise sequence. They may lead classes that use specific exercise equipment, such as stationary bicycles.

Specialized Fitness Instructors

Specialized fitness instructors teach popular conditioning methods, such as Pilates or yoga. In these classes, instructors show the different moves and positions of the particular method. They also watch students and correct those who are doing the exercises improperly.

Fitness Directors

Fitness directors oversee the fitness-related aspects of a gym or other type of health club. They often handle administrative duties, such as scheduling personal training sessions for clients and creating workout incentive programs. They may select and order fitness equipment for their facility.

WORK ENVIRONMENT

Immediate Physical Environment

Most fitness trainers and instructors work indoors at fitness centers, health clubs, and exercise studios. Others work in hospitals, country clubs, resorts, and clients' homes. Gym environments are generally cool, clean, and well ventilated. Fitness trainers and instructors who lead outdoor fitness classes tend to work in warm weather conditions.

Human Environment

Fitness trainers and instructors mostly interact with their clients, regularly seeing individuals at least once a week and often more. Many are self-employed; however, those who work in fitness or health

Transferable Skills and Abilities

Communication Skills
- Speaking effectively
- Writing concisely

Interpersonal/Social Skills
- Being sensitive to others
- Cooperating with others
- Motivating others
- Providing support to others
- Working as a member of a team

Organization & Management Skills
- Coordinating tasks
- Managing people/groups
- Organizing information or materials

Technical Skills
- Working with your hands

Unclassified Skills
- Being physically active

clubs typically report to fitness directors or gym managers.

Technological Environment

Fitness trainers and instructors commonly use balance boards and discs, exercise balls, fitness weights, pedometers, and first aid kits in their daily activities. In order to track sessions and schedule clientele, they may use accounting, calendar, and project management software.

EDUCATION, TRAINING, AND ADVANCEMENT

High School/Secondary

High school students who are interested in becoming fitness trainers and instructors can prepare by taking courses in sciences such as biology, physiology, and chemistry. They should also study mathematics, business, English, nutrition, psychology, and physical education. Interested students can join school sports teams, participate in local sports leagues, or take individual lessons to learn the fundamentals of physical activity. Aspiring fitness trainers and instructors can gain experience by volunteering or working part time for a private gym, resort, or health club, or the gym of a local hospital, country club, or university.

Suggested High School Subjects

- Applied Math
- Biology
- Business
- Chemistry
- English
- First Aid Training
- Foods & Nutrition
- Health Science Technology
- Mathematics
- Nurse Assisting
- Physics
- Physiology
- Psychology

Related Career Pathways/Majors

Education & Training Cluster

- Teaching/Training Pathway

Hospitality & Tourism Cluster

- Recreation, Amusements & Attractions Pathway

Human Services Cluster

- Consumer Services Pathway
- Family & Community Services Pathway
- Personal Care Services Pathway

Famous First

Jack LaLanne was a fitness, exercise, and nutrition expert. Long before other fitness gurus opened clubs, produced videos, and created lines of fitness equipment and apparel, LaLanne was already famous throughout the country as a result of his fitness show (1953-1985) and his motivational speaking. He is often referred to as the "Godfather of Fitness" and the "First Fitness Superhero."

Postsecondary

After high school, prospective fitness trainers and instructors may pursue various modes of training for their area of desired specialization. They often enroll in classes that will qualify them for professional certification. Once certified, many fitness trainers and instructors work with or shadow an experienced trainer to better understand the practical applications of fitness instruction. After a period of time, new fitness trainers and instructors begin to establish their own clientele. Instructors looking to teach group classes must usually audition to teach at a particular gym or club. Those specializing in a certain method of exercise may need additional training or specialty certification.

A bachelor's degree in physical education, kinesiology, health, or exercise science is becoming increasingly beneficial for new fitness trainers and instructors. In some cases, employers allow fitness trainers and instructors to substitute a postsecondary degree for professional licensure. Those looking to advance to management positions at health clubs or fitness centers should study exercise science, kinesiology, business administration, and accounting at the postgraduate level.

Related College Majors
- Exercise Science/Physiology/Movement Studies
- Health & Physical Education, General
- Parks, Recreation & Leisure Studies
- Physical Education Teaching & Coaching
- Sport & Fitness Administration/Management
- Sports Medicine & Athletic Training

Adult Job Seekers

Fitness trainers and instructors entering the job market should begin by contacting local health centers and other potential employers to determine their various needs. They are expected to be able to fulfill all of the job functions at the time of employment, without the need for on-the-job training. Many fitness trainers and instructors participate in part-time internships, apprenticeships, and job shadowing opportunities with experienced instructors at local health and fitness centers to gain necessary skills before beginning full-time work.

Professional Certification and Licensure

Certification in the fitness field is not always required; however, many employers prefer to hire fitness trainers and instructors who are certified. Candidates must have a high school diploma, maintain cardiopulmonary resuscitation (CPR) certification, and successfully complete an exam comprising both written and practical components related to physiology and exercise programs.

All certification exams have a written part, and some also have a practical part. The exams measure the candidate's knowledge of human physiology, understanding of proper exercise techniques, and ability to assess clients' fitness levels and develop appropriate exercise programs. Many certifying organizations offer study materials to prepare for the exam, including books, webinars, other audio and visual materials, and exam preparation workshops and seminars.

Fitness trainers and instructors must be recertified every two years. Because there are many certifying organizations within the fitness field, candidates should first verify an organization's validity with the National Association for Certifying Agencies.

Additional Requirements

Employers in the fitness industry look for outgoing, dynamic, and confident staff. Communication is one of the most important aspects of the job, so fitness trainers and instructors should be comfortable addressing, leading, and motivating individuals and larger groups. They should also be sensitive to the needs and concerns of their clients while inspiring them to challenge themselves and improve their physical health.

After becoming a certified personal trainer, new trainers typically work alongside an experienced trainer before they are allowed to train clients alone.

Training for specialized fitness instructors can vary greatly. For example, the duration of programs for yoga instructors can range from a few days to more than 2 years. The Yoga Alliance offers several credentials that require a minimum of between 200 and 500 hours, with a specified number of hours in techniques, teaching methods, anatomy, physiology, philosophy, and other areas.

Fun Fact

Trainers have their work cut out for them: 60 percent of New Year's resolution gym memberships are thought to go unused by mid-February.

Source: realbuzz.com

EARNINGS AND ADVANCEMENT

Individuals can advance by locating jobs in more prestigious settings and by obtaining jobs with more responsibilities. Those who continually improve their skills by attending workshops, seminars, training sessions and classes will advance more quickly.

Median annual wages, May 2017

Fitness trainers and aerobics instructors: $39,210

Total, all occupations: $37,690

Other personal care and service workers: $23,480

Note: All Occupations includes all occupations in the U.S. Economy. Source: U.S. Bureau of Labor Statistics, Occupational Employment Statistics

The median annual wage for fitness trainers and instructors was $39,210 in May 2017. The lowest 10 percent earned less than $19,640, and the highest 10 percent earned more than $74,520.

In May 2017, the median annual wages for fitness trainers and instructors in the top industries in which they worked were as follows:

Fitness and recreational sports centers	$41,480
Educational services; state, local, and private	38,010
Government	34,640
Civic and social organizations	32,390

Fitness trainers and instructors may work nights, weekends, or holidays. Some travel to different gyms or to clients' homes to teach classes or conduct personal training sessions. Some group fitness instructors and personal fitness trainers work other full-time jobs and teach fitness classes or conduct personal training sessions part time during evenings or weekends.

Fitness trainers and instructors may receive paid vacations, holidays, and sick days; life and health insurance; and retirement benefits. These are usually paid by the employer.

EMPLOYMENT AND OUTLOOK

Fitness trainers and instructors held about 299,200 jobs nationally in 2016. About ten percent were self-employed, mostly as personal trainers. As businesses, government, and insurance organizations continue to recognize the benefits of health and fitness programs for their employees, incentives to join gyms or other types of health clubs are expected to increase the need for fitness trainers and instructors. For example, some organizations may open their own exercise facilities onsite to promote employee wellness.

Other employment growth will come from the continuing emphasis on exercise to combat obesity and encourage healthier lifestyles for people of all ages. In particular, the baby-boom generation should continue to remain active to help prevent injuries and illnesses associated with aging.

Participation in yoga and Pilates is expected to continue to increase, driven partly by older adults who want low-impact forms of exercise and relief from arthritis and other ailments.

Job prospects should be best for workers with professional certification or increased levels of formal education in health or fitness. Overall opportunities are expected to be good because of the need to replace workers who leave the occupation.

Percent change in employment, Projected 2016-26

Other personal care and service workers: 23%

Fitness trainers and aerobics instructors: 10%

Total, all occupations: 7%

Note: All Occupations includes all occupations in the U.S. Economy. Source: U.S. Bureau of Labor Statistics, Employment Projections program

Related Occupations

This table shows a list of occupations with job duties that are similar to those of fitness trainers and instructors.

Occupation	Job Duties	Entry-Level Education	2017 Median Pay
Physical Therapist Assistants and Aides	Physical therapist assistants, sometimes called PTAs, and physical therapist aides work under the direction and supervision of physical therapists. They help patients who are recovering from injuries and illnesses regain movement and manage pain.	See How to Become One	$46,920
Physical Therapists	Physical therapists, sometimes called PTs, help injured or ill people improve their movement and manage their pain. These therapists are often an important part of the rehabilitation, treatment, and prevention of patients with chronic conditions, illnesses, or injuries.	Doctoral or professional degree	$86,850
Recreation Workers	Recreation workers design and lead activities to help people stay active, improve fitness, and have fun. They work with groups in summer camps, fitness and recreational sports centers, nursing care facilities, nature parks, and other settings. They may lead such activities as arts and crafts, sports, music, dramatics, or games.	High school diploma or equivalent	$24,540
Recreational Therapists	Recreational therapists plan, direct, and coordinate recreation-based treatment programs for people with disabilities, injuries, or illnesses. These therapists use a variety of modalities, including arts and crafts; drama, music, and dance; sports and games; aquatics; and community outings to help maintain or improve a patient's physical, social, and emotional well-being.	Bachelor's degree	$47,680

MORE INFORMATION

American Alliance for Health, Physical Education, Recreation & Dance
1900 Association Drive
Reston, VA 20192-1598
800.213.7193
www.aahperd.org

American Council on Exercise
4851 Paramount Drive
San Diego, CA 92123
888.825.3636
www.acefitness.org

American Fitness Professionals and Associates
1601 Long Beach Boulevard
P.O. Box 214
Ship Bottom, NJ 08008
800.494.7782
www.afpafitness.com

International Fitness Professionals Association
14509 University Point Place
Tampa, FL 33613
www.ifpa-fitness.com

National Board of Fitness Examiners
1650 Margaret Street, Suite 302-342
Jacksonville, FL 32204
www.nbfe.org

National Gym Association
P.O. Box 970579
Coconut Creek, FL 33097
954.344.8410
www.nationalgym.com

National Strength and Conditioning Association
1885 Bob Johnson Drive
Colorado Springs, CO 80906
800.815.6826
nsca@nsca.com
www.nsca.com

Society of State Directors of Health, Physical Educ. & Recreation
1900 Association Drive, Suite 100
Reston, VA 20191-1599
703.390.4599
billdatema@aahperd.org
www.thesociety.org

Briana Nadeau/Editor

Health Coach

OVERVIEW

Sphere of Work

Health coaches work their clients in an ongoing, collaborative manner in order to help improve their lifestyles for the better. They work to educate people so that they can make healthier food choices (like what and when to eat) as well as how to become more physically active. Their work can go well beyond fitness and nutrition to help clients with important behavioral modifications related to stress management, sleep, smoking cessation, and more.

Requirements

There are state or national accrediting organizations currently governing the practice of health coaching, which means that there is no standardized program of education or requirements to become licensed as a health coach. Employer-based requirements can vary widely. Despite the lack of national or state standards, there are several recognized health coaching certifications available for those who are interested in advancing their career.

Education

The majority of employers look for health coaches who have completed at least a bachelor's degree in a health-related subject. A clinical degree in nursing or dietetics may not be mandatory, but some employers do prefer or require those with formal healthcare education to better serve their clients.

Certification

Becoming certified in health coaching shows potential employers you're dedicated and are qualified to perform the duties and tasks they include in their job descriptions. Most organizations granting health coach certifications require you to have a degree, clinical background, or considerable work experience in health & fitness in order to sit for their exam.

The more education, experience, and credentials you have, the better your chances of being hired and earning a higher pay. Previous experience in the healthcare or fitness fields and/or a degree in any health-related subject as well as certification is a good way to improve your opportunities.

In some instances, a having a clinical background matters; you may be required to be a registered nurse (RN) or registered dietitian (RD), yet others require a bachelor's degree in a health-related major and health coach certification to be qualified. If you have a fitness background, but no clinical experience, you may consider offering health coaching services in addition to fitness training.

Work Settings

Most employment opportunities for health coaches fall within the healthcare sector working for health insurance companies, health & wellness solution businesses, physician groups/practices, and occupational health departments of hospitals. It's common for health coaches to be contracted on an hourly basis, although salaried positions do exist.

Those with an entrepreneurial spirit, loyal clients, and a solid network can success on their own with a consulting business, much like some registered dietitians and personal trainers do.

Large companies are also hiring health coaches to help their employees be healthier (and therefore, more productive). The commercial insurance offered to employees often includes health counseling and fitness training. And of course, Medicare and Medicaid programs may also provide work opportunities as a result of offering one-on-one coaching services.

Example of Health Coach Employers

- Insurance Companies
- Aetna
- Blue Cross Blue Shield
- Cigna
- Humana
- UnitedHealth Group
- Health & Wellness Solution Providers
- ActiveHealth Management
- American Specialty Health
- EngagementHealth
- Healthways
- Health Dialog
- Nurtur Health
- Provant Health
- Quantum Health
- WellCall

Digital Health: A New Wave

Digital health management and therapeutics companies are having a noticeable impact on the healthcare industry and those changes are opening up more opportunities for health coaches.

Duties

A large part of what health coaches do involves helping clients to develop healthier lifestyle behaviors, typically centered on weight and stress management plans that involve increased physical activity, proper nutrition, and healthy lifestyle changes. After a survey and review of a client's current behavior, health coaches create personalized goals and action plans to achieve the client's goals, whether it is simply to feel less tired or to become a triathlete. Some of their work can involve helping clients manage chronic conditions such diabetes, heart disease, or gastrointestinal complications like celiac disease, irritable bowel syndrome (IBS) or Crohn's disease. The plans often take advantage of multiple approaches such as dietary changes, exercise, meditation, or yoga.

Health coaches must be accessible to their patients/clients through in-person, phone, text message, and email communications. They may go food shopping with their clients to teach them make healthier food choices. They also may assist them at the gym (if the HC has a fitness background), or hold a collaborative meeting with a personal trainer on how to work with the client in developing a personalized plan, which once developed, the coach will help keep them motivated through ongoing encouragement and goal-tracking.

Salary

As of 2016, the nationwide average salary for health coaches was around $41,000 according to Indeed.com. A search for certified health coach returns a nationwide average salary figure of $68,000. This difference stresses the importance of certification, although it's important to note the greater pay may also involve clinical background or graduate level education requirements and more job responsibilities.

Job Outlook

An increased emphasis on health and wellness has put the focus on individual effort to make appropriate lifestyle changes to promote long term health and well-being. This increased awareness is showing up in workplaces, commercial and non-commercial health insurance organizations. Clinical professionals and the general public have made the role of health coach increasingly important.

While there is no official job growth rate specifically outlined for Health Coaches, the U.S. Bureau of Labor Statistics predicts Health Educators – who share some similar job duties and workplaces – to experience a 16% percent increase in employment opportunities from 2016-2026.

Fun Fact

The health coaching profession, while new, has become so popular that some insurance companies offer reimbursement for the practice, or even hire health coaches to deliver programs to their subscribers.

Source: huffingtonpost.com

Conversation With . . .
SUSAN SPANGLER, OWNER

Pilates Plus Wellness Center
Upper Marlboro, MD
Fitness and Coaching Industry, 25 years

1. What was your individual career path in terms of education/training, entry-level job, or other significant opportunity?

I've always had an interest in health and fitness going back to the Presidential Physical Fitness Awards in grade school. I was the fastest girl and the longest jumper. Phys ed was my absolute favorite thing—that, and, later, business classes. They were easy for me and made me feel good.

I graduated from high school at 16 because I hated it and wanted to work. I went into the U.S. Air Force at 19, ran their weight management program, came out four years later as a staff sergeant, went to work, and realized I could not climb the corporate ladder without a degree. I did corporate training for Digital Equipment Corporation and worked on my undergraduate degree part-time for nine years. I graduated from the University of Maryland with a degree in business management and technology.

Even doing corporate training, where I taught things like time management and presentation skills, I gravitated to health-oriented programs like stress management.

When I got pregnant with my twins, I developed a corporate entity to do corporate training. Part-way through that venture, I started my wellness studio. I had hurt my back and was desperate to get it fixed. Everything I did was fleeting until I found Pilates. I trained in three different Pilates systems. But I found people needed more than Pilates, or massage therapy. They started asking for yoga, so I hired a teacher and took training myself. The spiritual and meditative part of yoga attracted me. During my training, we had a section on foods—using a Vitamix, and healing from disease with various tools and methods. That got me into food, and I went on to get certified as a raw chef.

All of this was driven by my personal life, and what I saw at the studio. I was dealing with sick family members or clients who wanted to lose weight but had horrible diets. A yoga class wasn't enough to help them reach their goals. I'd always been interested in hypnosis, and I knew it helped people change their thinking patterns. So I trained in hypnosis and now I use it all the time when I'm teaching in the studio, or doing outside training with groups such as firefighters, to reinforce new thinking.

I'm also a certified reiki master because I think people's energy can be a big part of their stress and strife.

I underwent my own health problems several years ago, and ended up having surgery that did not correct the problem. To help, I hired a health coach who totally ignited the fire for me to be the best version of myself I could be. I worked with her for a number of years and my health improved.

About a year ago, I began formal training to become an integrated health coach through the Institute for Integrative Nutrition. I'm halfway through the curriculum, certified on the food part, and have clients.

My studio serves a diverse clientele of about 250 people each week and draws from a large area that has limited access to wellness facilities such as mine. Last week, I had a 90-year-old in a trampoline class and also worked with a third grader.

2. What are the most important skills and/or qualities for someone in your profession?

Listening, empathy and compassion are paramount. Business and administrative skills are also critical so that you have structure and organization, as are written and oral communication skills. It's difficult to find a healer who has it all, but you need both skill sets. I've been in customer service for 25 years and it matters to me.

3. What do you wish you had known going into this profession?

I don't feel like I went into this profession; I was led into this profession after my back was hurt. It was like I was getting pulled. I believe there's a lot to be said for understanding what your skills and natural abilities are and figuring out how to make a living from that. So many people hate what they do.

4. Are there many job opportunities in your profession? In what specific areas?

There's nothing but opportunity in the health coaching field. In the future, health coaches are going to be the first line on things like gastrointestinal or skin issues. Potential places of employment include doctor's offices, health clinics, individual practices, or corporations. I have worked with insurance companies to do all kinds of things, from a healthy back program to showing people how to make healthy soups and smoothies. Insurers are interested in preventative health programs.

5. How do you see your profession changing in the next five years as it relates to fitness and/or sports injuries? How will technology impact that change, and what skills will be required?

I think we'll see a focus on bringing the alternative health world together with the science world. Technology has already arrived: I Skype with a client in Canada; you can track what you're eating with an app. There will be more virtual support.

6. What do you enjoy most about your job? What do you enjoy least about your job?

For me, the whole thing is helping people get what they want to become happier and healthier. I least like that it takes a really strong constitution to stay personally balanced. It's not enough to know I need to practice self-care; it's a matter of consistently doing it.

7. Can you suggest a valuable "try this" for students considering a career in your profession?

Have a coaching session with a health coach. Until you've been a student of health coaching, you shouldn't have fantasies of doing it yourself. Also, align yourself with someone who will let you sit in, watch, and observe.

Health Educator & Community Health Worker

Snapshot

Career Cluster(s): Health Science, Science, Education
Interests: Science, mathematics, health and wellness, communication, problem-solving
Earnings (median in 2017): $45,360 per year; $21.81 per hour
Employment & Outlook through 2026: 16% (Much faster than average growth expected)

OVERVIEW

Sphere of Work

Health educators teach people about behaviors that promote wellness. They develop and implement strategies to improve the health of individuals and communities. Community health workers collect data and discuss health concerns with members of specific populations or communities.

Work Environment

Health educators and community health workers work in a variety of settings, including hospitals, nonprofit organizations, government, doctors' offices, private businesses, and colleges.

Most health educators and community health workers work full time. They may need to work nights and weekends to attend programs or meetings.

Profile

Working Conditions: Work indoors
Physical Strength: Light work
Education Needs: Bachelor's Degree, Master's Degree, Doctoral Degree
Licensure/Certification: Required
Opportunities for Experience: Military service, internships, part-time work
Holland Interest Score*: SEC

* See Appendix A

Occupation Interest

People interested in a career as a health educator or community health worker typically enjoy working with, communicating with, and teaching people. These occupations often involve helping or providing service to others. They must also be adept at starting up and carrying out projects. These occupations can involve leading people and making many decisions. Sometimes they require risk taking and often deal with business.

A Day in the Life—Duties and Responsibilities

Health educators teach people about behaviors that promote wellness. They develop and implement strategies to improve the health of individuals and communities. Community health workers provide a link between the community and healthcare professionals. They develop and implement strategies to improve the health of individuals and communities. They collect data and discuss health concerns with members of specific populations or communities. Although the two occupations often work together, responsibilities of health educators and community health workers are distinct.

Health educators, also known as *health education specialists*, have different duties depending on their work setting. Most work in healthcare facilities, colleges, public health departments, nonprofits, and private businesses. People who teach health classes in middle and high schools are considered teachers. For more information, see the profiles on middle school teachers and high school teachers.

The following are descriptions of duties for health educators, by work setting:

In *healthcare facilities*, health educators may work one-on-one with patients or with their families. They may be called *patient navigators* because they help consumers understand their health insurance options and direct people to outside resources, such as support groups or home health agencies. They teach patients about their diagnoses and about any necessary treatments or procedures. They lead hospital efforts in developing and administering surveys to identify major health issues and concerns of the surrounding communities and developing programs to meet those needs. Health educators also help organize health screenings, such as blood pressure checks, and classes on topics such as installing a car seat correctly. They also create programs to train medical staff to interact more effectively with patients.

In *colleges*, health educators create programs and materials on topics that affect young adults, such as smoking and alcohol use. They may train students to be peer educators and supervise the students' delivery of health information in person or through social media. Health educators also advocate for campus wide policies to promote health.

In *public health departments*, health educators administer public health campaigns on topics such as emergency preparedness, immunizations, proper nutrition, or stress management. They develop materials to be used by other public health officials. During emergencies, they may provide safety information to the public and the media. Some health educators work with other professionals to create public policies that support healthy behaviors and environments. They may also oversee grants and grant-funded programs to improve the health of the public. Some participate in statewide and local committees dealing with topics such as aging.

In *nonprofits*, health educators create programs and materials about health issues faced by the community that they serve. They help organizations obtain funding and other resources. They educate policymakers about ways to improve public health and work on securing grant funding for programs to promote health and disease awareness. Many nonprofits focus on a particular disease or audience, so health educators in these organizations limit programs to that specific topic or audience.

In *private businesses*, health educators identify common health problems among employees and create programs to improve health. They work to develop incentives for employees to adopt healthy behaviors, such as losing weight or controlling cholesterol. Health educators recommend changes in the workplace to improve employee health, such as creating smoke-free areas.

Community health workers have an in-depth knowledge of the communities they serve. Within their community, they identify health-related issues, collect data, and discuss health concerns with the people they serve. For example, they may help eligible residents of a neighborhood enroll in programs such as Medicaid or Medicare and explain the benefits that these programs offer. Community health workers address any barriers to care and provide referrals for such needs as food, housing, education, and mental health services.

Community health workers share information with health educators and healthcare providers so that health educators can create new programs or adjust existing programs or events to better suit the needs of the community. Community health workers also advocate for the health needs of community members. In addition, they conduct outreach to engage community residents, assist residents with health system navigation, and to improve care coordination.

Duties and Responsibilities

Health educators typically do the following:

- Assess the health needs of the people and communities they serve
- Develop programs, materials, and events to teach people about health topics
- Teach people how to manage existing health conditions
- Evaluate the effectiveness of programs and educational materials
- Help people find health services or information
- Provide training programs for community health workers or other health professionals
- Supervise staff who implement health education programs
- Collect and analyze data to learn about a particular community and improve programs and services
- Advocate for improved health resources and policies that promote health

Community health workers typically do the following:

- Discuss health concerns with community members
- Educate people about the importance and availability of healthcare services, such as cancer screenings
- Collect data
- Report findings to health educators and other healthcare providers
- Provide informal counseling and social support
- Conduct outreach programs
- Facilitate access to the healthcare services
- Advocate for individual and community needs

WORK ENVIRONMENT

Relevant Skills and Abilities

Analytical skills

- Collect and analyze data
- Evaluate programs
- Determine the needs of the people they serve
- Use databases and other types of software

Instructional skills

- Public speaking
- Lead programs
- Teach classes
- Facilitate discussion with clients and families
- Interpersonal skills
- Good listeners
- Culturally sensitive

Problem-solving skills

- Think creatively
- Improve health education programs

Writing skills

- Develop written materials to convey health-related information
- Write proposals to develop programs
- Apply for funding

Physical Environment

Although most health educators work in offices, they may spend a lot of time away from the office to carry out programs or attend meetings.

Community health workers may spend much of their time in the field, communicating with community members, holding events, and collecting data.

Human Environment

Health educators and community health workers report that the ability to work with work group or team and deal with external customers is extremely important." They also must be able to establish and maintain interpersonal relationships, communicate with persons outside organization including customers, the public, government, and other external sources. They develop formal educational or training programs or classes, and teaching or instructing others and provide information to supervisors, co-workers, and subordinates by telephone, in written form, e-mail, or in person.

Technological Environment

Health educators and community health workers use a variety of tools and technologies including software for data base user interface and queries, graphics or photo imaging, medical, spreadsheet web page creation and editing, social media. They use electronic mail, telephones, digital video disk players or recorders, liquid crystal display projectors, notebook or laptop computers, personal digital assistant PDAs or organizers, and photocopiers.

EDUCATION, TRAINING, AND ADVANCEMENT

Health educators need at least bachelor's degree. Many employers require the Certified Health Education Specialist (CHES) credential. Community health workers typically need to have at least a high school diploma and must complete a brief period of on-the-job training. Some states have certification programs for community health workers.

High School

Community health workers need at least a high school diploma, although some jobs may require some postsecondary education. Education programs may lead to a 1-year certificate or a 2-year associate degree and cover topics such as wellness, ethics, and cultural awareness.

Suggested High School Subjects

- Algebra
- Applied Biology/Chemistry
- Applied Communication
- Applied Math
- Applied Physics
- Biology
- Blueprint Reading
- Chemistry
- College Preparatory
- Composition

- Computer Science
- English
- Geometry
- Mathematics
- Science
- Trigonometry

College/Postsecondary

Health educators need at least a bachelor's degree in health education or health promotion. Students learn theories and methods of health behavior and health education and gain the knowledge and skills they will need to develop health education materials and programs. Most programs include an internship.

Some health educator positions require candidates to have a master's or doctoral degree. Graduate programs are commonly in community health education, school health education, public health education, or health promotion. A variety of undergraduate majors may be acceptable for entry to a master's degree program.

Adult Job Seekers

Adults seeking employment as a health educator or community health worker should have, at minimum, a bachelor's degree in an area related to health, wellness, and community policy. They will benefit from joining professional organizations to help with networking and job searches.

Training

Community health workers typically complete a brief period of on-the-job training. Training often covers core competencies, such as communication or outreach skills, and information about the specific health topics that they will be focusing on. For example, community health workers who work with Alzheimer's patients may learn about how to communicate effectively with patients dealing with dementia.

Licenses, Certifications, and Registrations

Some employers require health educators to obtain the Certified Health Education Specialist (CHES) credential, which is offered by the National Commission for Health Education Credentialing, Inc.

Candidates must pass an exam that is aimed at entry-level health educators who have completed at least a bachelor's degree. To maintain their certification, they must complete 75 hours of continuing education every 5 years. There is also the Master Certified Health Education Specialist (MCHES) credential for health educators with advanced education and experience.

Most states do not require community health workers to obtain certification, however, voluntary certification exists or is being considered or developed in a number of states. Requirements vary but may include completing an approved training program. For more information, contact your state's board of health, nursing, or human services.

Additional Requirements

Community health workers usually have some knowledge of a specific community, culture, medical condition, or disability. The ability to speak a foreign language may be helpful.

Fun Fact

Making healthy eating choices means reconsidering soda intake: one can contains 10 teaspoons of sugar, and the average American adult is estimated to consume about 52 pounds of sugar via soft drinks every year.

Source: dosomething.org

EARNINGS AND ADVANCEMENT

The median annual wage for community health workers was $38,370 in May 2017. The lowest 10 percent earned less than $25,150, and the highest 10 percent earned more than $64,500.

The median annual wage for health educators was $53,940 in May 2017. The lowest 10 percent earned less than $31,440, and the highest 10 percent earned more than $97,160.

In May 2017, the median annual wages for community health workers in the top industries in which they worked were as follows:

Hospitals; state, local, and private	$46,350
Religious, grantmaking, civic, professional, and similar organizations	41,110
Government	40,740
Individual and family services	36,470
Outpatient care centers	35,370

In May 2017, the median annual wages for health educators in the top industries in which they worked were as follows:

Hospitals; state, local, and private	$63,510
Government	55,420
Outpatient care centers	51,130
Religious, grantmaking, civic, professional, and similar organizations	48,640
Individual and family services	40,360

Median annual wages, May 2017

Health educators: $53,940

Health educators and community health workers: $45,360

Counselors, social workers, and other community and social service specialists: $43,860

Community health workers: $38,370

Total, all occupations: $37,690

Note: All Occupations includes all occupations in the U.S. Economy. Source: U.S. Bureau of Labor Statistics, Occupational Employment Statistics

EMPLOYMENT AND OUTLOOK

Overall employment of health educators and community health workers is projected to grow 16 percent from 2016 to 2026, much faster than the average for all occupations. Growth will be driven by efforts to improve health outcomes and to reduce healthcare costs by teaching people healthy behaviors and explaining how to use available healthcare services.

Community health workers held about 57,500 jobs in 2016. The largest employers of community health workers were as follows:

Individual and family services	18%
Government	16
Religious, grantmaking, civic, professional, and similar organizations	14
Hospitals; state, local, and private	10
Outpatient care centers	10

Health educators held about 61,000 jobs in 2016. The largest employers of health educators were as follows:

Hospitals; state, local, and private	23%
Government	22
Religious, grantmaking, civic, professional, and similar organizations	9
Outpatient care centers	8
Individual and family services	7

Overall employment of health educators and community health workers is projected to grow 16 percent from 2016 to 2026, much faster than the average for all occupations. Growth will be driven by efforts to improve health outcomes and to reduce healthcare costs by teaching people healthy behaviors and explaining how to use available healthcare services.

Governments, healthcare providers, social services providers want to find ways to improve the quality of care and health outcomes, while reducing costs. This should increase demand for health educators and community health workers because they teach people how to live healthy lives and how to avoid costly diseases and medical procedures.

Community health workers who have completed a formal education program and those who have experience working with a specific population may have more favorable job prospects. In addition, opportunities may be better for candidates who speak a foreign language and understand the culture of the community that they intend to serve.

Health educators may improve their job prospects by obtaining certification.

Percent change in employment, Projected 2016-26

Community health workers: 18%

Health educators and community health workers: 16%

Counselors, social workers, and other community and social service specialists: 16%

Health educators: 14%

Total, all occupations: 7%

Note: All Occupations includes all occupations in the U.S. Economy. Source: U.S. Bureau of Labor Statistics, Employment Projections program

Related Occupations

This table shows a list of occupations with job duties that are similar to those of health educators and community health workers.

Occupation	Job Duties	Entry-Level Education	2017 Median Pay
Dietitians and Nutritionists	Dietitians and nutritionists are experts in the use of food and nutrition to promote health and manage disease. They advise people on what to eat in order to lead a healthy lifestyle or achieve a specific health-related goal.	Bachelor's degree	$59,410
Epidemiologists	Epidemiologists are public health professionals who investigate patterns and causes of disease and injury in humans. They seek to reduce the risk and occurrence of negative health outcomes through research, community education, and health policy.	Master's degree	$69,660

(Continues on page 133)

Occupation	Job Duties	Entry-Level Education	2017 Median Pay
High School Teachers	High school teachers help prepare students for life after graduation. They teach academic lessons and various skills that students will need to attend college and to enter the job market.	Bachelor's degree	$59,170
Middle School Teachers	Middle school teachers educate students, typically in sixth through eighth grades. They help students build on the fundamentals they learned in elementary school and prepare them for the more difficult curriculum they will face in high school.	Bachelor's degree	$57,720
School and Career Counselors	School counselors help students develop the academic and social skills needed to succeed in school. Career counselors help people choose careers and follow a path to employment.	Master's degree	$55,410
Social and Human Service Assistants	Social and human service assistants provide client services, including support for families, in a wide variety of fields, such as psychology, rehabilitation, and social work. They assist other workers, such as social workers, and they help clients find benefits or community services.	High school diploma or equivalent	$33,120
Social Workers	Social workers help people solve and cope with problems in their everyday lives. Clinical social workers also diagnose and treat mental, behavioral, and emotional issues.	Master's degree	$47,980

(Continues on page 134)

Occupation	Job Duties	Entry-Level Education	2017 Median Pay
Substance Abuse, Behavioral Disorder, and Mental Health Counselors	Substance abuse, behavioral disorder, and mental health counselors advise people who suffer from alcoholism, drug addiction, eating disorders, mental health issues, or other mental or behavioral problems. They provide treatment and support to help clients recover from addiction or modify problem behaviors.	Master's degree	$43,300
Marriage and Family Therapists	Marriage and family therapists help people manage and overcome problems with family and other relationships.	Master's degree	$48,790

Conversation With . . .
KATHIE A. COX, CHES

Public Health Educator II, PIO
Health Department
Scotland County, NC
Health Educator, 19 years

1. What was your individual career path in terms of education/training, entry-level job, or other significant opportunity?

I started college at the University of Southern Mississippi determined to become my family's first female attorney, but wound up going to school part time, working full time, getting married, and moving to rural North Carolina. I went back to a community college and switched my major to psychology, hoping to help people with behavioral and mental health issues. But I landed in public health and community health education after I moved on to the University of North Carolina at Pembroke and met the chair of that department. I was inspired by her. I earned my BS, completed an internship at the local hospital, and was fortunate to find my passion. The hospital hired me right after graduation. I was responsible for employee wellness, grant-funded programs, community health and events—and learned a lot from my supervisor.

After five years, I moved to the county health department. Job responsibilities in public health are quite different from private settings like hospitals because you have to meet certain standards. I wore a number of hats and hit the ground running.

Today, I am responsible for both developing programming and for researching evidence-based programming that I implement and evaluate. A lot of community health and public health involves communicating with the public.

My job is to help improve the public's health by promoting healthy behaviors. I encourage people to make healthy choices through behavioral change and I educate them about how to make informed decisions regarding such things as heat-related illness. For example, do they know the signs and symptoms of the three health-related illnesses—heat stress, exhaustion, and heat stroke? Do they know heat stroke is deadly? We do a lot of information-sharing through media and social media, and we do community events at, say, a church's Community Day.

Professionally, I participate in ongoing continuing education. For instance, I'll complete my Chronic Care Professional Certification this year; it's one of a number of certifications I hold in different specialties.

2. What are the most important skills and/or qualities for someone in your profession?

Communication—language and writing skills—as well as people skills. Some people just don't have that. You need to be passionate, as any good teacher is. You need to show that you are compassionate and have empathy. You need to be able to engage individuals and diverse groups in order to educate them about positive lifestyle changes. People are at different levels where change is concerned. It takes practice and creativity to help people change.

3. What do you wish you had known going into this profession?

The wide range of opportunity. A health educator can work in a number of areas —business and industry, schools, hospitals—and educate in areas ranging from nutrition to diabetes. You often can make very good money, depending on the agency, or your specialty.

4. Are there many job opportunities in your profession? In what specific areas?

Many. Health educators are increasingly employed across business and industry; hospitals; doctors' offices; insurance agencies; and local, state, and federal public health offices. There are different certifications for different specialties. It's important to consider travel and the work setting, as well as the job responsibilities, when you're looking for a job. Most of that is learned through experience and not education.

5. How do you see your profession changing in the next five years as it relates to fitness and/or sports injuries? What role will technology play, and what skills will be required?

Social media is critical to engage younger people, and you've got to have up-to-date computer skills. Prevention will be key to health and fitness. Thinking outside the box to face challenges will continue to be important.

6. What do you enjoy most about your job? What do you enjoy least about your job?

I most enjoy working with people. I'm a talker, I'm a teacher, and encouraging people also encourages me to work on the changes I need to make. A lot of people need support; a buddy system.

I least enjoy all the specific requirements involved in public health that keep me at my desk rather than out in the community. This is not a five-day-a-week; 9-to-5 job. Health educators work weekday evenings, many Saturdays and some Sundays.

7. Can you suggest a valuable "try this" for students considering a career in your profession?

Shadow a health educator, volunteer at a local public health agency or hospital, and get an internship. Internships are important not only to gain hands-on experience, but to determine whether or not a profession is a good "fit."

MORE INFORMATION

For more information about health educators and community health workers, visit:

Society for Public Health Education
10 G Street N.E. Suite 605
Washington, DC 20002
PHONE 202-408-9804
https://www.sophe.org/

American Public Health Association
800 I Street, NW
Washington, DC 20001
202-777-2742
https://www.apha.org/

For more information about the Certified Health Education Specialist (CHES) credential, visit:

National Commission for Health Education Credentialing, Inc.
541 Alta Drive, Suite 303
Whitehall, PA 18052-5642
Phone: (484) 223-0770; (484) 223-0770
Toll-Free: (888) 624-3248; (888) 624-3248
Fax: (800) 813-0727
http://www.nchec.org

Massage Therapist

Snapshot

Career Cluster(s): Health Science
Interests: Anatomy and physiology, biology, anatomy, sports medicine, physical education, psychology, health science technology
Earnings (median in 2017): $39,990 per year; $19.23 per hour
Employment & Outlook through 2026: 26% (Much faster than average growth expected)

OVERVIEW

Sphere of Work

Massage therapists treat clients by using touch to manipulate the muscles and other soft tissues of the body. With their touch, therapists relieve pain, help heal injuries, improve circulation, relieve stress, increase relaxation, and aid in the general wellness of clients.

Massage therapists typically complete a postsecondary education program of 500 or more hours of study and experience, although standards and requirements vary by state or other jurisdictions. Most states regulate massage therapy and require massage therapists to have a license or certification.

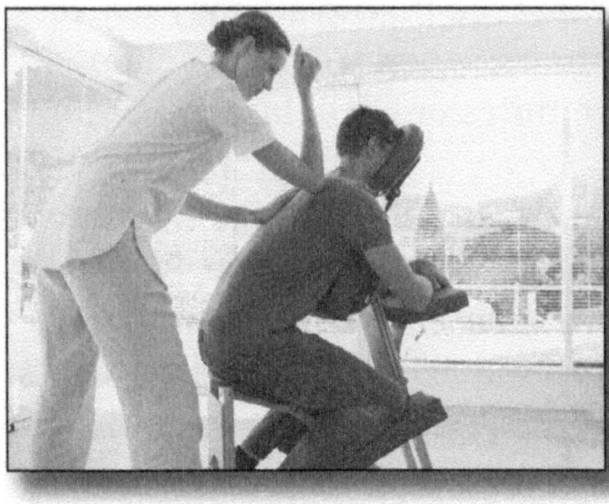

Work Environment

Massage therapists work in an array of settings, such as spas, franchised clinics, physicians' offices, hotels, and fitness centers. Some massage therapists also travel to clients' homes or offices to give a massage.

Profile

Interests: Data, people, things
Working Conditions: Work Inside
Physical Strength: Dynamic strength and manual dexterity
Education Needs: Training in vocational schools, related on-the-job experience, or an associate degree
Licensure/Certification: Required
Physical Abilities Not Required: Not climb
Opportunities for Experience: Internship, part-time work
Holland Interest Score*: SIE

* See Appendix A

Occupation Interest

Individuals attracted to the field of massage therapy tend to be physically strong people who enjoy hands-on work and close interaction with people from diverse backgrounds. Those who excel as massage therapists exhibit traits such as physical stamina, problem solving, empathy, patience, and caring. Massage therapists should enjoy learning, stay knowledgeable about changes in therapeutic techniques, and expect to work as part of a team to effectively address patient needs.

A Day in the Life—Duties and Responsibilities

Massage therapists use touch to treat clients' injuries and to promote the clients' general wellness. They use their hands, fingers, forearms, elbows, and sometimes feet to knead muscles and soft tissues of the body.

Massage therapists may use lotions and oils, and massage tables or chairs, when treating a client. A massage can be as short as 5–10 minutes or could last more than an hour.

Massage therapists talk with clients about what they hope to achieve through massage. They may suggest personalized treatment plans for their clients, including information about additional relaxation techniques to practice between sessions.

Massage therapists can specialize in many different types of massage or modalities. Swedish massage, deep-tissue massage, and sports massage are just a few of the many modalities of massage therapy. Most massage therapists specialize in several modalities, which require different techniques.

The type of massage given typically depends on the client's needs and physical condition. For example, massage therapists may use a special technique for elderly clients that they would not use for athletes. Some forms of massage are given solely to one type of client; for example, prenatal massage is given only to pregnant women.

Duties and Responsibilities

- **Talk with clients about their symptoms, medical history, and desired results**
- **Evaluate clients to locate painful or tense areas of the body**
- **Manipulate muscles and other soft tissues of the body**
- **Provide clients with guidance on stretching, strengthening, overall relaxation, and how to improve their posture**
- **Document clients' conditions and progress**

WORK ENVIRONMENT

Relevant Skills and Abilities

Communication Skills

- Massage therapists need to listen carefully to clients in order to understand what they want to achieve through massage sessions.

Decision-making skills

- Massage therapists must evaluate each client's needs and recommend the best treatment on the basis of that person's needs.

Empathy

- Massage therapists must give clients a positive experience, which requires building trust between therapist and client. Making clients feel comfortable is necessary for therapists to expand their client base.

Integrity

- Massage therapists often have access to client information such as medical histories. Therefore, they must be trustworthy and protect the privacy of their clients.

Physical stamina

- Massage therapists may give several treatments during a workday and have to stay on their feet throughout massage appointments.

Physical Environment

Some massage therapists travel to clients' homes or offices to give a massage. Others work out of their own homes. Many massage therapists, especially those who are self-employed, provide their own table or chair, sheets, pillows, and body lotions or oils.

A massage therapist's working conditions depend heavily on the venue in which the massage is performed and on what the client wants. For example, when giving a massage to help clients relax, massage therapists generally work in dimly lit settings and use candles, incense, and calm, soothing music. In contrast, a massage meant to help rehabilitate a client with an injury may be conducted in a well-lit setting with several other people receiving treatment in the same room.

Because giving a massage is physically demanding, massage therapists can injure themselves if they do not use the proper techniques. Repetitive-motion problems and fatigue from standing for extended periods are most common.

Physical strength and dexterity

- Massage therapists must be strong and able to exert pressure through a variety of movements of the arms and hands when manipulating a client's muscles.

Time-management skills

- Massage therapists must tailor an appointment to a client's specific needs. They must use their appointment time wisely to help each client accomplish his or her goals.

Therapists can limit these risks by using good body mechanics, spacing sessions properly, exercising, and, in many cases, receiving a massage themselves regularly.

Technological Environment

Massage therapists rely on a variety of tools: balance beams or boards or bolsters or rockers for rehabilitation or therapy, full body immersion hydrotherapy baths or tanks, mats or platforms for rehabilitation or therapy, massage chairs or stools; portable massage tables, treatment tables, medical heat lamps or accessories, therapeutic heating or cooling pads or compresses or packs, cupping sets; hot packs; massage stone sets.

EDUCATION, TRAINING, AND ADVANCEMENT

Education requirements for massage therapists vary greatly by state or locality. Education programs are typically found in private or public postsecondary institutions. Most programs require at least 500 hours of study for their completion; some programs require 1,000 or more hours.

Famous First

Archaeological evidence of massage has been found in many ancient civilizations including China, India, Japan, Korea, Egypt, Rome, Greece, and Mesopotamia. The Tomb of Akmanthor (also known as "The Tomb of the Physician") in Saqqara, Egypt, depicts two men having work done on their feet and hands, presumably massage, sometime around 2330 BCE.

College/Post Secondary

A high school diploma or equivalent is usually required for admission to a massage therapy program. Programs generally include both classroom study and hands-on practice of massage techniques. Programs cover subjects such as anatomy; physiology, which is the study of organs and tissues; kinesiology, which is the study of motion and body mechanics; pathology, which is the study of disease; business management; and ethics.

Programs may concentrate on certain modalities, or specialties, of massage. Several programs also offer job placement services and continuing education. Both full-time and part-time programs are available.

Professional Certification and Licensure

In 2016, 45 states and the District of Columbia regulated massage therapy. Although not all states license massage therapy, they may have regulations at the local level.

In states with massage therapy regulations, workers must get a license or certification before practicing massage therapy. State regulations typically require graduation from an approved massage therapy program and passing an exam.

The exam may be a state-specific exam or the Massage and Bodywork Licensing Examination (MBLEx) licensure exam, offered by the Federation of State Massage Therapy Boards.

Massage therapists also may need to pass a background check, have liability insurance, and be certified in cardiopulmonary resuscitation (CPR). Many states require massage therapists to complete continuing education credits and to renew their license periodically. Those wishing to practice massage therapy should look into legal requirements for the state and locality in which they intend to practice.

Fun Fact

The belief in the benefits of massage therapy go way back: Julius Caesar received massages to help treat his epilepsy, and ancient Egyptian tombs feature hieroglyphics of people giving massages.

Source: salterschool.com

EARNINGS AND ADVANCEMENT

The median annual wage for massage therapists was $39,990 in May 2017. The lowest 10 percent earned less than $20,300, and the highest 10 percent earned more than $77,470.

In May 2017, the median annual wages for massage therapists in the top industries in which they worked were as follows:

Offices of chiropractors	$51,240
Offices of all other health practitioners	42,860
Personal care services	38,200
Accommodation	28,050

Most massage therapists earn a combination of wages and tips and may receive free or discounted massages as a benefit.

About half of all massage therapists worked part time in 2016. Because therapists work by appointment in most cases, their schedules and the number of hours worked each week vary considerably. In addition to giving massages, therapists, especially those who are self-employed, may spend time recording clients' notes, marketing, booking clients, washing linens, and conducting other general business tasks.

Median annual wages, May 2017

Massage therapists: $39,990

Total, all occupations: $37,690

Other healthcare support occupations: $33,920

Note: All Occupations includes all occupations in the U.S. Economy. Source: U.S. Bureau of Labor Statistics, Occupational Employment Statistics

EMPLOYMENT AND OUTLOOK

Massage therapists held about 160,300 jobs in 2016. Employment of massage therapists is projected to grow 26 percent from 2016 to 2026, much faster than the average for all occupations. Continued growth in the demand for massage services will lead to new openings for massage therapists.

As more states adopt licensing requirements and standards for massage therapists, the practice of massage is likely to be respected and accepted by more people as a way to treat pain and to improve overall wellness.

Similarly, demand will likely increase as more healthcare providers understand the benefits of massage and these services become part of treatment plans. However, demand in some healthcare settings will be tempered by limited insurance coverage for massage services.

Massage also offers specific benefits to particular groups of people whose continued demand for massage services will lead to overall growth for the occupation. For example, many sports teams hire massage therapists to help their athletes rehabilitate from injuries and to relieve or manage pain.

The number of massage clinic franchises has increased in recent years. Many franchised clinics offer more affordable massages than those provided at spas and resorts, making massage services available to a wider range of customers.

The largest employers of massage therapists were as follows:

Self-employed workers	39%
Personal care services	29
Offices of all other health practitioners	12
Offices of chiropractors	7
Accommodation	6

About half of all massage therapists worked part time in 2016.

Because therapists work by appointment in most cases, their schedules and the number of hours worked each week vary considerably. Moreover, because of the strength and endurance needed to give a massage, many therapists cannot perform massage services 8 hours per day, 5 days per week.

In addition to giving massages, therapists, especially those who are self-employed, may spend time recording clients' notes, marketing, booking clients, washing linens, and conducting other general business tasks.

In states that regulate massage therapy, opportunities should be available to those who complete formal programs and pass a professionally recognized exam. However, new massage therapists should expect that it can take time to build a client base.

Because referrals are an important source of work for massage therapists, marketing and networking may help increase the number of job opportunities. Joining a professional association also can help build strong contacts and further increase the likelihood of steady work. In addition, massage therapists may be able to attract a wider variety of clients by completing education programs in multiple modalities.

Employment Trend, Projected 2016-26

Massage therapists: 26%

Other healthcare support occupations: 22%

Total, all occupations: 7%

Note: All Occupations includes all occupations in the U.S. Economy. Source: U.S. Bureau of Labor Statistics, Employment Projections program

Related Occupations

Occupation	Job Duties	Entry-Level Education	2017 Median Pay
Athletic Trainers	Athletic trainers specialize in preventing, diagnosing, and treating muscle and bone injuries and illnesses.	Bachelor's degree	$46,630
Exercise Physiologists	Exercise physiologists develop fitness and exercise programs that help patients recover from chronic diseases and improve cardiovascular function, body composition, and flexibility.	Bachelor's degree	$49,090
Physical Therapist Assistants and Aides	Physical therapist assistants, sometimes called PTAs, and physical therapist aides work under the direction and supervision of physical therapists. They help patients who are recovering from injuries and illnesses regain movement and manage pain.	High school degree	$46,920
Physical Therapists	Physical therapists, sometimes called PTs, help injured or ill people improve their movement and manage their pain. These therapists are often an important part of the rehabilitation, treatment, and prevention of patients with chronic conditions, illnesses, or injuries.	Doctoral or professional degree	$86,850

Conversation With . . .
JOHN WOOD, LMT

Annapolis, MD
Massage Therapist, 19 years

1. What was your individual career path in terms of education/training, entry-level job, or other significant opportunity?

I worked for the Washington, DC area electric company, Pepco, for over 20 years. More than a decade into my career, I got rear-ended in a car accident. I saw a chiropractor but that only helped a little. I ended up with a recommendation for a massage therapist. That made the difference in terms of my healing, and it made me believe in massage.

The therapist became a friend and mentor. I was curious about the cost and time involved in studying massage, and eventually decided to go for it.

The Potomac Massage Training Institute didn't take me right off the bat. They felt I needed more background and recommended I read more, practice more, and go to a six-week class at the school, which I did. After six weeks I called the registrar and started that fall. I attended twice a week, three hours a night, for a year and a half. Once I graduated, I took a national test to become a "certified massage therapist." At the time, Maryland used that test for licensure although now the state has its own requirements.

I kept my full-time job and did massage two nights a week at a gym. Then a guy I knew at Pepco who was very health conscious—a vegetarian who kept in shape—had a heart attack while cutting his grass and died. That resonated with me. I thought, "In 10 years if I don't do this, will I wonder 'what if?'"

I took a leap of faith. I worked full-time for a few months at a center for massage. I was the only guy and didn't do as well as the women therapists. I think this has changed but I had been told that it would be tougher because I'm a man.

I left and went to work for a chiropractor, which helped me get established. I moved to a wellness center and some clients followed me, while others were referred by people like the center's acupuncturist. It does take time to build a clientele.

Ongoing training to maintain your license is a fact of this career. My niche is clinical/orthopedic work. I take classes on sports massage, orthopedic massage, or classes focusing on just the hip or just the shoulder.

I see people with issues such as tennis elbow or frozen shoulder. A lot of people are sore from working out and massage is part of their recovery. People come in with stiff joints, like a hip or shoulder that needs to be moved, along with the related muscles. I also see a lot of neck issues caused by the forward head posture of computer and smartphone users who spend so much time looking down at their screens.

2. **What are the most important skills and/or qualities for someone in your profession?**

   Listen. Listen to what the client is telling you and you can get an idea of what's going on in their body. I always do a verbal as well as written intake.

3. **What do you wish you had known going into this profession?**

   I wish I had more of a background in business and marketing. I don't think most massage schools prepare you for that.

   Also, state licensing requirements are different. So, from a business standpoint, it's important to check to see what you will need to do every year or two and factor those costs into your earnings. For instance, here in Maryland you might need to think about whether you're better off paying rent for your own space or earning a percentage in an office.

4. **Are there many job opportunities in your profession? In what specific areas?**

   There's always going to be a place for massage. A lot of places, such as massage franchises and fitness centers, are offering massage now. Chiropractors and some physical therapy offices have massage therapists. You can still go out as an independent, rent your own space, and be your own boss. Another option is to be a mobile therapist, carry a table and work with sports teams, or do chair massage in corporate environments.

5. **How do you see your profession changing in the next five years as it relates to fitness and/or sports injuries, how will technology impact that change, and what skills will be required?**

   I see the independent massage therapist becoming a thing of the past, working instead in spas, salons, and wellness centers. Obviously, this will always be a hands-on profession, but there are some technological things—I've seen a robot massager.

6. **What do you enjoy most about your job? What do you enjoy least about your job?**

   I've always enjoyed working with my hands. Being of help to clients who are in need of manual therapy is very satisfying.

Being an independent without a guaranteed income means I have fluctuations. There's a drop-off in the summer when people leave town on weekends and spend money elsewhere.

7. Can you suggest a valuable "try this" for students considering a career in your profession?

Get massages from different therapists. Get in their head; see what they do. Do you think you can replicate that? Talk to them about massage therapy and how they got to be where they are. Serious students must practice, practice, practice—which means you must be prepared to give away massage so you get good at what you do. Every person on the table is going to teach you something.

MORE INFORMATION

For more information about careers in massage therapy, visit:

Associated Bodywork & Massage Professionals
25188 Genesee Trail Road, Suite 200
Golden, CO 80401
expectmore@abmp.com
Phone: 800-458-2267
Fax: 800-667-8260
https://www.abmp.com/

National Certification Board for Therapeutic Massage & Bodywork
1333 Burr Ridge Pkwy #200
Burr Ridge, IL 60527
Phone: (630) 627-8000
https://www.ncbtmb.org

American Massage Therapy Association
500 Davis St #900
Evanston, IL 60201
Phone: (877) 905-0577
https://www.amtamassage.org

For more information about national testing and national certification, visit:

Federation of State Massage Therapy Boards
Massage & Bodywork Licensing Examination (MBLEx) Office
P.O. Box 198748, Nashville, TN 37219
Phone: 866.962.3926 Email: mblex@fsmtb.org
FSMTB Executive Office
7111 West 151st Street, Suite 356, Overland Park, KS 66223
Phone: 913.681.0380 Email: info@fsmtb.org
https://www.fsmtb.org/

For more information about accredited massage therapy programs, visit:

Commission on Massage Therapy Accreditation
2101 Wilson Blvd, Suite 302
Arlington, VA 22201
Phone: 202-888-6790
Fax: 202-888-6787
Email: Info@comta.org
https://comta.org/

Neurologist

Snapshot

Career Cluster(s): Health Science
Interests: Medicine, solving problems, working with sick or injured people, communicating with others
Earnings (median in 2017): equal to or greater than $208,000 per year or $100.00 per hour
Employment & Outlook through 2026: 13% (Faster than average growth expected)

OVERVIEW

Sphere of Work

Neurologists are physicians who specialize in treating patients with neurological disorders. Neurology is a branch of medicine concerned with the human nervous system, which includes the brain, spinal cord, and outlying nerves. Neurologists are highly trained and are able to test, diagnose, and treat patients with a wide variety of neurological disorders. They can prescribe medicine based on results of blood work, x-rays, and other tests. Some neurologists, known as neurosurgeons, specialize in performing related surgeries.

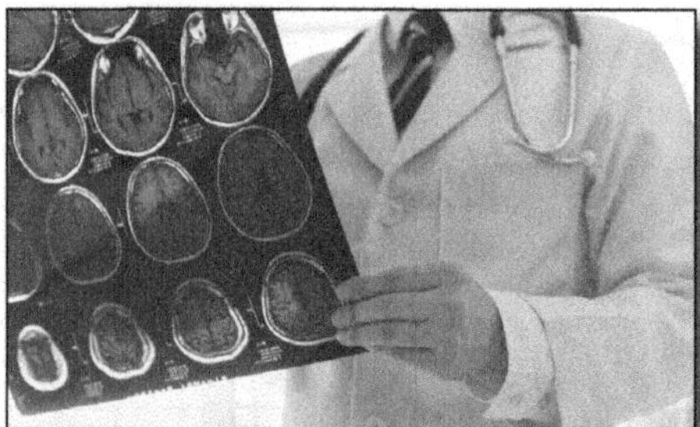

Work Environment

Neurologists work in a variety of inpatient and outpatient medical facilities. Some work out of private offices or clinics, while many others work out of group practices, health care organizations, or hospitals. At larger institutions, neurologists share patients with other physicians and nurses. These facilities are frequently well lit and sterile. Neurologists may be required to stand for extended periods of time and work long and irregular hours.

Profile

Interests: Data, People, Things
Working Conditions: Work Inside
Physical Strength: Light Work
Education Needs: Doctoral Degree
Licensure/Certification: Required
Physical Abilities Not Required: Not Climb
Opportunities for Experience: Military Service, Volunteer Work, Part Time Work
Holland Interest Score*: ISR

* See Appendix A

Occupation Interest

Like many professionals in the medical field, neurologists come from a broad range of medical backgrounds, but the majority of them have made neurology the focus of their education. They need to be very empathetic and understanding, as they must frequently interact with patients who are sick or injured. Neurologists must also be very detail oriented and ensure that their patients are receiving the proper treatment and diagnosis. This also requires excellent problem-solving skills.

A Day in the Life—Duties and Responsibilities

Like other physicians, neurologists are primarily responsible for examining, diagnosing, and treating the injuries or ailments of their patients. While these procedures can lead to similar day-to-day activities, each patient is unique. A neurologist will also record a patient's medical history, prescribe appropriate medications, and perform or order diagnostic tests. These tests may include blood tests, x-rays, and computed axial tomography (CAT) scans. Neurologists also examine patients' reflexes, vision, strength, sensations, and coordination, which are all related to the nervous system. Nurses typically assist in the administration of these tests. Other duties of the profession may include making hospital rounds, filling out paperwork, and teaching, usually at the college level.

Some neurologists specialize in certain areas of the field, such as research, clinical trials, or neurosurgery. All of these specializations require additional training. They can also specialize in diagnosing and treating specific disorders, such as dementia, epilepsy, or insomnia. Neurologists also spend a great amount of time educating their patients and patients' families about appropriate precautions, treatments, and medications. It is common for a neurologist to see a dozen or more patients per day.

Research can also be a part of a neurologist's day. Many neurologists publish articles in medical and scientific journals and present findings of case studies throughout their careers. It is common for neurologists to travel to related conferences to network, present findings, and compare research.

Duties and Responsibilities

- **Examining patients**
- **Diagnosing diseases and conditions of the brain and nervous system**
- **Ordering or performing various tests and procedures**
- **Prescribing and administering medications and treatments**
- **Teaching patients about preventative medicine**

WORK ENVIRONMENT

Transferable Skills and Abilities

Communication Skills
- Speaking effectively
- Writing concisely
- Listening attentively
- Reading well
- Expressing thoughts and ideas

Interpersonal/Social Skills
- Being able to remain calm
- Being able to work independently
- Cooperating with others
- Providing support to others
- Working as a member of a team
- Being sensitive to others
- Being patient
- Having good judgment
- Being objective
- Being objective

Organization & Management Skills
- Handling challenging situations
- Making decisions
- Managing people/groups
- Paying attention to and handling details
- Performing duties which change frequently
- Managing time
- Demonstrating leadership

Research & Planning Skills
- Developing evaluation strategies
- Using logical reasoning
- Identifying problems
- Identifying resources
- Gathering information
- Solving problems
- Analyzing information

Immediate Physical Environment

Neurologists work in health facilities alongside others in the profession. These facilities include hospitals, group practices, health care organizations, clinics, and private practices.

Human Environment

Neurologists work with a variety of professionals as well as patients. They frequently communicate and collaborate with others in the medical field, including other neurologists, surgeons, and researchers. The nature of their work requires them to make physical contact with and be very close to patients with various ailments throughout the day.

Technological Environment

Neurologists use a broad range of tools, from small instruments to large, sophisticated medical apparatuses. Basic instruments include digital thermometers, eye charts, and stethoscopes. To examine a patient's neurological system further, a neurologist may use functional magnetic resonance imaging (MRI), lumbar

Technical Skills
- Performing scientific, mathematical and technical work

Work Environment Skills
- Working in a medical setting

punctures, and electrodiagnostic tests. Neurologists must follow safety procedures when operating medical machinery.

EDUCATION, TRAINING, AND ADVANCEMENT

High School/Secondary

A high school diploma is required in order to enroll in the postsecondary courses required of a neurologist. At the high school level, basic and advanced courses in subjects such as biology, chemistry, and mathematics would greatly benefit an individual interested in pursuing a career in the field.

Suggested High School Subjects
- Algebra
- Biology
- Chemistry
- College Preparatory
- English
- Geometry
- Health Science Technology
- Humanities
- Mathematics
- Physics
- Physiology
- Psychology
- Science
- Sociology
- Statistics
- Trigonometry

Related Career Pathways/Majors

Health Science Cluster

- Therapeutic Services Pathway

Famous First

Edward Flatau published the influential *Atlas of the Human Brain and the Course of the Nerve-Fibres* in 1894 when he was just 26 years old. The book was written in Polish, and then was translated into German, English, French, and Russian by 1896. The atlas was based on long-exposure photographs of fresh brain sections (up to 10 minutes for flat and 30 minutes for uneven surfaces).

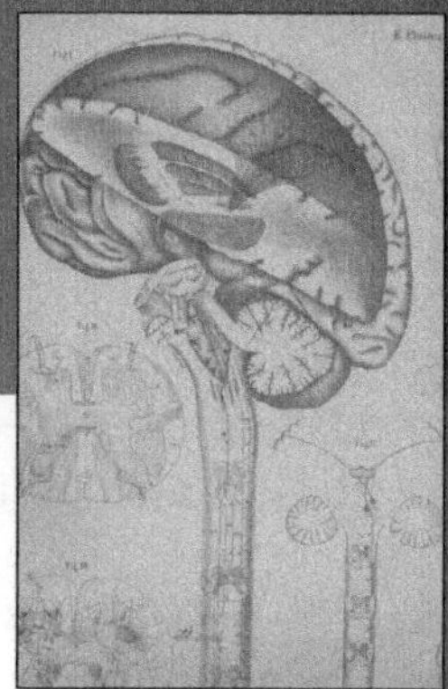

Postsecondary

Neurologists typically complete four years of undergraduate schooling followed by four years of medical school. Depending on a neurologist's specialty, further education may be required. Undergraduates planning to continue on to medical school are typically not required to major in a specific subject, but they should excel in courses such as biology, chemistry, and physics. Undergraduates are also encouraged to volunteer at local hospitals or medical facilities. This is an effective way to gain valuable experience and observe experienced professionals.

To enroll in medical school, an individual must submit transcripts and letters of recommendation and pass the Medical College Admission Test (MCAT). Medical schools are very competitive, so undergraduate students should do their best to excel in all aspects of their education. An applicant will typically have to interview with an admissions board, which will also consider extracurricular activities, volunteer work, and various qualities of the applicant's personality.

The first two years of medical school typically combine instruction in classrooms and laboratories. Courses required for neurologists include anatomy, medical ethics, biochemistry, and, since their work involves the human brain, psychiatry. They are also instructed in necessary skills such as how to record a patient's medical history, examine a patient, and diagnose problems.

For the final two years of medical school, students are given hands-on instruction alongside experienced professionals in hospitals or other medical facilities. Students are observed throughout the examination, diagnosis, and treatments of patients. After completing medical school, students then enter an internship or a residency program, which can last three to eight years. These take place in hospitals or other medical facilities.

Related College Majors

- Anatomy
- Human & Animal Physiology
- Medicine (M.D.)
- Osteopathic Medicine
- Pre-Medicine Studies

Adult Job Seekers

Adult job seekers interested in pursuing careers in neurology should take into account the length and cost of medical school as well as the irregular hours required of many medical professionals. Neurologists usually pursue their careers immediately after leaving high school, so if an adult is considering this profession, he or she is encouraged to contact a local medical school and inquire how to begin the process.

Professional Certification and Licensure

All neurologists must be licensed by the states in which they wish to practice medicine. The requirements for this license vary by state but typically involve taking written and practical exams. After receiving the license, a neurologist can test to become a board-certified doctor in neurology. This can be done through the American Board of Medicinal Specialties, which offers a test incorporating both written and oral sections.

Additional Requirements

Neurologists must be able to communicate with patients and their families compassionately. To examine and diagnose patients accurately, neurologists must be very detail oriented and be good problem solvers. They should also be persistent, as some patients require extra attention, treatment, and monitoring. Neurologists who own their own practices should be very organized.

Fun Fact

Human brains contain more than 100 billion cells, outnumbering the 7.8 billion human beings on the planet.

Source: www.bioexplorer.net

EARNINGS AND ADVANCEMENT

Wages for physicians and surgeons are among the highest of all occupations, with a median wage equal to or greater than $208,000 per year. Median wages showing the differences in pay between types of physicians and surgeons are not available, but mean (average) annual wages for physicians and surgeons in May 2017 were as follows:

Anesthesiologists	$265,990
Surgeons	251,890
Obstetricians and gynecologists	235,240
Psychiatrists	216,090
Physicians and surgeons, all other	211,390
Family and general practitioners	208,560
Internists, general	198,370
Pediatricians, general	187,540

Many physicians and surgeons work long, irregular, and overnight hours. Physicians and surgeons may travel between their offices and hospitals to care for their patients. While on call, a physician may need to address a patient's concerns over the phone or make an emergency visit to a hospital or nursing home.

Neurologists may receive paid vacations, holidays, and sick days; life and health insurance; and retirement benefits. Self-employed neurologists must arrange for their own health insurance and retirement programs. Some employers provide for paid educational leave.

Median annual wages, May 2017

Physicians and surgeons: This wage is equal to or greater than $208,000 per year.

Health diagnosing and treating practitioners: $79,480

Total, all occupations: $37,690

Note: All Occupations includes all occupations in the U.S. Economy. Source: U.S. Bureau of Labor Statistics, Occupational Employment Statistics

EMPLOYMENT AND OUTLOOK

Overall employment of physicians and surgeons is projected to grow 13 percent from 2016 to 2026, faster than the average for all occupations.

The growing and aging population is expected to drive overall growth in the demand for physician services. As the older population grows and rates of chronic illnesses increase, consumers will seek high levels of care that use the latest technologies, diagnostic tests, and therapies.

Demand for physicians and surgeons is expected to increase despite factors that can temper growth. New technologies, such as improved information technologies or remote monitoring, are expected to allow physicians to treat more patients in the same amount of time. If adopted, new technologies can reduce the number of physicians who would be needed to complete the same tasks. In addition, physician assistants and nurse practitioner can do many of the routine duties of physicians and may be used to reduce costs at hospitals and doctor's offices.

Demand for physicians' services is sensitive to changes in healthcare reimbursement policies. Consumers may seek fewer physician services if changes to health coverage result in higher out-of-pocket costs for them.

Job prospects are expected to be very good because almost all graduates of domestic medical schools are matched to residencies (their first jobs as physicians) immediately after graduating.

Prospects should be especially good for physicians who are willing to practice in rural and low-income areas, because these areas tend to have difficulty attracting physicians. Job prospects also should be good for physicians in specialties dealing with health issues that mainly affect aging baby boomers. For example, physicians specializing in cardiology and radiology will be needed because the risks for heart disease and cancer increase as people age

Percent change in employment, Projected 2016-26

Health diagnosing and treating practitioners: 16%

Physicians and surgeons: 13%

Total, all occupations: 7%

Note: All Occupations includes all occupations in the U.S. Economy. Source: U.S. Bureau of Labor Statistics, Employment Projections program

Related Occupations

- Allergist & Immunologist
- Anesthesiologist
- Cardiologist
- Neuropsychologist
- Ophthalmologist
- Pediatrician
- Podiatrist
- Psychiatrist
- Radiologist
- Surgeon

Related Military Occupations

- Physician & Surgeon

Conversation With . . .
NICOLE REAMS, MD

Section Head, Concussion
Associate Director, Sports Concussion Program
NorthShore University HealthSystem
Chicago region, IL
Sports Neurologist, 3 years

1. What was your individual career path in terms of education/training, entry-level job, or other significant opportunity?

I went to college at the University of Notre Dame and double-majored in Science Pre-Professional Studies (pre-med) and psychology, then went on to medical school at St. Louis University. After my internship at the University of Michigan, I did a neurology residency at the University of Michigan, followed by a Sports Neurology Fellowship. I studied under concussion expert Dr. Jeffrey Kutcher and served as team physician for Eastern Michigan University's 19 Division 1 teams.

Today, I am a sports neurologist and serve on the neurology faculty at the Chicago-area NorthShore University HealthSystem and as section head of the system's concussion program. I serve as medical director and concussion specialist for the U.S. Intercollegiate Boxing Association and as a neurologic consultant for the NFL's Chicago Bears, the Chicago Force Women's Tackle Football, the Chicago Blackhawks, and Northwestern University athletics.

2. What are the most important skills and/or qualities for someone in your profession?

An interest in caring for others; patience and compassion; passion for science, exercise, and anatomy; and a passion for returning others to their passions.

Specifically, you need expertise in concussion and neurologic conditions, as well as a unique understanding of exercise physiology, the physical and psychological demands on athletes, and how that affects the neurological care of an athlete.

3. What do you wish you had known going into this profession?

That the road to becoming a physician is very long and can be arduous and expensive. There are other roles in healthcare that one should explore before they commit to an MD/DO track, such as a physician's assistant, nurse practitioner, physical therapist, or occupational therapist. That being said, the autonomy and independence of a physician is unparalleled and very rewarding.

In sports neurology, a large part of my job is media-facing, so obtaining media training and getting comfortable speaking to the media is important. Concussion is a hot topic, so professionals and experts are often interviewed for their perspectives on athletes' injuries or careers, new medical devices, or innovations in the field.

4. **Are there many job opportunities in your profession? In what specific areas?**

Sports neurologists and concussion specialists are highly sought after. There are very few fellowship-trained sports neurologists in the country, which makes those who are very marketable. Fellowship training is rigorous additional training that boosts specialization among the most promising doctors in their field.

5. **How do you see your profession changing in the next five years, how will technology impact that change, and what skills will be required?**

There is tremendous attention to and research in the field of concussion presently. In coming years, there are likely to be new diagnostic modalities for concussion, including imaging and blood biomarkers that will help us confirm both the diagnosis of concussion and when a concussion is resolved to assist in our decision-making for returning an athlete to play. We are hopeful that technology will advance to allow us to learn more about chronic traumatic encephalopathy (CTE) in a living person, so that we can counsel athletes about their risk of continued participation in contact sports.

6. **What do you enjoy most about your job? What do you enjoy least about your job?**

I love working on the sidelines of games and providing coverage for football and boxing events. This allows me to assess athletes immediately at the time of possible injury and make minute-to-minute decisions about their ability to return to play or not. This can be challenging, but is an exciting aspect of my specialty. What I enjoy least is the public's misperception of the negative aspects of concussion and the CTE epidemic. Myself and others in the field work hard to correct the messages that concussion is a death sentence and that every concussion will result in dementia, as well as the belief that we know a lot about CTE. We don't. We have a lot more questions than answers about CTE.

7. **Can you suggest a valuable "try this" for students considering a career in your profession?**

Try shadowing a sports neurologist or someone in a concussion clinic for a day. If possible, shadow a sports medicine doctor who sidelines for football games to see what the experience is like.

MORE INFORMATION

American Academy of Neurology
1080 Montreal Avenue
Saint Paul, MN 55116
800.879.1960
memberservices@aan.com
www.aan.com

American Board of Medical Specialties
222 North LaSalle Street, Suite 1500
Chicago, IL 60601
312.436.2600
www.abms.org

American Medical Association
515 N. State Street
Chicago, IL 60654
800.621.8335
www.ama-assn.org

American Neurological Association
5841 Cedar Lake Road, Suite 204
Minneapolis, MN 55416
952.545.6284
ana@llmsi.com
www.aneuroa.org

Federation of State Medical Boards
400 Fuller Wiser Road, Suite 300
Euless, TX 76039
817.868.4000
www.fsmb.org

Patrick Cooper/Editor

Neuropsychologist

Snapshot

Career Cluster(s): Education & Training, Health Science
Interests: Neurology, psychology, working with sick or injured people
Earnings (median in 2017): $77,030 per year; $37.03 per hour
Employment & Outlook through 2026: 14% (Faster than average growth expected)

OVERVIEW

Sphere of Work

Neuropsychologists are psychologists who diagnose and treat patients with neuropsychological problems. These problems include behavioral and cognitive issues that affect the brain. Neuropsychologists observe and perform tests on patients to properly diagnose issues caused by brain injuries, disorders, or diseases. Common causes of these issues include Parkinson's disease, multiple sclerosis, and strokes. Neuropsychologists use their knowledge and observational ability to find the best way to treat the problem, often working closely with physicians and other medical professionals.

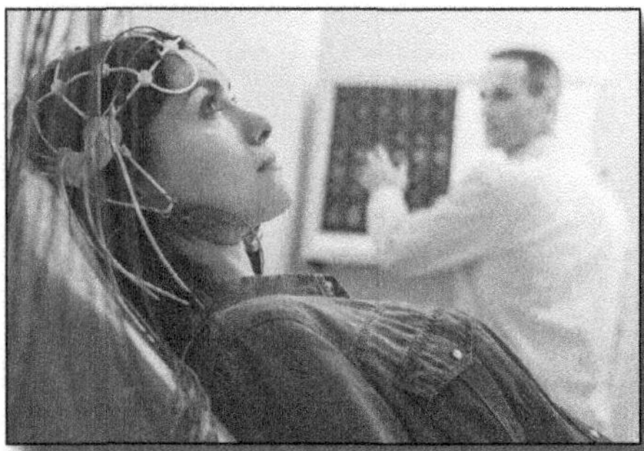

Work Environment

Neuropsychologists can work independently or as part of a health-care facility. Those who work in private practices perform research and normally work strictly with clients and patients. They are able to make their own schedules. Neuropsychologists who work in health-care facilities communicate and collaborate with other medical professionals, physicians, and social workers. Usually neuropsychologists work in an office or a sterile medical environment such as a hospital or rehabilitation center.

Profile

Interests: Data, People
Working Conditions: Work Inside
Physical Strength: Light Work
Education Needs: Doctoral Degree
Licensure/Certification: Required
Physical Abilities Not Required: Not Climb, Not Kneel
Opportunities for Experience: Military Service, Volunteer Work
Holland Interest Score*: ISA

* See Appendix A

Occupation Interest

Neuropsychologists come from a wide range of educational backgrounds, but the majority of them have a degree in some form of neurology or psychology. They need to be very sympathetic and persistent in order to handle patients suffering from a disease, disorder, or injury. Neuropsychologists understand that they will have to continue their education and training throughout their career. They are typically very personable and excellent problem solvers who know how to reach the best possible conclusion.

A Day in the Life—Duties and Responsibilities

Typically, neuropsychologists spend the majority of their day working closely with patients. Their primary responsibilities involve the examination, testing, diagnosing, and treatment of patients suffering from neurological disorders, diseases, or injuries. This process involves similar duties that recur often, but since each patient is different, a neuropsychologist must treat each case as unique. While examining a patient, a neuropsychologist will look at the patient's history and, through observation and assessment, decide what further tests need to be performed.

Neuropsychological tests help neuropsychologists diagnose a patient through a series of specifically designed tasks that measure a particular brain function, such as concentration, language, or memory. Neuropsychologists also use neuroimaging to examine patients. This involves the use of various forms of computer-aided imaging to capture images of the structure and function of a patient's brain.

Neuropsychologists work with a broad range of patients of all ages, including children suffering from an early developmental disability and elderly patients struggling with dementia. If the patient has a neurological disorder, the neuropsychologist works to identify the root of the problem and helps provide psychotherapy, behavior therapy, or other forms of therapy. During therapy and treatment, he or she monitors the patient's progress.

Neuropsychologists should keep up with current literature and research in their field. Many also perform research and publish clinical neuropsychological reports themselves.

Duties and Responsibilities

- **Examining patients**
- **Diagnosing neuropsychological problems, such as cognitive and behavioral disorders**
- **Administering and interpreting psychological tests**
- **Counseling individuals**
- **Conferring with other medical and mental health professionals**

WORK ENVIRONMENT

Transferable Skills and Abilities

Communication Skills
- Speaking effectively
- Writing concisely
- Listening attentively
- Reading well
- Reporting information

Interpersonal/Social Skills
- Being sensitive to others
- Counseling others
- Cooperating with others
- Perceiving others' feelings
- Working as a member of a team
- Being able to work independently
- Being patient
- Being objective

Organization & Management Skills
- Paying attention to and handling details
- Managing time
- Making decisions
- Organizing information or materials
- Performing duties which change frequently

Research & Planning Skills
- Identifying problems
- Gathering information
- Solving problems
- Analyzing information
- Developing evaluation strategies
- Using logical reasoning

Technical Skills
- Performing scientific, mathematical and technical work

Immediate Physical Environment

Neuropsychologists work in either private practices or at other health-care facilities, such as hospitals or rehabilitation centers. These facilities are normally sterile and very well lit. Some parts of the facilities may contain complex medical equipment, while other areas may be a more formal office environment.

Human Environment

Neuropsychologists communicate and collaborate with a wide variety of patients, clients, and other medical professionals, including psychologists, therapists, and physicians. Examining and diagnosing patients requires a neuropsychologist to be in frequent close contact.

Technological Environment

Neuropsychologists utilize an assortment of technologies in their profession. Standardized neurological tests are used to link specific neurocognitive processes. These tests include the Wechsler Adult Intelligence Scale (WAIS), the Halstead-Reitan Neuropsychological Battery, and the Benton Visual Retention Test. Neuropsychologists also use magnetic resonance imaging (MRI) and other computer-aided imaging to scan the brain structure and function of patients. Basic tools such as stethoscopes and digital thermometers are also used.

EDUCATION, TRAINING, AND ADVANCEMENT

High School/Secondary

A high school diploma or an equivalent is required in order to move on to a postsecondary education. High schools normally offer several basic and advanced courses that can benefit a student interested in neuropsychology, such as chemistry, psychology, and biology. Students planning on pursuing a career as a neuropsychologist should do as well as they can on their SAT in order to get into a reputable college.

Suggested High School Subjects

- Algebra
- Applied Biology/Chemistry
- Applied Physics
- Biology
- Chemistry
- College Preparatory
- Composition
- English
- Health Science Technology
- Physics
- Physiology
- Psychology
- Science
- Social Studies
- Sociology
- Statistics

Related Career Pathways/Majors

Education & Training Cluster

- Professional Support Services Pathway

Health Science Cluster

- Therapeutic Services Pathway

Postsecondary

Neuropsychologists are typically required to possess a doctoral degree. Most neuropsychologists receive their undergraduate degree in applied behavior analysis, cognitive psychology, applied psychology, or one of many other related fields. If a neuropsychologist wishes to specialize in a specific field of the profession, further education may be necessary. Many students volunteer at a local health facility or rehabilitation center while completing their undergraduate degree. This is a great way to learn from experienced professionals in the field.

Most master's programs do not require a student's undergraduate degree to be in a psychology-related field. The programs are competitive, however, so students should be sure they have completed some course work in psychology. Master's degree programs typically include courses in research design, applied psychology, and industrial-organizational psychology. Individuals with a master's degree in psychology can work as psychological assistants in clinical, counseling, or research locations.

In order to be accepted in a doctoral program, most schools require an individual to have a master's degree in psychology. Neuropsychologists can get their PhD in psychology or a doctor of psychology (PsyD) degree. Completing a comprehensive exam and an original research dissertation completes the PhD in psychology. In a clinical or health-service setting, students will sometimes have to complete a one-year internship in order to get their PhD. Students going for their PsyD often have to successfully complete comprehensive exams and perform practical work rather than write a dissertation.

Related College Majors

- Clinical Psychology
- Psychology, General

Adult Job Seekers

Those who do not have the necessary education to pursue a career as a neuropsychologist are encouraged to research reputable school in the area. They can seek out professionals in the field and inquire how best to start pursuing their career. Many schools will help individuals find the proper way to begin their education based on what they wish to pursue as a career.

Professional Certification and Licensure

Many states require neuropsychologists to be licensed; these licensing laws vary by state. In order to become licensed, neuropsychologists must typically pass an oral and written examination, demonstrate their professional experience, or have a doctorate in psychology. Other typical requirements include an internship, postdoctoral supervised experience, or a residency program.

The American Board of Professional Psychology offers licensing in a number of areas of psychology, including clinical neuropsychology.

Additional Requirements

Due to the variety of diseases, injuries, and disorders that neurologists can encounter, they must be very empathetic and possess a great understanding of patients' needs. They must also be able to thoroughly communicate to patients and their families the nature of specific ailments. Being able to collaborate with others in the profession is necessary to ensure patients get the appropriate diagnosis and treatment. If a neuropsychologist runs a private practice, he or she should be highly organized.

Fun Fact

Different types of intellect peak at different stages of life. Information processing speed peaks around age 18 or 19, while vocabulary skills peak when people are in their 60s and early 70s.

Source: Association of Psychological Science

EARNINGS AND ADVANCEMENT

The median annual wage for psychologists was $77,030 in May 2017. The lowest 10 percent earned less than $42,330, and the highest 10 percent earned more than $124,520.

Median annual wages for psychologists in May 2017 were as follows:

Psychologists, all other	$97,740
Industrial-organizational psychologists	87,100
Clinical, counseling, and school psychologists	75,090

In May 2017, the median annual wages for psychologists in the top industries in which they worked were as follows:

Government	$94,910
Hospitals; state, local, and private	83,910
Ambulatory healthcare services	77,030
Elementary and secondary schools; state, local, and private	74,470

Psychologists in private practice often set their own hours, and many work part time as independent consultants. They may work evenings or weekends to accommodate clients. Those employed in hospitals or other healthcare facilities also may have evening or weekend shifts. Most psychologists in clinics, government, industry, or schools work full-time schedules during regular business hours.

Median annual wages, May 2017

Psychologists, all other: $97,740

Industrial-organizational psychologists: $87,100

Social scientists and related workers: $76,970

Clinical, counseling, and school psychologists: $75,090

Total, all occupations: $37,690

Note: All Occupations includes all occupations in the U.S. Economy. Source: U.S. Bureau of Labor Statistics, Occupational Employment Statistics

EMPLOYMENT AND OUTLOOK

Employment of clinical, counseling, and school psychologists is projected to grow 14 percent from 2016 to 2026, faster than the average for all occupations. Greater demand for psychological services in schools, hospitals, mental health centers, and social service agencies should drive employment growth.

Demand for clinical and counseling psychologists will increase as people continue to turn to psychologists for help with their problems. Psychologists also will be needed to provide services to an aging population, helping people deal with the mental and physical changes that happen as they grow older. Psychological services will also be needed for veterans suffering from war trauma, for survivors of other trauma, and for individuals with autism.

Employment of school psychologists will continue to grow because of the raised awareness of the connection between mental health and learning and because of the increasing need for mental health services in schools. School psychologists will be needed to work with students, particularly those with special needs, learning disabilities, and behavioral issues. Schools rely on school psychologists to assess and counsel students. In addition, school psychologists will be needed to study how factors both in school and outside of school affect learning. Once aware of those factors, teachers and administrators can use them to improve education. Job opportunities may be limited, however, because employment of school psychologists in public schools and universities is contingent on state and local budgets.

Employment of industrial–organizational psychologists is projected to grow 8 percent from 2016 to 2026, about as fast as the average for all occupations. Organizations will continue to use industrial–organizational psychologists to help select and retain employees, increase organizational productivity and efficiency, and improve office morale.

Competition for jobs for psychologists will vary by specialty and level of education obtained.

Industrial–organizational psychologists are expected to face competition for positions because of the large number of qualified applicants. Industrial–organizational psychologists with extensive training in quantitative research methods may have a competitive edge.

Candidates with a doctoral or education specialist degree and postdoctoral work experience will have the best job opportunities in clinical, counseling, or school psychology positions.

There are expected to be better opportunities for psychologists who specialize in working with the elderly and in rehabilitation psychology.

Percent change in employment, Projected 2016-26

Clinical, counseling, and school psychologists: 14%

Social scientists and related workers: 11%

Psychologists, all other: 11%

Industrial-organizational psychologists: 8%

Total, all occupations: 7%

Note: All Occupations includes all occupations in the U.S. Economy. Source: U.S. Bureau of Labor Statistics, Employment Projections program

Related Occupations

- Neurologist
- Physician
- Psychiatrist
- Psychologist

Related Military Occupations

- Psychologist

Conversation With . . .
ALICIA SUFRINKO

Neuropsychologist/Assistant Professor
University of Pittsburgh Medical Center
Pittsburgh, PA
Neuropsychology, 5 years

1. What was your individual career path in terms of education/training, entry-level job, or other significant opportunity?

I obtained an undergraduate degree in psychology and biological sciences from Marquette University, and my doctorate in clinical health psychology at East Carolina University. I received specialty training in neuropsychology through a predoctoral internship/residency at the University of Florida. After that, I went on to complete a two-year post-doctoral fellowship with the University of Pittsburgh Medical Center (UPMC) Sports Medicine Concussion Program, specializing in sports neuropsychology, which primarily deals with athletes who have sustained sport concussions. I use testing to assess concussions, make treatment recommendations, and determine when it is safe for athletes to return to play. I communicate with athletic trainers, sports medicine doctors, school personnel, and others to coordinate the treatment plan.

My research interests include the role of sleep in recovery from concussion, and identifying risk factors for injury and poor outcomes following concussion.

The path that I took—starting general, then specializing as I got more experience—is the typical progression to become a professional neuropsychologist. The training is very specific, and necessary for licensure and credentialing as a licensed psychologist.

2. What are the most important skills and/or qualities for someone in your profession?

Good listening skills, empathy, and patience. You must be assertive, confident in decision-making, and detail-oriented. It's important to have good research skills, including reading and writing skills, as that is a big part of the job! In addition to seeing patients, most sports neuropsychologists conduct research. Finally, it is important to be a good communicator, as the neuropsychologist is one provider within a team of doctors, athletic trainers, physical therapists, and other healthcare professionals.

3. What do you wish you had known going into this profession?

Unlike other areas of neuropsychology, where patients typically are seen for evaluations to help with diagnoses (think going to the doctor for testing for ADHD or dementia), working with athletes with concussions is different. There's a lot of pressure to get athletes back to play, sometimes before they are fully recovered. It's important to be in control and confident even when athletes and their parents and coaches are in disagreement with your healthcare recommendations and decisions.

4. Are there many job opportunities in your profession? In what specific areas?

My focus is so specialized that there are less job opportunities than for a neuropsychologist who has a more generalized practice. However, the need for concussion management continues to grow and I expect an increase in the need for sports neuropsychologists.

5. How do you see your profession changing in the next five years as it relates to fitness and/or sports injuries? What role will technology play, and what skills will be required?

As research continues to develop new tests and tools to measure concussion impairments, we are always learning and adopting new technology. In the future, specialized brain imaging and other new technology may influence our decisions on when an athlete is ready to return to play following a concussion.

6. What do you enjoy most about your job? What do you enjoy least about your job?

I love seeing the excitement of athletes getting cleared from their concussion and getting back to their sport and passion, as well as having their normal social life back. At the same time, I do not enjoy having to deliver the opposite news. I am often the bearer of bad news when an athlete has to miss a big competition, social event, or school due to the injury. Working with people who have injuries that are causing them significant pain and interfering with their life can get emotionally exhausting. Therefore, it's important for the sport neuropsychologist to have his or her own form of stress relief or stress management to deal with the job.

7. Can you suggest a valuable "try this" for students considering a career in your profession?

Try to shadow a neuropsychologist for a day. Also, there are a few qualities or traits that are important to possess to be a successful professional psychologist. Are you the type who likes to truly listen to other people when they're stressed and have an issue? Try talking to a friend who's having a problem. Are you patient? Do you enjoy helping them problem solve or cope with the stress? If the answer is no, then you most likely will not like being any type of psychologist.

MORE INFORMATION

American Board of Clinical Neuropsychology
Dept. of Psychiatry (F6248, MCHC-6)
University of Michigan
1500 E. Medical Center Drive
SPC 5295
Ann Arbor, MI 48109-5295
734.936.8269
linas@umich.edu
www.theabcn.org

American Board of Professional Psychology
600 Market Street, Suite 300
Chapel Hill, NC 27516
919.537.8031
office@abpp.org
www.abpp.org

American Psychological Association
750 First Street NE
Washington, DC 20002-4242
800.374.2721
www.apa.org

National Academy of Neuropsychology
7555 East Hampden Avenue
Suite 525
Denver, CO 80231
303.691.3694
www.nanonline.org

Patrick Cooper/Editor

Orthotist & Prosthetist

Snapshot

Career Cluster(s): Health Science, Manufacturing
Interests: Science, anatomy, applied technology, biomechanics, medical appliances
Earnings (median in 2017): $66,240 per year; $31.85 per hour
Employment & Outlook through 2026: 22% (Much faster than average growth expected)

OVERVIEW

Sphere of Work

Orthotists and prosthetists are health care professionals who treat patients by developing, crafting, producing, fitting, maintaining, repairing, and servicing orthotic and prosthetic devices. Orthotists and prosthetists help optimize movement and increase independence for individuals who have lost part or all of a limb due to birth defects, accidents, or disease. They assess patient conditions, design treatment devices, and evaluate treatment efficacy. They may follow prescriptions from medical professionals, such as podiatrists, orthopedic surgeons, occupational therapists, and rehabilitation specialists, when fabricating

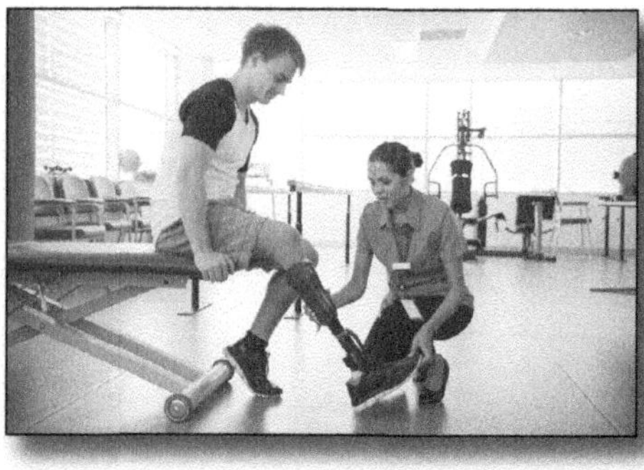

medical braces, arch supports, splints, stabilizers, joints, and artificial arms, hands, legs, and feet.

Work Environment

Orthotists and prosthetists spend their workdays in hospitals, doctors' offices, rehabilitation facilities, medical technology businesses, educational facilities, and independent medical laboratories. These settings tend to be clean and well ventilated. Human interaction in medical labs tends to be limited to communication with laboratory staff, doctors, and patients. Orthotists and prosthetists generally work forty-hour weeks or more.

Profile

Interests: Data, People, Things
Working Conditions: Work Inside
Physical Strength: Medium Work
Education Needs: Bachelor's Degree
Licensure/Certification: Required
Physical Abilities Not Required: Not Climb
Opportunities for Experience: Internship, Apprenticeship, Military Service, Volunteer Work, Part Time Work
Holland Interest Score*: RSE

* See Appendix A

Occupation Interest

Individuals drawn to the professions of orthotist and prosthetist tend to be intelligent and detail oriented. Successful orthotists and prosthetists possess strong hand-eye coordination and focus, problem-solving skills, mechanical aptitude, and concern for others. Orthotists and prosthetists should enjoy spending time in laboratory settings and have a strong background in science and machine fabrication.

A Day in the Life—Duties and Responsibilities

The orthotist's or prosthetist's specialty area and work environment determine the individual's daily occupational duties and responsibilities. Specialty areas in orthotics and prosthetics include pediatrics, geriatrics, and sports.

The fabrication of orthoses and prostheses involves multiple steps and patient appointments. Orthotists and prosthetists do initial measuring and casting on patients. Additional appointments are required for patient fittings, patient instruction, and device maintenance and repair. Orthotists and prosthetists use patient feedback to achieve optimum comfort and flexibility.

Orthotists and prosthetists make an initial plaster cast or digital impression of the effected limb or body area and then use thermoplastics, carbon fiber, and acrylic and epoxy resins to fabricate a brace or limb. Once the brace or artificial limb is made, the orthotists and prosthetists use tools to grind, polish, buff, and finish the piece. The brace or limb is covered with a soft material, such as leather or felt, to create a barrier between human skin and the artificial limb. Dyes and coverings are used in some instances to give the orthoses and prostheses a lifelike appearance. Orthotists and prosthetists test all fabricated limbs and braces for stability and proper alignment. When necessary, they also service and repair orthoses and prostheses.

In addition, all orthotists and prosthetists are responsible for routine set up, calibration, and sterilization of all laboratory equipment and materials. Orthotists and prosthetists also discuss patient progress and goals with patient care teams.

Duties and Responsibilities

- **Consulting with physicians, surgeons and occupational or physical therapists**
- **Measuring patients**
- **Planning devices, including materials and tools**
- **Making casts and models**
- **Fitting and aligning orthotic and prosthetic devices**
- **Modifying, maintaining, and repairing devices**

OCCUPATION SPECIALTIES

Orthotics Assistants

Orthotics assistants help orthotists make and fit orthopedic braces for patients with disabling conditions of limb and spine by making casts, measurements, models, and layouts; performing fitting and alignments; evaluating fit, function, appearance, and workmanship of orthoses; and repairing and maintaining orthoses.

Prosthetics Assistants

Prosthetics assistants help prosthetists make and fit prostheses for patients with partial or total absence of limbs by making cast measurements and model modifications; performing fitting and alignments; evaluating fit, function, appearance, and workmanship of prostheses; and repairing and maintaining prostheses.

Orthotics Technicians

Orthotics technicians make, fit, repair, and maintain orthoses under the direction of an orthotist or orthotics assistant.

Prosthetics Technicians

Prosthetics technicians make, fit, maintain and repair prostheses under the direction of a prosthetist or prosthetics assistant.

WORK ENVIRONMENT

Transferable Skills and Abilities

Interpersonal/Social Skills
- Cooperating with others
- Working as a member of a team

Organization & Management Skills
- Coordinating tasks
- Making decisions
- Managing people/groups
- Paying attention to and handling details
- Performing duties which change frequently

Research & Planning Skills
- Developing evaluation strategies

Technical Skills
- Performing scientific, mathematical and technical work
- Working with machines, tools or other objects
- Working with your hands

Immediate Physical Environment

The immediate physical environment of orthotists and prosthetists vary based on their employer and specialization. Orthotists and prosthetists spend their workdays in laboratory settings located in hospitals, doctors' offices, medical businesses, educational facilities, and independent medical laboratories.

Orthotists and prosthetists are at higher than average risk for such job-related injuries as eyestrain, backache, and machine accidents. Their work frequently requires them to wear protective gear.

Human Environment

Orthotists and prosthetists should be comfortable meeting with laboratory staff, physicians, and patients. Orthotists and prosthetists are often a key part of patient care teams that consist of podiatrists, orthopedic surgeons, occupational therapists, and rehabilitation specialists.

Technological Environment

Tools used to construct orthoses and prostheses include drills, hammers, anvils, and saws. Materials used in the fabrication of orthoses and prostheses include wood, metal, fabric and leather, plastics and thermoplastics, lamination, plaster, carbon fiber, and acrylic and epoxy resins. Some orthotists and prosthetists may need additional knowledge of computerized systems as more advanced prosthetic devices require electronic input to function.

EDUCATION, TRAINING, AND ADVANCEMENT

High School/Secondary

High school students interested in pursuing a career as an orthotist and prosthetist should prepare themselves by developing good study habits. High school-level study of biology, chemistry, anatomy, and mathematics can provide a strong foundation for college-level work in the field. Courses in art, draft, technology, and metalworking can also build necessary skills for work with orthotics and prosthetics. High school students interested in this career path may benefit from seeking internships or part-time work that exposes the students to laboratory and medical settings and procedures.

Suggested High School Subjects

- Applied Biology/Chemistry
- Applied Math
- Applied Physics
- College Preparatory
- English
- Science
- Welding

Related Career Pathways/Majors

Health Science Cluster

- Support Services Pathway

Manufacturing Cluster

- Production Pathway

Famous First

The Cairo Toe or the Greville Chester Great Toe is believed to be around 3,000 years old and the earliest example of a functioning, practical prosthesis. Studies of the toe have revealed that it was carefully fitted to the owner, most likely the daughter of an Egyptian priest.

Postsecondary

Postsecondary students interested in becoming orthotists and prosthetists should work towards a bachelor's or master's degree in prosthetics, orthotics, clinical sciences, applied technology, or a related field. Coursework in biomechanics, biology, kinesiology, anatomy, and mathematics may also prove useful in their future work. Postsecondary students can gain work experience and potential advantage in their future job searches by securing internships or part-time employment in laboratory and medical settings.

Related College Majors

- Anatomy
- Exercise Science/Physiology/Movement Studies
- Orthotics & Prosthetics

Adult Job Seekers

Adults seeking employment as an orthotist and prosthetist should have at least completed an undergraduate degree and one year of training in a prosthetics or orthotics residency or internship program. Many medical appliance technicians and assistants eventually become orthotists and prosthetists. Adult job seekers should educate themselves about the educational and professional license requirements of their home states and the organizations where they seek employment.

Adult job seekers may benefit from joining professional associations to help with networking and job searching. Professional medical associations, such as the American Academy of Orthotists &

Prosthetists and the American Orthotic & Prosthetic Association, generally offer career workshops and maintain lists and forums of available jobs.

Professional Certification and Licensure

Orthotists and prosthetists are typically required to be certified and licensed as a condition of employment. The American Board for Certification in Orthotics and Prosthetics offers certifications for orthotists and prosthetists. Candidates may earn the Certified Prosthetist (CP), Certified Orthotist (CO), or Certified Orthotist/Prosthetist (CPO) designation by completing accredited training programs and passing national exams. These exams require test takers to demonstrate their knowledge through hands-on, practical evaluations as well as written comprehension and problem-solving sections.

At the state level, certification and licensing requirements for orthotists and prosthetists vary. Specific state-level certification and licensing requirement information should be sought directly from state departments of health. In general, state-level certification for orthotists and prosthetists requires successfully completing both a national exam and a bachelor's degree in orthotics and prosthetics as well as engaging in ongoing professional development.

Additional Requirements

Individuals who find satisfaction, success, and job security as orthotists and prosthetists will be knowledgeable about the profession's requirements, responsibilities, and opportunities. Orthotists and prosthetists must have integrity and professional ethics as professionals in this role have access to private medical information and are responsible for their patients' safety. Membership in professional medical associations is encouraged among all orthotists and prosthetists as a means of building status in the professional community and networking.

Fun Fact

3D printing is bringing prosthetic care to millions of people around the world who previously had none. It was also good news for Millie, a greyhound in Australia, whose owners 3D printed a paw for her.

Source: www.autodesk.com

EARNINGS AND ADVANCEMENT

The median annual wage for orthotists and prosthetists was $66,240 in May 2017. The lowest 10 percent earned less than $36,050, and the highest 10 percent earned more than $104,900.

In May 2017, the median annual wages for orthotists and prosthetists in the top industries in which they worked were as follows:

Medical equipment and supplies manufacturing	$70,240
Federal government, excluding postal service	68,440
Health and personal care stores	66,190
Ambulatory healthcare services	64,430
Hospitals; state, local, and private	57,470

Most orthotists and prosthetists work full time.

Orthotists and prosthetists may receive paid vacations, holidays, and sick days; life and health insurance; and retirement benefits. These are usually paid by the employer.

Median annual wages, May 2017

Orthotists and prosthetists: $66,240

Health technologists and technicians: $43,590

Total, all occupations: $37,690

Note: All Occupations includes all occupations in the U.S. Economy. Source: U.S. Bureau of Labor Statistics, Occupational Employment Statistics

EMPLOYMENT AND OUTLOOK

Nationally, there were about 7,800 orthotists and prosthetists employed in 2016. Employment of orthotists and prosthetists is projected to grow 22 percent from 2016 to 2026, much faster than the average for all occupations. However, because it is a small occupation, the fast growth will result in only about 1,700 new jobs over the 10-year period.

The large baby-boom population is aging, and orthotists and prosthetists will be needed because both diabetes and cardiovascular disease, two leading causes of limb loss, are more common among older people. In addition, older people will continue to need other devices designed and fitted by orthotists and prosthetists, such as braces and orthopedic footwear.

Advances in technology are allowing more people to survive traumatic events. Patients with traumatic injuries, such as some veterans, will continue to need orthotists and prosthetists to create devices that allow the patients to regain or improve mobility and functionality.

Job prospects should be best for orthotists and prosthetists with professional certification. Although it is not required in all states, certification shows a specific level of educational knowledge and training that employers may prefer.

Percent change in employment, Projected 2016-26

Orthotists and prosthetists: 22%

Health technologists and technicians: 14%

Total, all occupations: 7%

Note: All Occupations includes all occupations in the U.S. Economy. Source: U.S. Bureau of Labor Statistics, Employment Projections program

Related Occupations
- Physical Therapist

Related Military Occupations
- Medical Care Technician

Conversation With . . .
PHILLIP HESS

Certified Orthotist/Board Eligible Prosthetist
Ability Prosthetics and Orthotics
York, PA
Orthotist/Prosthetist, 2 years

1. What was your individual career path in terms of education/training, entry-level job, or other significant opportunity?

I lost my leg in a boating accident at age 8 and I've known that this was what I wanted to do since I was 10. I wanted to help individuals who had gone through a similar experience.

I received my bachelor's degree from Penn State University, where I majored in kinesiology. Most people entering this field study either kinesiology or exercise science as an undergraduate. After completing my bachelor's, I pursued a Master of Science in prosthetics and orthotics from California State University, Dominguez Hills. After completing the degree, you're required to do additional field education, which is called a residency. During my 18-month residency, I focused on both orthotics and prosthetics. I did my residency here at Ability Prosthetics and Orthotics and they offered me a full-time job.

2. What are the most important skills and/or qualities for someone in your profession?

You have to be able to communicate with patients, doctors, fabricators, and other staff—and be able to do it effectively. You have to be patient. Some individuals that you're treating have just had a life-altering event and you may have to explain something two or three times in different ways before they grasp the concept.

3. What do you wish you had known going into this profession?

I wish I had known that talking to people and building relationships was a large part of the job. Prior to entering the field, I thought that the patients just showed up at the office and you made a device. I didn't think about the work required to get doctors to refer patients to you, or about building relationships with them. From patients to therapists to doctors, the people you interact with every day can have a great impact on how successful you will be.

4. Are there many job opportunities in your profession? In what specific areas?

There's a great need for individuals in the field across the country. Only 13 schools offer a master's degree in orthotics and prosthetics. That limited number of schools produces only about 500 individuals a year who are qualified to do this work. There's a deficit, so prosthetists and orthotists are in demand.

5. How do you see your profession changing in the next five years as it relates to fitness and/or sports injuries? What role will technology play, and what skills will be required?

The profession will likely go a route similar to physical therapy, in that assistants will be more prevalent. Currently, a Certified Prosthetist/Orthotist (CPO) sees most of the patients. However, once prosthetist/orthotist assistants become more available, they will likely do patient follow ups, whereas the CPOs will do evaluations and deal with more complicated patients. Assistants must have a bachelor's degree and must have taken courses in human anatomy, physics, and medical terminology.

Technology is always changing the field, as new high-tech devices become available. Microprocessor knees and feet that provide powered motion to patients who have lost a limb are becoming more prevalent. Same thing with powered exoskeletons, a similar device that provides powered motion to someone who has had a spinal cord injury or a stroke.

Typically, most of our involvement with sports injuries is providing bracing for those who have torn an ACL. We also help Paralympic athletes with prostheses and braces.

6. What do you enjoy most about your job? What do you enjoy least about your job?

I enjoy being able to make a difference for people on a daily basis. Patients who come to me are usually somehow debilitated. They may have had an amputation, or a stroke. We're providing them with a device that allows them to get back up and moving, doing everyday activities that they haven't been able to do in quite some time.

My least favorite part of the job is dealing with insurance and paperwork. Insurance companies limit what devices can be provided to the patients, which sometimes leads to sub-optimal outcomes.

7. Can you suggest a valuable "try this" for students considering a career in your profession?

Find a local orthotics and prosthetics facility and job shadow. I think that's the best way to find out about the field and see what it's like on a day-to day-basis. Most places that I've been to are very open to letting interested individuals check things out.

MORE INFORMATION

American Academy of Orthotists & Prosthetists
1331 H Street NW, Suite 501
Washington, DC 20005
202.380.3663
cblondes@oandp.org
www.oandp.org

Offers scholarships for students majoring in orthotics and prosthetics: www.oandp.org/education/professional_development/scholarships.asp

American Board for Certification in Orthotics, Prosthetics & Pedorthics, Inc.
330 John Carlyle Street, Suite 210
Alexandria, VA 22314
703.836.7114
info@abcop.org
www.abcop.org

American Orthotic Prosthetic Association
330 John Carlyle Street, Suite 200
Alexandria, VA 22314
571.431.0876
info@aopanet.org
www.aopanet.org

Simone Isadora Flynn/Editor

Personal Trainer

Snapshot

Career Cluster(s): Education & Training, Hospitality & Tourism, Human Services
Interests: Exercise, being active, motivating others
Earnings (median in 2017): $39,210 per year; $18.85 per hour
Employment & Outlook through 2026: 10% (Faster than average growth expected)

OVERVIEW

Sphere of Work

Personal trainers design, organize, and lead exercise and sports programs that allow individuals to improve their health through cardiovascular activity, strength training, and stretching exercises. They usually offer private lessons as well as group instruction. They teach the fundamentals of fitness by presenting clients with various techniques, helping them set individually tailored fitness goals, and motivating them physically and mentally to reach those goals. Personal trainers often focus on multiple areas of fitness, such as aerobics, weight lifting, yoga, or Pilates.

Work Environment

Personal trainers work in a variety of settings, from health clubs and exercise studios to resorts and universities. Some travel to clients' homes to provide regular instruction, while others organize fitness programs for large businesses. The majority of Personal trainers work indoors in cool climates; however, some offer instruction in pleasant outdoor environments. Most personal trainers work full time with irregular hours, as they must cater to the schedules of their clients. They often work early in the morning, at night, on weekends, and during holidays. Personal trainers spend most of their time standing, walking, and participating in physical activities.

Profile

Interests: People, Things
Working Conditions: Work Inside, Work Outside, Work Both Inside and Outside
Physical Strength: Medium Work
Education Needs: Bachelor's Degree
Licensure/Certification: Recommended
Physical Abilities Not Required: Not Climb
Opportunities for Experience: Internship, Volunteer Work
Holland Interest Score*: ESR

* See Appendix A

Occupation Interest

Those looking to become personal trainers must be in excellent physical condition and have natural athletic ability. They should have a passion for instructing and motivating individuals. Sometimes clients are reluctant or unwilling to participate in specified activities, so personal trainers should be firm, persuasive, and encouraging. Creativity and patience are also valuable traits. Personal trainers must have strong customer service skills in order to find and maintain their clientele.

A Day in the Life—Duties and Responsibilities

A personal trainer works one-on-one with a client to create and follow a fitness training plan that is customized to the client's specific goal(s): strength training, weight loss, improved performance, disease management, or enhanced health. Trainers introduce individualized exercise plans and should always keep current with the latest trends and professional recommendations in fitness and nutrition.

Professional personal trainers have a national certification coupled with advanced knowledge of human anatomy and physiology, nutrition and exercise science. They create and lead individual and group exercise sessions tailored to the health needs of their clients. Fitness trainers conduct client assessments to develop these plans, help establish healthy nutritional behaviors and motivate their clients to succeed.

EDUCATION, TRAINING, AND ADVANCEMENT

High School/Secondary

Most national certification bodies require candidates to have a high school diploma or equivalent to sit for a certifying examination. Although postsecondary education, in the form of a certificate, training course or formal degree is highly recommended, completing the minimum educational requirement is important.

Vocational and technical schools typically offer either short-term personal training programs or courses that focus on a specific personal training certification program, such as the Certified Personal Trainer (CPT) examination from the National Academy of Sports Medicine. Vocational programs are career-focused, allowing students to concentrate their studies in an area of interest (e.g. aerobics), without completing the requirements for an entire degree.

Postsecondary

Community college programs are designed to be short, professionally oriented instruction that prepares graduates for direct entry into a career field. Community college students may select from several types of training, including stand-alone certificate programs, personal training programs, and formal associate degree programs in majors such as exercise science, kinesiology, and personal training. The goal of each of these programs is to prepare graduates for national certification examinations.

Four-year universities and colleges offer undergraduate (bachelor's) and graduate (master's/PhD) programs for individuals interested in expanding their knowledge of personal fitness, wellness, and health. These programs are much broader in scope, with curriculum that covers both general education and courses in specialized fields, such as exercise science.

Professional Certification and Licensure

Prospective trainers can select a specialization that matches their skill sets, personal interests, and professional goals such as the following: group exercise, individualized personal training, fitness programming. Once you decide on your path, you should review various fitness certifying bodies and the fitness certifications they offer to find the program that makes the most sense to prepare you for the career you envision for yourself.

Once you have determined the certification that is best for you, whether Certified Personal Trainer from the American Council on Exercise or National Academy of Sports Medicine, you can start to prepare for the certification examination by taking exam prep courses, multi-session training classes, undergraduate degrees in exercise science, or even graduate degrees in kinesiology.

Personal training courses are offered directly by certifying bodies, such as the American College of Sports Medicine. These live clinics last one to three days in length, serving as exam preparation workshops that include lectures and practical instruction from experienced and certified trainers. At the conclusion, graduates are prepared to take national certification examinations.

Personal trainers must be ready to deal with physical emergencies when working with clients and should complete cardiopulmonary resuscitation (CPR) and automated external defibrillator (AED) certification programs to be ready for them. These programs teach trainers how to recognize a medical emergency, deal appropriately with cardiac or breathing emergencies, and act swiftly to help a client until professional first responders arrive. AED and CPR certifications are required by nearly every national personal training certification organization.

You should register for the selected certification examination, which typically includes an application and fee. Most personal training certifications are computer-based tests that include between 120 and 150 multiple-choice questions. For example, the Certified Personal Trainer Certification from the National Academy of Sports Medicine has questions across four sections: Program Planning; Client Consultation and Fitness Assessment; Exercise Techniques; and Safety/Emergency Issues.

The National Commission for Certifying Agencies (NCCA) is the primary accrediting body for personal training certifications. Individuals interested in personal trainer careers should ensure they select accredited programs as most employers prefer accredited candidates. The four major certifying bodies include the following:

- American College of Sports Medicine
- National Academy of Sports Medicine
- American Council on Exercise
- National Strength and Conditioning Association

EARNINGS AND ADVANCEMENT

Across the US In 2015, the national median salary for fitness trainers was slightly above $36,000, according to the Bureau of Labor Statistics. However, earning potential varies greatly, depending on place of employment, specialization and credentials, clientele, and location. Use the map below to learn more personal trainer pay throughout the US.

Certified personal trainers may be self-employed, work for a gym or fitness center, or even work for corporations. As the fitness industry evolves, trainers need to learn about new products and trends. This means that not only are current trainers able to grow in their work, new positions for new trainers are also opening up. The Bureau of Labor Statistics projects more than 23,000 job openings nationally for fitness trainers between 2016 and 2026.

Fitness and health are expansive industries with multiple possible career paths available.

EMPLOYMENT AND OUTLOOK

The fitness industry is large with a number of different personal trainer careers to consider in the areas of nutrition, conditioning, performance, sports medicine and more. Below are five examples of potential career specializations for individuals seeking to go beyond personal training.

Exercise Physiologist

Exercise physiologists work with diverse populations, ranging from world-class athletes to individuals with chronic diseases to maintain, improve, or enhance their clients' overall fitness, health, and physical performance. An undergraduate degree in kinesiology or exercise science is usually required, along with national certification from the American College of Sports Medicine and a master's degree and board certification from the American Society of Exercise Physiologists for clinical positions.

Sports Nutritionist

Sports nutritionists understand how the body uses food to fuel physical activity and they work with clients including sports teams or as part of corporate wellness programs to develop nutritionally sound menus, implement education programs, and assist in one-on-one nutritional counseling. State educational requirement vary, but a bachelor's degree in nutrition, kinesiology, exercise science, or related field is the typical minimum educational requirement. Certification from the American Dietetics Association or board certification from the Commission on Dietetic Registration is commonly required.

Group Exercise Instructor

Group exercise instructors design, develop, and lead group personal training sessions in specialty exercise modalities including yoga, aerobics, cycling, Pilates, and more. Instructors lead the class, doing the exercises along with their clients to provide motivation as well as to teach and model proper technique. Professional certification from organizations such as the American College of Sports Medicine and American Council on Fitness are typically required for employment.

Corrective Exercise Specialist

Corrective exercise specialists use their knowledge of posture and the mechanics of body movement to help clients deal with flexibility issues, joint pain, or muscle through individualized corrective exercise programs to restore full body movement in clients. Professional experience and a Certified Personal Trainer certification are generally required before earning a Corrective Exercise Specialist certification from the National Academy of Sports Medicine.

Strength and Conditioning Coach

Strength and conditioning coaches generally have two goals for their clients: Improved athletic performance and fewer athletic injuries. They traditionally work with sports teams, but may also work in physical therapy clinics, fitness clubs, and high schools. A bachelor's degree, previous fitness experience, and certification from the National Strength and Conditioning Association are typically required.

Conversation With . . . BRIAN JOHNSON

Fitness Trainer, 3 years

1. **What was your individual career path in terms of education/training, entry-level job, or other significant opportunity?**

   I was in corporate America for almost 20 years. I became unemployable because I topped out on the rate scale. My last job was running a Safeway distribution center. I asked myself: what's the one thing I've always done? And that's go to the gym. So I got my certification and started training people. I had enough money saved up so I was living off my savings, but the motivating piece was, I didn't want to work for anybody else ever again. I did a 12-week online course to get my certification in 8 weeks. I joined networking groups, which is how I got my clients.

   I have my own gym. I trained my first client outside at the park across the street. I used an eight foot chain TRX and a five dollar fitness map. I migrated from individual clients into boot camps, which just makes sense because you're leveraging your time and working with 20 people for $15 each, as opposed to one person at $80.

   Through all my marketing and networking, I got hooked up with a couple of wedding vendors. The clients walk in there, see my business cards, and the next thing you know I'll have a bridal party boot camp that usually lasts about two months. I also am starting a two-hour ultimate boot camp challenge, that also has a 5K mudrun, live music, vendors...a fitness festival. We have one coming up in May in Annapolis, and I'm talking about doing one with a guy on Long Island, NY, and a guy in Raleigh, NC. My goal is to do one a month across the nation.

2. **What are the most important skills and/or qualities for someone in your profession?**

   The ability to inspire, motivate and hold people accountable, that's the most important piece. Without that, whether you're working in a gym or doing your own gig, you're never going to retain people.

3. What do you wish you had known going into this profession?

How difficult it would be to get clients. I thought it would be easy. In the fitness industry, word of mouth is everything, networking and social media. You've got to get your name out there. I do Business Networking International and other local area mixers. You have to identify the best social media for your industry. For mine, it's Facebook. For a banker, it's LinkedIn. At the end of the day, I have a very extensive and elaborate website but the majority of my clients come from word of mouth.

Also, in hindsight, I would have trained at a gym for two or three months to gain that confidence level to train people. I only charged my first client $30 a session. Now, I charge $80 for a private session. You need to research what other people are charging. You don't want to devalue yourself, or overprice yourself out of business. You've got to find that balance and test the market.

4. Are there many job opportunities in your profession? In what specific areas?

Yes. I say that because I've seen constant turnover at the gyms. They're always looking for quality instructors.

5. How do you see your profession changing in the next five years? What role will technology play in those changes, and what skills will be required?

I think a lot of it's going to go online. I can already see that shift happening. My vision is, you have this ten-by-ten room, you have a nice camera in there, people log in every day, and I instruct them for an hour. For $1, I have 1,000 people logging in for an hour.

6. What do you enjoy most about your job? What do you enjoy least?

Getting people to their goals, whether somebody is morbidly obese or somebody is already fit and training for a tough event. At my gym, we have a whiteboard where everybody writes their goals. I have a 61-year-old lady flipping a 200-pound tractor tire. It helps to motivate everyone.

What I like least is that you're always on. It's hard to shut it off. Not that I ever would, but God forbid if I ever wanted to go to McDonalds and have a cheeseburger. Too many people in this town know me! But it's a blessing. If I was working for a gym training someone, I would leave there at the end of the day and be done.

7. Can you suggest a valuable "try this" for students considering a career in your profession?

Try it at a gym first. Don't try it on your own. Write out all the pros and cons and make sure it's right for you, because it's not right for everybody.

[Note: This interview was conducted in 2014.]

MORE INFORMATION

Academy of Applied Personal Training Education (AAPTE)
NCCA Accredited Programs: Certified Personal Fitness Trainer (CPFT)
Requirements: Be at least 18 years old, have NCCA-accredited personal training certification, OR pass a human anatomy course
# of Exam Questions: NA

ACTION Certification (ACTION)
NCCA Accredited Programs: Certified Personal Trainer (CPT)
Requirements: NA
# of Exam Questions: 60
Exam Cost: $150

American College of Sports Medicine (ACSM)
NCCA Accredited Programs: ACSM Certified Personal Trainer (CPT)
Requirements: Must be at least 18 years of age; have a high school diploma or GED; Must have current CPR and AED certification.
# of Exam Questions: 150

American Council on Exercise (ACE)
NCCA Accredited Programs: Personal Trainer (ACE-CPT)
Requirements: Must be at least 18 years of age; have a high school diploma or GED; Must have current CPR and AED certification.
# of Exam Questions: 150

International Fitness Professionals Association (IFPA)
NCCA Accredited Programs: International Fitness Professionals Association Personal Fitness Training Certification (IFPA – PFT)
Requirements: Must be CPR/First-Aid certified.
# of Exam Questions: 150

National Academy of Sports Medicine (NASM)
NCCA Accredited Programs: Certified Personal Trainer (CPT)
Requirements: Must be at least 18 years of age, possess active Automated External Defibrillator (AED) and Emergency Cardiac Care (CPR) certification.
# of Exam Questions: 120

National Council on Strength and Fitness (NCSF)
NCCA Accredited Programs: National Certified Personal Trainer (NCSF-CPT)
Requirements: Must be at least 18 years of age and have a high school degree or equivalent
# of Exam Questions: 150

National Exercise and Sports Trainers Association (NESTA)
NCCA Accredited Programs: Personal Fitness Trainer (PFT)
Requirements: Must be at least 18 years old, have a high school diploma/GED, have CPR certification, and a valid driver's license or passport.
# of Exam Questions: 125

National Exercise Trainers Association (NETA)
NCCA Accredited Programs:
Certified Personal Trainer (NETA-CPT)
Requirements: Must be at least 18 years of age; have a high school diploma or GED; Must have current CPR and AED certification.
# of Exam Questions: 120

National Federation of Professional Trainers (NFPT)
NCCA Accredited Programs:
Certified Personal Fitness Trainer (CPT)
Requirements: Must be 18 years of age or older, have a high school diploma or equivalent, and have at least two years of physical fitness experience
# of Exam Questions: 120

National Strength and Conditioning Association (NSCA)
NCCA Accredited Programs:
Certified Personal Trainer (NSCA-CPT)
Requirements: Must be at least 18 years of age; have a high school diploma or GED; Must have current CPR and AED certification.
# of Exam Questions: 140

PTA Global, Inc. (PTA Global, Inc.)
NCCA Accredited Programs:
Personal Training Academy Global Certified Personal Trainer (PTA Global CPT)
Requirements: Must be at least 18 years of age; have a high school diploma or GED; Must have current CPR and AED certification
# of Exam Questions: 100

The Cooper Institute (CI)
NCCA Accredited Programs:
Personal Trainer Certification (CPT)
Requirements: Must be at least 18 years old and have current adult CPR certification.
# of Exam Questions: 100

Physical Therapist

Snapshot

Career Cluster(s): Health Science
Interests: Anatomy and physiology, biology, anatomy, sports medicine, physical education, psychology, health science technology
Earnings (median in 2017): \$86,850 per year; \$41.76 per hour
Employment & Outlook through 2026: 28% (Much faster than average growth expected)

OVERVIEW

Sphere of Work

Physical therapists (PTs) provide therapeutic services to patients who have temporary and chronic physical conditions or illnesses that limit physical movements and mobility, thereby negatively affecting patients' life and work. When working with patients, a physical therapist may use techniques such as therapeutic exercise, manual therapy techniques, assistive devices, adaptive devices, hydrotherapy, and electrotherapy. Physical therapists develop patient treatment plans designed to help maintain or recover a patient's physical mobility, lessen pain, increase productivity and independence, and improve quality of life.

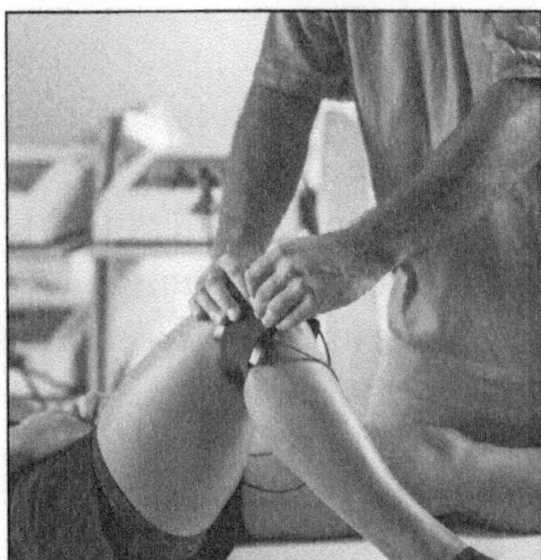

Work Environment

Physical therapists work in rehabilitation facilities, hospitals, nursing homes, physical therapy clinics, and schools. In medical environments, physical therapists work with a team of medical and social service professionals to increase a patient's physical abilities and overall independence. In school settings, physical therapists partner with educational professionals, such as teachers and special education coordinators, to address a student's physical issues. Physical therapists generally work a standard forty-hour workweek, and scheduled appointments are the norm.

Profile

Interests: Data, People, Things
Working Conditions: Work Inside
Physical Strength: Medium Work, Heavy Work
Education Needs: Bachelor's Degree, Master's Degree
Licensure/Certification: Required
Physical Abilities Not Required: Not Climb
Opportunities for Experience: Internship, Military Service, Volunteer Work, Part Time Work
Holland Interest Score*: SIE

* See Appendix A

Occupation Interest

Individuals attracted to the field of physical therapy tend to be physically strong people who enjoy hands-on work and close interaction with people from diverse backgrounds. Those who excel as physical therapists exhibit traits such as physical stamina, problem solving, empathy, patience, and caring. Physical therapists should enjoy learning, stay knowledgeable about changes in therapeutic techniques, and expect to work as part of a team to effectively address patient needs.

A Day in the Life—Duties and Responsibilities

A physical therapist's daily duties and responsibilities include full days of hands-on patient interaction and treatment, as well as administrative duties. Physical therapists' patients include those experiencing physical limitations and effects from neck and spinal cord injuries; traumatic brain injury; arthritis; burns; cerebral palsy; muscular dystrophy; strokes; limb or digit amputation; or work- or sports-related injuries.

As a medical or therapeutic professional, physical therapists interact with patients or clients on a daily basis and strive to understand the particular challenges faced by each individual. Treatment typically includes a blend of physical techniques and emotional encouragement, since the patient may be in the process of adjusting to a major life change. Some of a physical therapist's daily responsibilities include conducting patient assessments, developing patient treatment plans, and providing physical treatment to patients with severe physical limitations. Physical therapists frequently advise patients on the use of adaptive equipment, such as wheelchairs and orthopedic aids. Some provide early intervention services to young children experiencing physical delays and limitations. Others may offer consultation on or participate in building customized adaptive equipment for patients with special needs not met by existing options. Physical therapists also instruct individuals and groups on physical exercises to prevent injury, lead fitness and health classes and workshops, and counsel patients on physical adaptations that can help the patient to continue to work at his or her chosen occupation. They may also supervise the activities of physical therapy assistants and aides.

During the course of treatment, a physical therapist will consult with a team of physicians, educators, social workers, mental health professionals, occupational therapists, speech therapists, and other medical professionals to help ensure that each patient receives comprehensive care.

A physical therapist's administrative responsibilities include documenting treatment sessions and ongoing patient evaluation. Physical therapists must draft treatment plans, record notes following patient treatment sessions, provide written updates to the other members of a patient's treatment team, and provide insurance companies with patient records and progress notes as required. Independent physical therapists who do not work as part of a school or medical clinic may also be responsible for scheduling appointments and for submitting bills to insurance companies or patients.

Duties and Responsibilities

- **Recording patients' treatments, responses and progress**
- **Evaluating the physician's referral and the patient's medical records to determine the treatment required**
- **Performing tests, measurements and evaluations such as range-of-motion and manual-muscle tests, gait and functional analyses and body-parts measurements**
- **Administering manual therapeutic exercises to improve or maintain muscle function**
- **Administering treatments involving the application of such agents as light, heat, water, and ice massage techniques**

OCCUPATION SPECIALTIES

Directors of Physical Therapy

Directors of physical therapy plan, direct and coordinate physical therapy programs and make sure the program complies with state requirements.

WORK ENVIRONMENT

Transferable Skills and Abilities

Communication Skills
- Expressing thoughts and ideas
- Speaking effectively
- Writing concisely

Interpersonal/Social Skills
- Being patient
- Being sensitive to others
- Cooperating with others
- Working as a member of a team

Organization & Management Skills
- Coordinating tasks
- Managing people/groups
- Paying attention to and handling details
- Performing duties which change frequently

Research & Planning Skills
- Analyzing information
- Developing evaluation strategies
- Using logical reasoning

Technical Skills
- Performing scientific, mathematical and technical work
- Working with your hands

Immediate Physical Environment

Physical therapists work in rehabilitation facilities, hospitals, nursing homes, therapy clinics, and schools. Therapeutic office settings used by physical therapists may be shared with other therapeutic professionals, such as occupational, recreational, or speech and language therapists.

Human Environment

Physical therapists work with patients who use physical therapy to improve their strength and mobility, as well as their independence and quality of life. This may include people experiencing balance and strength issues caused by cerebral palsy, spinal cord injuries, or muscular dystrophy; stroke victims experiencing coordination problems or paralysis; and children or adults suffering the physical effects of injuries, abuse, or accidents. Physical therapists usually work as part of a patient treatment team that includes patient families, social workers, teachers, doctors, and additional therapists.

Technological Environment

Physical therapists use a wide variety of technology in their work. Computers and Internet communication tools are widely used in physical therapy work and practice. Specialized therapies, such as electrotherapy, hydrotherapy, and ultrasound therapy, require technical equipment and training. In addition, physical therapists must learn how to use and teach the use of adaptive devices, such as wheelchairs and orthopedic aids.

EDUCATION, TRAINING, AND ADVANCEMENT

High School/Secondary

High school students interested in pursuing the profession of physical therapy in the future should develop good study habits. High school courses in biology, psychology, anatomy, sociology, and mathematics will prepare students for college- and graduate-level studies. Students interested in the physical therapy field will benefit from seeking internships or part-time work with physical therapists or with people who have physical issues that affect their range of movement or daily life.

Suggested High School Subjects

- Algebra
- Applied Communication
- Applied Math
- Applied Physics
- Biology
- Chemistry
- College Preparatory
- English
- Geometry
- Health Science Technology
- Humanities
- Physical Education
- Physics

- Physiology
- Psychology
- Science
- Trigonometry

Related Career Pathways/Majors

Health Science Cluster

- Therapeutic Services Pathway

Famous First

Per Henrik Ling, known as the "Father of Swedish Gymnastics," founded the Royal Central Institute of Gymnastics (RCIG) in 1813 as a professional organization that promoted use of spinal manipulative therapy and exercise as a means of treating physical injuries. By 1887, PTs were given official registration by Sweden's National Board of Health and Welfare. Other countries soon followed: In 1894, Britain's' Chartered Society of Physiotherapy was formed; in 1913, New Zealand's School of Physiotherapy at the University of Otago; in 1914, United States' Reed College in Portland, Oregon.

Postsecondary

Postsecondary students interested in becoming physical therapists should complete coursework in physical therapy, if possible, as well as courses on occupational therapy, special education, biology, psychology, anatomy and physiology, sociology, and mathematics. Prior to graduation, college students interested in joining the physical therapy profession should apply to graduate-level physical therapy programs or secure physical therapy-related employment. Those who choose to pursue a master's degree tend to have better prospects for employment and advancement in the field. Membership in the American Physical Therapy Association may help provide postsecondary students with networking opportunities and connections.

Related College Majors

- Adapted Physical Education/Therapeutic Recreation
- Anatomy
- Art Therapy
- Exercise Science/Physiology/Movement Studies
- Health & Physical Education, General
- Human & Animal Physiology
- Physical Therapy
- Sports Medicine & Athletic Training

Adult Job Seekers

Adult job seekers in the physical therapy field should have a master's degree in physical therapy from a college or university accredited by the Commission on Accreditation in Physical Therapy Education. They must also earn the necessary professional licensure. Physical therapists seeking employment may benefit from the networking opportunities, job workshops, and job lists offered by professional physical therapy associations, such as the American Physical Therapy Association and American Board of Physical Therapy Specialties. Advancement in the physical therapy field often depends on the individual's education and specialty certification.

Professional Certification and Licensure

Physical therapists are required to have earned a professional physical therapy (PT) license prior to beginning their professional practice. Upon completion of an accredited master's or doctoral program in physical therapy, candidates take the National Physical Therapy Examination (NPTE) administered by the Federation of State Boards of Physical Therapy. In addition to passing the NPTE, physical therapists are required to register with their state health board, pass a state exam, and engage in continuing education as a condition of their PT license.

Physical therapists may choose to pursue additional, specialized physical therapy certification from the American Board of Physical Therapy Specialties. Certification is available for the following specialties: cardiovascular and pulmonary, clinical electrophysiology, geriatrics, neurology, pediatrics, sports, and women's health.

Additional Requirements

Individuals who find satisfaction, success, and job security as physical therapists will be knowledgeable about the profession's requirements, responsibilities, and opportunities. Successful physical therapists engage in ongoing professional development related to changes in therapeutic techniques, ethical standards, and new technology. Because physical therapists work with vulnerable people and share confidential patient information with other medical professionals, adherence to strict professional and ethical standards is required. Both entry-level and senior-level physical therapists may find it beneficial to join professional associations as a means of building professional community and networking.

Fun Fact

Physical therapy originated during World War I and the first physical therapists were known as "reconstruction aides."

Source: www.apta.org/History/

EARNINGS AND ADVANCEMENT

Earnings of physical therapists depend on the type and size of the employer and the physical therapist's length of employment and level of responsibility. Physical therapists in private practice tend to earn more than salaried workers. Salaries are usually higher in rural areas as employers try to attract physical therapists to where there are severe shortages.

Median annual earnings of physical therapists were $86,850 in May 2017. The lowest 10 percent earned less than $59,080, and the highest 10 percent earned more than $122,650.

Physical therapists may receive paid vacations, holidays, and sick days; life and health insurance; and retirement benefits. These are usually paid by the employer. Some employers also provide for paid educational leave.

Most physical therapists work full time. About 1 in 5 worked part time in 2016. Although most therapists work during normal business hours, some may work evenings or weekends.

Median annual wages, May 2017

Physical therapists: $86,850

Health diagnosing and treating practitioners: $79,480

Total, all occupations: $37,690

Note: All Occupations includes all occupations in the U.S. Economy. Source: U.S. Bureau of Labor Statistics, Occupational Employment Statistics

EMPLOYMENT AND OUTLOOK

There were approximately 239,800 physical therapists employed nationally in 2016. Employment of physical therapists is projected to grow 28 percent from 2016 to 2026, much faster than the average for all occupations.

Demand for physical therapy will come in part from the large number of aging baby boomers, who are staying more active later in life than their counterparts of previous generations. Older people are more likely to experience heart attacks, strokes, and mobility-related injuries that require physical therapy for rehabilitation.

In addition, a number of chronic conditions, such as diabetes and obesity, have become more prevalent in recent years. More physical therapists will be needed to help these patients maintain their mobility and manage the effects of chronic conditions.

Advances in medical technology have increased the use of outpatient surgery to treat a variety of injuries and illnesses. Medical and technological developments also are expected to permit a greater percentage of trauma victims and newborns with birth defects to survive, creating additional demand for rehabilitative care. Physical therapists will continue to play an important role in helping these patients recover more quickly from surgery.

Job opportunities are expected to be good for licensed physical therapists in all settings. Job prospects should be particularly good in acute-care hospitals, skilled-nursing facilities, and orthopedic settings, where the elderly are most often treated. Job prospects should be especially favorable in rural areas because many physical therapists live in highly populated urban and suburban areas.

Related Occupations

- Activities Therapist
- Athletic Trainer
- Chiropractor
- Occupational Therapist
- Occupational Therapy Assistant
- Orthotist and Prosthetist
- Recreational Therapist
- Respiratory Therapist

Related Military Occupations

- Physical & Occupational Therapist

Conversation With . . .
ARACELLY LATINO-FELIZ, DPT

Founder/Director of Physical Therapy
The Movement Institute, Dania Beach, FL
Physical Therapist, 10 years

1. What was your individual career path in terms of education/training, entry-level job, or other significant opportunity?

Originally, I planned to go to medical school and was pre-med at Florida State University. I did some observation hours in a hospital and realized that the profession is geared toward prescribing medicine. I wanted to prescribe a healthy lifestyle, to prescribe movement. For a year, I did a lot of soul searching, volunteering, and talking to professionals. I thought maybe I'd be a nurse, maybe a physician's assistant, a respiratory therapist, or an occupational therapist.

I was 19 and worked as a personal trainer and group exercise instructor at a recreation center while I pursued my degree. I was promoted to senior instructor and assistant director of the group exercise program. It was a great opportunity to be on the health and wellness side of preventing injuries and promoting healthy habits.

When I met a physical therapist who ran the gym's clinic, I felt that I had met a soulmate. She introduced me to the world of sports medicine.

I graduated from FSU with a Bachelor of Science in human sciences, then got a master's in physical therapy from Florida International University in 2007. Five years later, I got my Ph.D. in physical therapy.

I'm the owner of The Movement Therapy Institute, a physical therapy private practice. I'm also a professor at the University of St. Augustine for Health Sciences Doctoral Physical Therapy Program in Miami and really value the importance of evidence-based research. Last but not least, I recently started work as a consultant for a corporate wellness company, Livewell 1440. I educate the staff of about 350 people on how a physical therapist can help with wellness and with injuries and stress management; I perform movement assessments; and I do onsite treatment.

Before starting my own business, I was clinical director/physical therapist at Sports and Orthopedic Leaders Physical Therapy and Performance in the San Francisco area.

I've worked with collegiate, Olympic-level and professional athletes from the NFL, MLB, and USA Men's Bobsled Team. I'm an athlete myself—track and field, soccer, cheerleading, and an avid runner—so I really understand proper body mechanics and how to optimize performance.

2. What are the most important skills and/or qualities for someone in your profession?

Compassion, patience, grit, resilience, perseverance and a commitment to growth and education.

3. What do you wish you had known going into this profession?

I wish I had known how to become an entrepreneur. I also wish I had known how to effectively pay off student loans. Fortunately, scholarships paid for my undergrad education, but I had to pay for graduate school, including room and board. That was definitely a challenge, coming from a family with very little money. My mother was a single mom of four and worked cleaning homes for a living. I came out of school about $100,000 in debt and am still paying off those loans.

Finally, I wish I had understood compassion fatigue and how to balance work and personal health. Early in my career, I was working in an outpatient clinic seeing 15 to 20-something patients a day. Although I love what I do, it was taking a toll emotionally and on my body. There were many days when I was so exhausted from work that I had little energy left for my own personal well-being. I learned how to overcome this on my own, but it would have been useful to have some help along the way. They mention it in physical therapy school, but not to the extent of saying, "These are the signs to look for." It's something that I make sure I educate my students about.

4. Are there many job opportunities in your profession? In what specific areas?

Yes, many. Physical therapists can work in outpatient orthopedic centers, hospitals, home health, skilled nursing facilities, and private practice or for sports teams, either at a school or at the professional level. And they can teach.

5. How do you see your profession changing in the next five years as it relates to fitness and/or sports injuries? What role will technology play, and what skills will be required?

Teleheath is becoming popular as the internet continues to bring the world together. In the next five years, I see more physical therapists opening private practices and the public becoming more educated about and comfortable with seeing PTs as the practitioner of choice for musculoskeletal injuries. Technology will play a huge role in educating the public and connecting patients with providers.

6. **What do you enjoy most about your job? What do you enjoy least about your job?**

   I love that I get to be a key player in transforming patients' lives. I love seeing patients be empowered to take care of themselves as they heal and go back to their jobs and families. It makes the world a healthier and happier place. I love how physically active our profession is. Teaching is very rewarding. I've always been a clinical instructor, but actually teaching future physical therapists has been extremely rewarding as well.

   What I enjoy least is doing administrative paperwork and learning about payroll, marketing, and business planning, though I'm learning to embrace it. It's part of being a business owner.

7. **Can you suggest a valuable "try this" for students considering a career in your profession?**

   Spend a day with a physical therapist and ask yourself if you see yourself doing what a PT does.

MORE INFORMATION

American Physical Therapy Association
1111 N. Fairfax Street
Alexandria, VA 22314-1488
800.999.2782
www.apta.org

Federation of State Boards of Physical Therapy
124 West Street S, 3rd Floor
Alexandria, VA 22314
703.299.3100
www.fsbpt.org

Simone Isadora Flynn/Editor

Physical Therapy Assistant

Snapshot

Career Cluster(s): Health Science
Interests: Anatomy and physiology, exercise science, biology, physical therapy, health science technology, physical education
Earnings (median in 2017): $46,920 per year; $22.56 per hour
Employment & Outlook through 2026: 30% (Much faster than average growth expected)

OVERVIEW

Sphere of Work

Physical therapy assistants help licensed physical therapists provide therapeutic services to patients who have acute or chronic physical conditions or illnesses that limit physical movement and mobility. They implement the patient care and services as described in a patient treatment plan devised by a physical therapist. These services are aimed at helping patients maintain or recover physical mobility and strength, lessen pain, increase productivity, and improve quality of life.

Work Environment

Physical therapy assistants work in medical settings, such as rehabilitation facilities, hospitals, nursing homes, and physical therapy clinics, and in schools. In medical environments, physical therapy assistants generally partner with medical and social service professionals, such as doctors and social workers, to increase a patient's physical strength and overall independence. In school settings, they work with educational professionals, such as teachers and special education coordinators, to address a student's physical issues. Physical therapy assistants generally work a standard forty-hour week, and scheduled work hours and appointments are the norm.

Profile

Interests: People, Things
Working Conditions: Work Inside
Physical Strength: Medium Work
Education Needs: Junior/Technical/ Community College
Licensure/Certification: Required
Physical Abilities Not Required: Not Climb
Opportunities for Experience: Internship, Military Service, Part Time Work
Holland Interest Score*: SCR

* See Appendix A

Occupation Interest

Individuals attracted to the field of physical therapy tend to be people who find fulfillment in hands-on work and close interaction with others. Those who excel as physical therapy assistants exhibit traits such as physical strength and stamina, good problem-solving abilities, patience, caring, and a desire to help. Physical therapy assistants must be good at science and able to work as part of a team to meet patient needs. Strong communication skills are also essential.

A Day in the Life—Duties and Responsibilities

A physical therapy assistant's daily duties and responsibilities include full days of hands-on patient interaction and care as well as clerical and administrative duties. Patients treated by physical therapy assistants include those experiencing physical limitations and effects from neck and spinal cord injuries, traumatic brain injuries, arthritis, burns, cerebral palsy, muscular dystrophy, strokes, limb or digit amputation, or work- or sport-related injuries.

As medical or therapeutic workers, physical therapy assistants regularly interact with patients. Daily work responsibilities may include participating in patient assessments, consulting with patient teams, contributing to treatment plans, and preparing the equipment and materials that will be used in a physical therapy session. Some skills and techniques a physical therapy assistant may use with patients include therapeutic exercise, manual therapy techniques, assistive and adaptive devices, hydrotherapy, and electrotherapy. Physical therapy assistants support physical therapists in their treatment of patients who have severe physical limitations; this might involve lifting patients in wheelchairs, providing early intervention services to young children with physical delays and limitations, and helping to build adaptive equipment for patients with special needs not met by existing options. They also provide therapies using water, heat, touch, sound, electricity, or light to patients as directed, and report any improvements or setbacks during the course of treatment. They may instruct individuals and groups on physical exercises to prevent injury, teach patients to use assistive or adaptive equipment, or provide counsel on physical adaptations that will allow the patient to continue to work at his or her chosen occupation.

A physical therapy assistant's daily administrative and clerical responsibilities include the record keeping involved with patient evaluation and treatment. Physical therapy assistants must record notes following patient treatment sessions and provide insurance companies with patient records and progress notes as required. They may also be responsible for the daily tasks of patient appointment scheduling and billing.

Duties and Responsibilities

- **Completing therapy treatments as per the orders of a supervising physical therapist**
- **Working with patients in acute pain**
- **Reporting to supervisors any progress or regress in therapy**
- **Fitting and training patients in the use of therapeutic equipment or appliances**

OCCUPATION SPECIALTIES

Physical Therapy Technicians

Physical Therapy Technicians specialize in one or more corrective physical therapy treatments.

Physical Therapy Aides

Physical Therapy Aides prepare patients for physical therapy treatments by either a physical therapist or assistant.

WORK ENVIRONMENT

Immediate Physical Environment

Physical therapy assistants work in rehabilitation facilities, hospitals, nursing homes, therapy clinics, and schools. Office settings used by physical therapy assistants and their supervisors may be shared with other therapeutic professionals, such as occupational, recreational, or speech and language therapists.

Human Environment

Patients who need physical therapy include those with balance and strength issues caused by cerebral palsy, spinal cord injuries, or muscular dystrophy, as well as stroke victims experiencing coordination problems or paralysis and children or adults suffering the physical effects of injuries, abuse, or accidents. Physical therapy assistants usually work as part of a patient treatment team that includes patient families, social workers, teachers, doctors, and other therapists.

Transferable Skills and Abilities

Communication Skills
- Listening attentively
- Speaking effectively
- Writing concisely

Interpersonal/Social Skills
- Being patient
- Being sensitive to others
- Providing support to others
- Working as a member of a team

Organization & Management Skills
- Following instructions
- Making decisions

Research & Planning Skills
- Using logical reasoning

Technical Skills
- Working with machines, tools or other objects
- Working with your hands

Work Environment Skills
- Working in a medical setting

Technological Environment

Physical therapy assistants use a wide variety of technology in their work. Computers and Internet communication tools are a ubiquitous part of physical therapy work and practice. Specialized therapies, such as electrotherapy, hydrotherapy, and ultrasound therapy, require technical equipment and training. In addition, physical therapy assistants generally learn how to use and teach the use of adaptive devices, such as wheelchairs and orthopedic aids.

EDUCATION, TRAINING, AND ADVANCEMENT

High School/Secondary

High school students interested in pursuing the profession of physical therapy assistant should take courses in biology, psychology, anatomy, sociology, and mathematics. They may benefit from seeking internships or part-time work with physical therapists or people who have physical problems that limit their movement or daily life.

Related High School Subjects
- Applied Math
- Applied Physics
- Biology

- Chemistry
- English
- Foods & Nutrition
- Health Science Technology
- Mathematics
- Medical Assisting
- Physical Education
- Physics
- Physiology
- Science

Related Career Pathways/Majors

Health Science Cluster

- Therapeutic Services Pathway

Postsecondary

Interested postsecondary students should complete at least an associate degree in physical therapy, as well as classes in physics, chemistry, biology, psychology, anatomy and physiology, pathology, sociology, communications, and mathematics. Programs in physical therapy provide hands-on clinical instruction, CPR certification, and first aid training in addition to classroom learning. Membership in the American Physical Therapy Association may provide networking opportunities and connections.

Related College Majors

- Anatomy
- Exercise Science/Physiology/Movement Studies
- Human & Animal Physiology
- Physical Therapy Assistant Training

Adult Job Seekers

Adults seeking jobs as physical therapy assistants should have, at a minimum, an associate or bachelor's degree from a school or university accredited by the Commission on Accreditation of Physical Therapy Education. They may benefit from the networking opportunities, job workshops, and job lists offered by professional physical therapy associations such as the American Physical Therapy Association and the American Board of Physical Therapy Specialties.

Professional Certification and Licensure

Physical therapy assistants are required to have obtained a professional physical therapy assistant (PTA) license prior to beginning their professional practice. Upon completion of an accredited educational program in physical therapy, candidates take the National Physical Therapy Assistant Examination administered by the Federation of State Boards of Physical Therapy. In addition to passing the national exam, physical therapy assistants are required to register with their state health board, pass a state jurisprudence exam in physical therapy, and engage in continuing education as a condition of their license.

Additional Requirements

Successful physical therapy assistants engage in ongoing professional development. High levels of integrity and ethics are required, as physical therapy assistants work with vulnerable people and have access to confidential patient information. Membership in professional physical therapy associations is encouraged.

EARNINGS AND ADVANCEMENT

Physical therapy assistants earn an hourly rate which depends on the type of employer and years of experience. Those working in hospitals tended to earn less than those working in private practice. Yet, many hospitals offer physical therapy assistants a structured path of advancement. It is possible for physical therapy assistants to continue their education and become physical therapists.

The median annual wage for physical therapist aides was $25,730 in May 2017. The lowest 10 percent earned less than $19,620, and the highest 10 percent earned more than $38,490.

The median annual wage for physical therapist assistants was $57,430 in May 2017. The lowest 10 percent earned less than $35,930, and the highest 10 percent earned more than $79,380.

In May 2017, the median annual wages for physical therapist aides in the top industries in which they worked were as follows:

Nursing care facilities (skilled nursing facilities)	$30,240
Hospitals; state, local, and private	28,670
Government	26,580
Offices of physicians	26,460
Offices of physical, occupational and speech therapists, and audiologists	24,250

In May 2017, the median annual wages for physical therapist assistants in the top industries in which they worked were as follows:

Nursing care facilities (skilled nursing facilities)	$66,280
Home healthcare services	62,630
Hospitals; state, local, and private	55,770
Offices of physical, occupational and speech therapists, and audiologists	55,560
Offices of physicians	54,480

Physical therapy assistants may receive paid vacations, holidays, and sick days; life and health insurance; and retirement benefits. These are usually paid by the employer.

Most physical therapist assistants and aides work full time. Some night and weekend work may be required because many physical therapy offices and clinics have extended hours to accommodate patients' schedules.

Median annual wages, May 2017

Physical therapist assistants: $57,430

Occupational therapy and physical therapist assistants and aides: $50,510

Physical therapist assistants and aides: $46,920

Total, all occupations: $37,690

Physical therapist aides: $25,730

Note: All Occupations includes all occupations in the U.S. Economy. Source: U.S. Bureau of Labor Statistics, Occupational Employment Statistics

EMPLOYMENT AND OUTLOOK

Physical therapy assistants held about 88,300 jobs nationally in 2016 and physical therapy assistants held 52,000 jobs.

Employment of physical therapist assistants is projected to grow 31 percent from 2016 to 2026, much faster than the average for all occupations. Employment of physical therapist aides is projected to grow 29 percent from 2016 to 2026, much faster than the average for all occupations.

Demand for physical therapy is expected to increase in response to the health needs of an aging population, particularly the large baby-boom generation. This group is staying more active later in life than previous generations did. However, many baby boomers also are entering the prime age for heart attacks, strokes, and mobility-related injuries, increasing the demand for physical therapy needed for rehabilitation.

In addition, a number of chronic conditions, such as diabetes and obesity, have become more prevalent in recent years. More physical therapist assistants and aides will be needed to manage the effects of such conditions and help patients maintain their mobility. Moreover, medical and technological developments should permit an increased percentage of trauma victims and newborns with birth defects to survive, creating added demand for therapy and rehabilitative services.

Physical therapists are expected to increasingly use physical therapist assistants, particularly in long-term care environments, in order to reduce the cost of physical therapy services. Once the physical therapist has evaluated a patient and designed a plan of care, the assistant can provide many parts of the treatment, as directed by the therapist.

Opportunities for physical therapist assistants are expected to be good. Physical therapist assistants will be needed to help physical therapists care for and manage more patients. However, physical therapist aides may face strong competition from the large pool of qualified people because requirements for entry are low.

Job opportunities should be particularly good in settings where the elderly are most often treated, such as skilled-nursing homes, home health, and outpatient orthopedic facilities. Job prospects should be especially favorable in rural areas because many physical therapists cluster in highly populated urban and suburban areas.

Related Occupations

- Activities Therapist
- Occupational Therapy Assistant

Related Military Occupations

- Physical & Occupational Therapy Specialist

MORE INFORMATION

American Physical Therapy Association
1111 North Fairfax Street
Alexandria, VA 22314
800.999.2782
www.apta.org

Federation of State Boards of Physical Therapy
124 West Street South, 3rd Floor
Alexandria, VA 22314
703.299.3100
www.fsbpt.org

Simone Isadora Flynn/Editor

Physician

Snapshot

Career Cluster(s): Health Science
Interests: Biology, physiology, chemistry, working with the sick or injured, making decisions quickly, communicating with others
Earnings (median in 2017): equal to or greater than $208,000 per year or $100.00 per hour
Employment & Outlook through 2026: 13% (Faster than average growth expected)

OVERVIEW

Sphere of Work

Physicians are doctors who care for sick and injured people. In addition to diagnosing illnesses through interpretation of medical tests, physicians treat injuries that occur accidentally or as a result of disease or illness. Physicians in the United States are divided into two specialties: medical doctors (MDs), who use pharmaceutical and surgical methods to treat patients, and doctors of osteopathic medicine (DOs), who use similar procedures and also incorporate preventative techniques and holistic medical care.

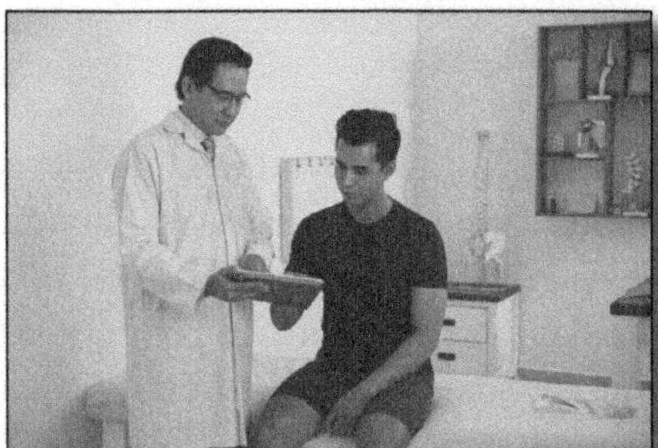

Work Environment

Physicians work in medical office settings and in hospitals. Depending on experience and area of specialization, physicians may divide their time between treating patients, conducting medical research, and offering educational instruction to medical students in both classroom and laboratory settings. The location in which a physician works varies based on whether he or she has a private medical practice, is a researcher for a hospital or a university, or is employed by a pharmaceutical or health organization.

Profile

Interests: Data, People, Things
Working Conditions: Work Inside
Physical Strength: Light Work
Education Needs: Doctoral Degree
Licensure/Certification: Required
Physical Abilities Not Required: Not Climb
Opportunities for Experience: Military Service, Volunteer Work
Holland Interest Score*: ISR

* See Appendix A

Occupation Interest

Medicine attracts students with demonstrated academic success in biology, physiology, and chemistry. Many professionals who are drawn to the field are those who have excelled academically and want to put their knowledge to use for the benefit of others. Becoming a physician necessitates more than a decade of academic study.

A Day in the Life—Duties and Responsibilities

The day-to-day duties of physicians vary depending on their employers and medical specialties. Physicians who operate their own private medical practices spend their days visiting with patients to diagnose and treat illness and injuries. Private physicians instruct patients on strategies to prevent disease by leading healthier lives. They also prescribe medicines both to treat illness and disease and to prevent future disease.

Physicians employed in the field of medical research spend their days evaluating new treatments, primarily in a laboratory setting. Medical research involves both clinical investigation of the effects of medical treatment on humans over time and investigation of trends in sickness and disease through extensive evaluation of public-health records.

Hospital- and university-employed physicians divide their time between treating patients and instructing medical students while also making occasional forays into medical research. Unlike private practices, in which physicians are also charged with overseeing the administrative and financial aspects of their operations, hospitals and universities offer physicians the assistance of large administrative bodies comprising both medical health professionals and medical students.

Duties and Responsibilities

- **Examining patients**
- **Ordering or performing various tests, analyses and x-rays**
- **Prescribing and administering drugs and treatments**

OCCUPATION SPECIALTIES

General Practitioners

General Practitioners diagnose and treat a variety of diseases and injuries in general practice. They order or execute various tests to obtain information on the patient's condition. They analyze the findings and prescribe drugs and other treatments. They make house or emergency calls, refer patients to specialized physicians, and perform minor surgery.

Osteopathic Physicians

Osteopathic Physicians diagnose and treat diseases and injuries of the human body, and examine patients to determine symptoms attributable to impairments of the musculoskeletal system. They treat disorders of bones, muscles, nerves and other body systems through surgical procedures or manipulative therapy.

Surgeons

Surgeons perform operations to correct deformities, repair injuries, prevent diseases, and improve body functions in patients.

Pediatricians

Pediatricians specialize in the diagnosis and treatment of children's diseases and in preventive medicine for children from birth through adolescence.

Obstetricians

Obstetricians and Gynecologists (070.101-034) specialize in the care and treatment of women during and immediately following pregnancy and in diseases of the female reproductive organs.

Cardiologists

Cardiologists diagnose and treat diseases of the heart.

Psychiatrists

Psychiatrists study, diagnose, and treat mental, emotional, and behavioral disorders.

Podiatrists

Podiatrists diagnose and treat disorders and diseases of the foot and lower leg.

Neurologists

Neurologists diagnose and treat organic diseases and disorders of the human nervous system.

Internists

Internists diagnose and treat diseases and injuries of human internal organ systems.

Family Practitioners

Family Practitioners provide comprehensive medical services for all members of a family, regardless of age or sex, on a continuing basis.

WORK ENVIRONMENT

Transferable Skills and Abilities

Communication Skills
- Speaking effectively
- Writing concisely

Interpersonal/Social Skills
- Being able to remain calm
- Being able to work independently
- Cooperating with others
- Providing support to others
- Working as a member of a team

Organization & Management Skills
- Handling challenging situations
- Making decisions
- Managing people/groups
- Paying attention to and handling details
- Performing duties which change frequently

Research & Planning Skills
- Developing evaluation strategies
- Using logical reasoning

Technical Skills
- Performing scientific, mathematical and technical work

Immediate Physical Environment

Physicians work in a wide variety of academic and medical settings, including laboratories, hospitals, and university classrooms.

Human Environment

Physicians must be excellent interpersonal communicators possessing the capability to explain intricate medical concepts in an understandable manner. As physicians must often discuss sensitive topics with patients, they must be capable of exhibiting tremendous compassion.

Technological Environment

Physicians use a vast array of traditional and contemporary medical devices and diagnostic technology, ranging from complex computer software to highly specialized instruments.

EDUCATION, TRAINING, AND ADVANCEMENT

High School/Secondary

High school students can best prepare to enter the medical field by taking high-level courses in algebra, calculus, geometry, biology, chemistry, and physics. Students who become medical doctors usually demonstrate high levels of achievement in each of these courses as well as extensive extracurricular involvement in high school events such as science fairs and national scholastic science competitions. Volunteerism and charitable work also help high school students attain and hone the interpersonal communication skills relevant to the position.

Suggested High School Subjects

- Algebra
- Biology
- Chemistry
- College Preparatory
- English
- Geometry
- Health Science Technology
- Humanities
- Mathematics
- Physical Education
- Physics
- Physiology
- Psychology
- Science
- Sociology
- Statistics
- Trigonometry

Related Career Pathways/Majors

Health Science Cluster

- Therapeutic Services Pathway

Famous First

Frank Hammond Krusen is considered the first "sports medicine" physiatrist. He is thought to have become interested in the use of what are now widely used physical therapy treatments such as hydrotherapy and hyperbaric oxygen in the treatment of injured athletes due to his own experience as a patient receiving treatment for tuberculosis in the 1920s.

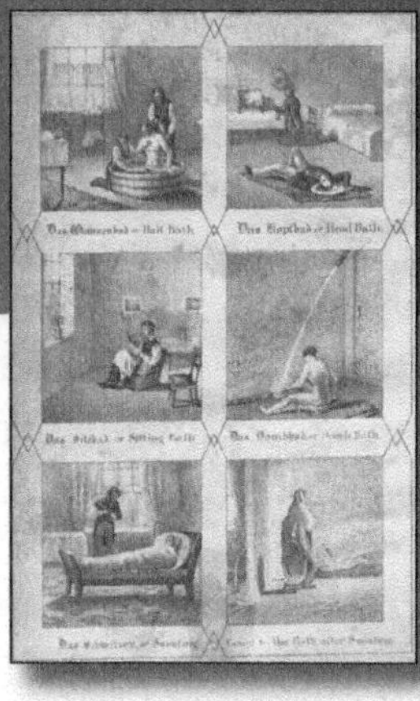

Postsecondary

Few professions require as much postsecondary education as that of physician. Aspiring physicians first complete four years of premedicine collegiate courses. Premed students must successfully complete collegiate-level courses in organic chemistry, physics, and biology. Such coursework involves investigations into complex topics such as cell biology, genetics, and biochemistry.

Upon the completion of premed studies, aspiring physicians are required to apply and be accepted to a four-year program at one of numerous accredited medical schools. In medical school, students dedicate themselves to a particular realm of medicine while completing coursework in anatomy, internal medicine, and general surgery.

Aspiring physicians must then successfully complete a three- to four-year doctoral program in which they investigate the historical development of and contemporary issues related to their particular realm of medical expertise. Specific medical fields pursued by medical students may include pathology, radiology, clinical medicine, and neurophysiology. Such programs are usually supplemented with hospital residency programs and thesis presentations outlining specific field or laboratory research.

Related College Majors

- Anatomy
- Human & Animal Physiology
- Medicine (M.D.)

- Osteopathic Medicine
- Pre-Medicine Studies

Adult Job Seekers

The enormous educational commitment required to become a physician makes adult job seekers who have dedicated a significant portion of their careers to other disciplines a rarity in medicine. Medical students often rely on the contacts and professional networks they construct during their lengthy period of education to lay the groundwork for future professional opportunities. There remain several medicine-centric avenues for adult job seekers to begin new careers in the medical field, particular in the realms of nursing, research analytics, and record keeping.

Professional Certification and Licensure

All physicians must hold and subsequently renew a state medical license, which grants them the right to practice medicine in that state. Medical license applications are reviewed annually by state medical boards.

Additional Requirements

Intense dedication to academics and perseverance in the face of challenging coursework are necessary for completion of the numerous years of study required to become a physician. In addition to the desire to help others, aspiring physicians must also be patient communicators who possess the ability to motivate themselves and those around them in the face of adversity.

Fun Fact

A wearable device called Catapult is tracking the heart rates, movements, and energy levels of pro athletes in the NFL, NBA, and NHL, not to mention college, high school and independent league athletes.

Source: www.beckersspine.com

EARNINGS AND ADVANCEMENT

Wages for physicians and surgeons are among the highest of all occupations, with a median wage equal to or greater than $208,000 per year. Median wages showing the differences in pay between types of physicians and surgeons are not available, but mean (average) annual wages for physicians and surgeons in May 2017 were as follows:

Anesthesiologists	$265,990
Surgeons	251,890
Obstetricians and gynecologists	235,240
Psychiatrists	216,090
Physicians and surgeons, all other	211,390
Family and general practitioners	208,560
Internists, general	198,370
Pediatricians, general	187,540

Many physicians and surgeons work long, irregular, and overnight hours. Physicians and surgeons may travel between their offices and hospitals to care for their patients. While on call, a physician may need to address a patient's concerns over the phone or make an emergency visit to a hospital or nursing home.

Neurologists may receive paid vacations, holidays, and sick days; life and health insurance; and retirement benefits. Self-employed neurologists must arrange for their own health insurance and retirement programs. Some employers provide for paid educational leave.

Median annual wages, May 2017

Physicians and surgeons: This wage is equal to or greater than $208,000 per year.

Health diagnosing and treating practitioners: $79,480

Total, all occupations: $37,690

Note: All Occupations includes all occupations in the U.S. Economy. Source: U.S. Bureau of Labor Statistics, Occupational Employment Statistics

Physicians may receive paid vacations, holidays, and sick days; life and health insurance; and retirement benefits. These are usually paid by the employer. Most physicians, however, are self-employed and must arrange for their own health insurance and retirement programs. Some employers also provide for paid educational leave.

EMPLOYMENT AND OUTLOOK

Overall employment of physicians and surgeons is projected to grow 13 percent from 2016 to 2026, faster than the average for all occupations.

The growing and aging population is expected to drive overall growth in the demand for physician services. As the older population grows and rates of chronic illnesses increase, consumers will seek high levels of care that use the latest technologies, diagnostic tests, and therapies.

Demand for physicians and surgeons is expected to increase despite factors that can temper growth. New technologies, such as improved information technologies or remote monitoring, are expected to allow physicians to treat more patients in the same amount of time. If adopted, new technologies can reduce the number of physicians who would be needed to complete the same tasks. In addition, physician assistants and nurse practitioner can do many of the routine duties of physicians and may be used to reduce costs at hospitals and doctor's offices.

Demand for physicians' services is sensitive to changes in healthcare reimbursement policies. Consumers may seek fewer physician services if changes to health coverage result in higher out-of-pocket costs for them.

Job prospects are expected to be very good because almost all graduates of domestic medical schools are matched to residencies (their first jobs as physicians) immediately after graduating.

Prospects should be especially good for physicians who are willing to practice in rural and low-income areas, because these areas tend to have difficulty attracting physicians. Job prospects also should be good for physicians in specialties dealing with health issues that mainly affect aging baby boomers. For example, physicians specializing in cardiology and radiology will be needed because the risks for heart disease and cancer increase as people age.

Percent change in employment, Projected 2016-26

Health diagnosing and treating practitioners: 16%

Physicians and surgeons: 13%

Total, all occupations: 7%

Note: All Occupations includes all occupations in the U.S. Economy. Source: U.S. Bureau of Labor Statistics, Employment Projections program

Related Occupations

- Allergist & Immunologist
- Anesthesiologist
- Neurologist
- Ophthalmalogist
- Pediatrician
- Physician
- Podiatrist
- Radiologist
- Surgeon

Related Military Occupations

- Physician & Surgeon

Conversation With . . .
DR. JEANNE DOPERAK, DO

Sports Medicine Physician
University of Pittsburgh Medical Center
Sports Medicine Physician, 12 years

1. **What was your individual career path in terms of education/training, entry-level job, or other significant opportunity?**

In high school, I took an anatomy and physiology course and was amazed. It was hard but it was my favorite class. That prompted me to take a first-aid course, and I got my lifeguard certification. I liked understanding the human body, but I also liked helping people as a lifeguard.

As I studied biology at Allegheny College, I also took an EMT course at a local community college and spent summers as an EMT. That reaffirmed that this was work I really loved.

I went on to Philadelphia College of Osteopathic Medicine with the idea that I would be a family doctor. In osteopathic medicine—as opposed to the typical "allopathic" model—we are taught to consider all parts of an illness: it's not just a broken arm, but it's a right arm and the person is a carpenter and how is their mental health because they can't work? The two models often take the same boards and go to the same residencies.

I needed to fill an elective near the end of my fourth year and a fellow student told me he'd done an elective in sports medicine at Pennsylvania State University, so I emailed them. It was life changing.

During college, I was a soccer player and I loved being on a team. I dreamed of the Olympics when I was young, but was never remotely good enough. But, wow, sports medicine was a way I got to be part of the team! I like the patients because athletes want to get better.

In sports medicine, I would argue we are saving lives every day because our patients are exercising, and we are helping keep them from illnesses such as heart disease and diabetes.

My residency was in family medicine at Latrobe Area Hospital in Pennsylvania, and I went on to a primary care sports medicine fellowship at UPMC Shadyside. You can take several residency pathways to sports medicine. I think family medicine residents are often the most prepared for sports medicine.

As a clinician, I see patients with injuries a few days a week. I also teach medical students and fellows and residents as an assistant professor. I'm a team physician for the athletic departments at the University of Pittsburgh, St. Vincent College, and others. I am responsible for the health and safety of all of Pitt's Olympic-sports teams, such as soccer, tennis, and gymnastics. As their primary care doctor, I sometimes travel with the team and am on the sidelines working with athletic trainers. This is a profession where you never get bored; every morning or afternoon I'm doing something different.

2. What are the most important skills and/or qualities for someone in your profession?

You need to be a collaborator; I'm part of a big team of people that provides care. When you're working with a group you have to be able to communicate your thoughts and ideas.

Being a good teacher is helpful with patients. Teaching them about their problem lets them be part of the process and buy into our plan.

You need to be willing to help. Three weeks ago, I was watching my daughter play softball. A girl fell and fractured her leg; I didn't get to see my daughter's softball game because I was on the next field helping. To be a physician is a life commitment.

3. What do you wish you had known going into this profession?

I wish I had known that I didn't have to major in biology. I loved human anatomy, not environmental science. In hindsight, I love psychology. I research mind-body wellness. I wish I had known all I had to do were the prerequisite classes.

4. Are there many job opportunities in your profession? In what specific areas?

Sports medicine is starting to get flooded. It's a fairly young field. Most of us aren't going to retire for awhile. There's always a need for people who are good at musculoskeletal care, and there is opportunity for sports medicine within a town or community. But there's not a plethora of team openings, and few positions with professional athletes.

5. How do you see your profession changing in the next five years, how will technology impact that change, and what skills will be required?

The newest thing is musculoskeletal ultrasound as a diagnostic tool, which requires hand-eye coordination. Biologics, including stem cell therapy, is up and coming in sports medicine. Sports is a huge business and keeping athletes healthy is integral to that business. With new technology, the challenge is determining evidence-based technologies that actually help.

6. What do you enjoy most about your job? What do you enjoy least about your job?

By far, I most love the people I work with. I get to meet and work with the most talented and smart people in the country—nutritionists, strength training coaches, surgeons. In the NCAA, I get to interact with physicians from all over the country.

Sometimes it would be nice to step away. This is a 24/7, 365-day-a-year job. I feel bad sometimes that my family has to wait for me. I've missed a lot of weddings. If it's a Saturday in the fall and you're a sports medicine doctor, you're on the football field.

7. Can you suggest a valuable "try this" for students considering a career in your profession?

A lot of high schools have a student athletic trainer program where a student can help the athletic trainer. That's a good peek inside what we do. Take courses like anatomy. Get first aid or CPR certification. For high school students 18 or over, being an EMT is good money and a good experience. There are also junior EMT programs for students 14-17.

MORE INFORMATION

American Medical Association
515 N State Street
Chicago, IL 60654
800.621.8335
www.ama-assn.org

American Medical Women's Association
Attn: Career Information
100 North 20th Street, 4th Floor
Philadelphia, PA 19103
215.320.3716
info@amwa-doc.org
www.amwa-doc.org

American Osteopathic Association
Public Relations Department
142 East Ontario Street
Chicago, IL 60611
800.621.1773
www.aoa-net.org

American Podiatric Medical Association
9312 Old Georgetown Road
Bethesda, MD 20814
301.581.9200
askapma@apma.org
www.apma.org

Association of American Medical Colleges
2450 N Street, NW
Washington, DC 20037-1126
202.828.0400
amcas@aamc.org
www.aamc.org

National Medical Association
8403 Colesville Road, Suite 920
Silver Spring, MD 20910
202.347.1895
www.nmanet.org

John Pritchard/Editor

Podiatrist

Snapshot

Career Cluster(s): Health Science
Interests: Medicine, podiatry, anatomy, biology, physiology, clinical science
Earnings (median in 2017): $127,740 per year; $61.41 per hour
Employment & Outlook through 2026: 10 % (Faster than average growth expected)

OVERVIEW

Sphere of Work

Podiatrists are physicians trained in the diagnosis and treatment of foot and lower leg disorders, injuries, and deformities. They provide general foot care, which can include the treatment or removal of bunions, corns, and calluses, as well as treatment of diabetes- or arthritis-related complications. They may choose to specialize in surgery, preventive care, sports medicine, orthopedics, or physical therapy. In addition, podiatrists may assist prosthetists and orthotists in the development, fitting, and maintenance of devices such as prosthetic feet and custom-made shoe inserts.

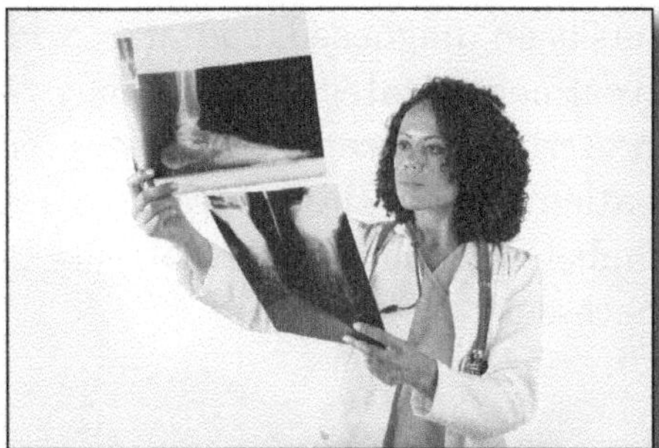

Work Environment

Podiatrists spend their workdays in hospitals and medical practices. They generally work forty-hour weeks but may work between thirty and sixty hours depending on patient need. In order to provide patients with convenient appointment times, podiatrists may work days, evenings, weekends, and on-call. However, self-employed podiatrists are typically able to set their own schedules. Due to the medical nature of the work, podiatrists may risk exposure to infectious disease.

Profile

Interests: Data, People, Things
Working Conditions: Work Inside
Physical Strength: Light Work
Education Needs: Doctoral Degree
Licensure/Certification: Required
Physical Abilities Not Required: Not Climb
Opportunities for Experience: Internship, Volunteer Work, Part Time Work
Holland Interest Score*: SIR

* See Appendix A

Occupation Interest

Individuals drawn to the profession of podiatrist tend to be intelligent, dexterous, analytical, and detail oriented. They must be able to identify and solve problems quickly, particularly because the early signs of several potentially life-threatening health problems manifest in the feet and lower legs. Podiatrists should enjoy working in a medical environment and be calm and tactful when discussing medical issues with patients.

A Day in the Life—Duties and Responsibilities

Podiatrists examine and treat patients with a variety of foot and lower leg injuries, disorders, and deformities. They begin by interviewing patients about their foot, lower leg, and general health history, determining the origin of the problem in question. Once the condition has been diagnosed, podiatrists identify and carry out one or more treatment strategies. They may remove bunions, corns, or calluses, or prescribe medication to treat infections or pain. Podiatrists educate patients about the progression and complications of arthritis and diabetes and may refer patients for x-rays or laboratory tests when necessary.

Depending on their area of specialty, podiatrists may perform surgeries to correct conditions such as tendonitis, tumors, or fractures, or they may refer patients to a specialist. Likewise, podiatrists may prescribe a physical therapy regimen to patients with chronic muscle or joint problems, or they may provide therapeutic treatments themselves. They also frequently provide preventive care or referrals to specialists in preventive care. These services may include footwear analysis, foot screenings for diabetic patients, and stride and gait analysis. Podiatrists may use techniques such as plaster casting to correct physical deformities in growing children and assist prosthetists and orthotists in the creation and maintenance of artificial feet or legs, corrective shoes, and ankle braces.

In addition, podiatrists frequently work with office staff to plan and schedule appointments, greet patients and explain the role of podiatry in their medical care, and participate in the daily operations of the facility as needed. Self-employed podiatrists are responsible for overseeing all aspects of business, including bookkeeping and advertising. Maintaining the confidentiality of patient information is essential, so all podiatrists must educate themselves about the administrative, physical, and technical patient privacy safeguards included in the federal Health Insurance Portability and Accountability Act.

Duties and Responsibilities

- **Examining the foot, leg and toe structures**
- **Diagnosing foot ailments, such as tumors, ulcers, fractures, skin or nail diseases and congenital or geriatric deformities**
- **Treating deformities such as flat or weak feet, and foot imbalance, by mechanical and electrical methods**
- **Treating conditions such as corns, calluses, ingrown nails, tumors, shortened tendons, cysts, bone disorders and abscesses by surgical methods**
- **Prescribing drugs**
- **Correcting deformities by means of plaster casts and strapping**

OCCUPATION SPECIALTIES

Orthopedic Podiatrists

Orthopedic podiatrists treat bone, muscle and joint disorders of the leg and foot.

Podopediatricians

Podopediatricians are concerned with foot ailments affecting children. They treat congenital foot disorders and work toward prevention of foot diseases.

Podiatric Surgeons

Podiatric surgeons perform foot surgery.

WORK ENVIRONMENT

Immediate Physical Environment

Podiatrists typically diagnose and treat patients in hospitals and private medical offices. They may occasionally travel between clinics or other medical facilities.

Human Environment

Podiatrists should be comfortable interacting with patients, physicians, laboratory technicians, nurses, and office staff. Due to the sensitive nature of medical diagnosis and treatment, podiatrists should be tactful, empathetic, and committed to patient confidentiality.

Transferable Skills and Abilities

Communication Skills
- Speaking effectively
- Writing concisely

Interpersonal/Social Skills
- Being able to remain calm
- Cooperating with others
- Working as a member of a team

Organization & Management Skills
- Handling challenging situations
- Making decisions

Research & Planning Skills
- Developing evaluation strategies

Technical Skills
- Performing scientific, mathematical and technical work

Technological Environment

Podiatrists may use a wide variety of tools and equipment to complete their work, including computers, Internet communication tools, medical tape, plaster casting, prosthetic devices, ultrasound machines, whirlpools, bandages, x-ray machines, and surgical tools.

EDUCATION, TRAINING, AND ADVANCEMENT

High School/Secondary

High school students interested in pursuing a career in podiatry should study anatomy, physiology, biology, and mathematics. Students interested in this career path will benefit from seeking volunteer opportunities, internships, or part-time work in medical settings. Aspiring podiatrists should apply to college or university programs following graduation.

Suggested High School Subjects
- Algebra
- Applied Math
- Biology
- Chemistry
- College Preparatory
- English

- Geometry
- Health Science Technology
- Physiology
- Trigonometry

Related Career Pathways/Majors

Health Science Cluster

- Therapeutic Services Pathway

Famous First

Clubfoot is a birth defect where one or both feet are rotated inwards and downwards. Juho "Nätti-Jussi" Nätti, a storyteller, lived in Lapland from 1890-1964. He was known as much for his stories as his untreated left clubfoot. A story tells that "not even the devil himself could tell which way Nätti has gone" by his footprints in the snow.

Postsecondary

Postsecondary students interested in becoming podiatrists should earn a bachelor's degree and apply for admission into a graduate training program accredited by the Council on Podiatric Medical Education (CPME). These four-year programs are similar to medical school and award the Doctor of Podiatric Medicine (DPM) degree. Coursework in anatomy, computer skills, clinical science, and medical ethics may also prove useful for aspiring podiatrists. Postsecondary students can gain work experience and potential advantage in their future job searches by securing internships or part-time employment in medical settings.

Related College Majors

- Anatomy
- Human & Animal Physiology
- Podiatry (DPM, DP, PodD)

Adult Job Seekers

Adults seeking employment as podiatrists should have a Doctor of Podiatric Medicine (DPM) degree from a CPME-accredited college. Professional podiatry associations, such as the American Podiatric Medical Association (APMA) and the American Association of Colleges of Podiatric Medicine (AACPM), may offer workshops, job listings, and networking opportunities.

Professional Certification and Licensure

Licensure is required of podiatrists as a condition of professional practice. Podiatry licenses are state-based and generally require that applicants earn a DPM from a CPME-accredited program, pass an examination offered by the National Board of Podiatric Medical Examiners (NBPME), complete a two-year postgraduate residency program, and participate in continuing education efforts. Due to differences in state licensing requirements, podiatrists should consult with the department of health in their home state for specific regulations.

Additional Requirements

Professionals in this role have access to confidential medical information; therefore, a high level of integrity and professional ethics is essential.

Fun Fact

A quarter of the bones in the human body are found in the feet—twenty-six bones, to be exact—plus 33 joints, 107 ligaments, 19 muscles, and tendons.

Source: www.foot.com

EARNINGS AND ADVANCEMENT

The median annual wage for podiatrists was $127,740 in May 2017. The lowest 10 percent earned less than $50,930, and the highest 10 percent earned more than $208,000.

In May 2017, the median annual wages for podiatrists in the top industries in which they worked were as follows:

Offices of physicians	$175,510
Federal government, excluding postal service	125,400
Offices of other health practitioners	123,160
Hospitals; state, local, and private	106,240

Most podiatrists work full time. Podiatrists' offices may be open in the evenings or on weekends to accommodate patients. Self-employed podiatrists or those who own their practice may set their own hours. In hospitals, podiatrists may have to work occasional nights or weekends, or may be on call.

Podiatrists may receive paid vacations, holidays, and sick days; life and health insurance; and retirement benefits. These are usually paid by the employer. Most podiatrists are self-employed and must provide for their own life and health insurance and retirement benefits.

Median annual wages, May 2017

Podiatrists: $127,740

Health diagnosing and treating practitioners: $79,480

Total, all occupations: $37,690

Note: All Occupations includes all occupations in the U.S. Economy. Source: U.S. Bureau of Labor Statistics, Occupational Employment Statistics

EMPLOYMENT AND OUTLOOK

There were approximately 11,000 podiatrists employed nationally in 2016. Employment of podiatrists is projected to grow 10 percent from 2016 to 2026, faster than the average for all occupations.

As the U.S. population ages, the number of people expected to have mobility and foot-related problems will rise, and podiatrists will be needed to treat these conditions. For example, older patients who remain active may incur injuries through exercise, and require foot and ankle care from podiatrists.

Growing rates of chronic conditions, such as diabetes and obesity, also may limit mobility of those with these conditions, and lead to problems such as foot ulcers and poor circulation in the feet and lower extremities. More podiatrists will be needed to provide care for these patients.

Job prospects for trained podiatrists should be good, given that there are a limited number of colleges of podiatry. In addition, the retirement of currently practicing podiatrists in the coming years is expected to increase the number of job openings for podiatrists.

Percent change in employment, Projected 2016-26

Health diagnosing and treating practitioners: 16%

Podiatrists: 10%

Total, all occupations: 7%

Note: All Occupations includes all occupations in the U.S. Economy. Source: U.S. Bureau of Labor Statistics, Employment Projections program

Related Occupations

- Allergist & Immunologist
- Cardiologist
- Medical Scientist
- Neurologist
- Ophthalmalogist
- Optometrist
- Pediatrician
- Physician
- Radiologist
- Surgeon

Conversation With . . .
DR. LISA SCHOENE

Podiatrist
Gurnee Podiatry & Sports Medicine Associates
Chicago, IL
Podiatrist, 28 years

1. What was your individual career path in terms of education/training, entry-level job, or other significant opportunity?

I am both a board-certified sports podiatrist and a certified athletic trainer. Ever since elementary school, I knew I wanted to be a doctor. In college, I worked as an EMT. A co-worker told me about a new class, basic athletic training. I thought it was like boot camp, but he said, "Oh, no, you take care of athletes." As soon as I walked into the training room, I knew it was the place for me. I decided to go into podiatry because I was already entrenched in taking care of athletes and really loving it and figured that as a podiatrist, I could see many types of athletes. I never looked back. After college, you complete four years of podiatry school. Many classes are identical to traditional medical school classes. You do a three-year residency program and then you're a foot and ankle surgeon and can specialize in areas like sports medicine or wound care. I graduated from the Dr. William M. Scholl College of Podiatric Medicine in Chicago. Podiatrists are like the primary care physicians of the lower extremities, because we have to know about everything that affects that part of the body: dermatology, vascular disease, rheumatological issues, biomechanics, and orthopedics. On any given day, I might treat wounds, see a runner who has back and hip pain, treat infected toenails, or do a biopsy on a suspicious mole.

I've worked with numerous professional, semi-professional and elite athletes—runners, skaters, football players, basketball players, triathletes and more. I was an athletic trainer at the World Cup Games in Chicago in 1994 and one of the podiatrists at the 1996 Olympic Games in Atlanta. I've treated athletes at the Olympic Training Center in Colorado Springs. For the last 18 years, I've treated many dancers around Chicagoland. And I've worked with the DePaul University Blue Demons basketball team for more than 26 years.

2. What are the most important skills and/or qualities for someone in your profession?

You have to be empathetic. You have to want to help patients. It can't just be about money. There's a high level of satisfaction in the podiatry field and all of my friends are happy with their practices and the lifestyle that podiatry affords us.

If you want to have a practice, you need to have an entrepreneurial streak. You have to be a self-starter. Many podiatrists practice in solo or small group practices, which allows us to have control over how our practice runs and to have that nice one-on-one contact with patients.

3. **What do you wish you had known going into this profession?**

   It would have been good to have a little bit of business know-how. Be aware that you may have to sell yourself. You have to get out there and really work hard. It may be unrealistic to think you're going to graduate and work for a clinic from 9 to 5 and make a lot of money.

4. **Are there many job opportunities in your profession? In what specific areas?**

   There's always going to be opportunity in podiatry, especially sports podiatry. A portion of our society is getting more and more obese, which comes with a plethora of medical issues like diabetes, hypertension, and related foot problems. On the flip side, there are always going to be people who are into fitness and working out. And if they're competing, they have higher demands and higher stakes. There are more foot and ankle injuries in the pediatric population, as kids are playing sports as if they're going to the Olympics tomorrow. We've got a lot of injuries that we didn't see in years past, because kids weren't playing sports 30-plus hours a week and they weren't playing the same sport all year long, which leads to repetitive injuries.

5. **How do you see your profession changing in the next five years as it relates to fitness and/or sports injuries, how will technology impact that change, and what skills will be required?**

   They're putting chips in shoes that will help determine what's happening with gait and pressure points. That will affect how we treat runners and other athletes. Video technology will be a tool for evaluating form and function. In regards to telemedicine, I doubt it will be prevalent in podiatry. As podiatrists, we use our hands on every patient; we pad, we do tapings, we use scissors, we use clippers, we use instruments, we make orthotics, give injections, and do office and operation room surgery.

6. **What do you enjoy most about your job? What do you enjoy least about your job?**

   I love when I can help one of my patients and they say, "Dr. Schoene saved my life because I can run now, I can walk, I can exercise, I can dance." I say to myself, "Well, I'm not curing cancer, but . . ." It's a nice thank you that you get. And it's really very, very rewarding.

What I like least is the bureaucracy. The insurance industry is just wreaking havoc on everyone's practice with so many regulations and rules. It has increased most physicians' stress levels, as well as the cost of running a practice.

7. Can you suggest a valuable "try this" for students considering a career in your profession?

Because we make orthotics and do padding, a little bit of a crafty nature can help you in podiatry. Contact local podiatrists and see if you can shadow for a day. Try going to more than one, as we all have different practices. That will give you a good look at what we do.

MORE INFORMATION

American Association of Colleges of Podiatric Medicine
15850 Crabbs Branch Way, Suite 320
Rockville, MD 20855
301.948.9760
info@aacpm.org
www.aacpm.org

American Podiatric Medical Association
9312 Old Georgetown Road
Bethesda, MD 20814
301.581.9200
askapma@apma.org
www.apma.org

National Board of Podiatric Medical Examiners
P.O. Box 510
Bellefonte, PA 16823
814.357.0487
NBPMEOfc@aol.com
www.nbpme.org

Simone Isadora Flynn/Editor

Rehabilitation Counselor

Snapshot

Career Cluster(s): Human Services
Interests: Counseling, mental health, physical rehabilitation, disability management, sociology, psychology
Earnings (median in 2017): $34,860 per year; $16.76 per hour
Employment & Outlook through 2026: 13% (Faster than average growth expected)

OVERVIEW

Sphere of Work

Rehabilitation counselors (also called case managers, rehabilitation specialists, and human services counselors) provide vocational, medical, housing, employment, and personal support services to individuals and groups with disabilities. In general, they work to help their clients become more independent, employable, and productive. Rehabilitation counselors support clients living with disabilities present since birth or impairments resulting from illness, disease, addiction, accident, or injury. For instance, individuals experiencing employment, housing, or social complications and challenges related to HIV/

AIDS, schizophrenia, or intellectual disability are generally eligible for rehabilitation counseling under the Rehabilitation Act and the Americans with Disabilities Act. The range of counseling services provided by rehabilitation counselors includes coordinating counseling activities at residential facilities, overseeing job training and vocational counseling programs, and creating rehabilitation plans for clients.

Work Environment

Rehabilitation counselors spend their workdays seeing clients in a wide variety of settings, including public or private rehabilitation facilities, mental health facilities, schools and universities, insurance companies, job training and placement programs, prisons and hospitals, and private counseling practices. Rehabilitation counselors may have an office or may travel to see clients. Given the diverse demands of rehabilitative counseling, rehabilitation counselors may need to work days, evenings, weekends, and on-call hours to meet client or caseload needs.

Profile

Interests: Data, People
Working Conditions: Work Inside
Physical Strength: Light Work
Education Needs: Bachelor's Degree, Master's Degree
Licensure/Certification: Required
Physical Abilities Not Required: Not Climb, Not Kneel
Opportunities for Experience: Military Service, Volunteer Work, Part Time Work
Holland Interest Score*: SEC

* See Appendix A

Occupation Interest

Individuals drawn to the rehabilitation counseling profession tend to be intelligent and socially conscious and able to quickly assess situations, find resources, demonstrate caring, and solve problems. Successful rehabilitation counselors display traits such as time management, knowledge of human behavior, initiative, and concern for individuals and society. Rehabilitation counselors should find satisfaction in spending time with a wide range of people, including those considered at-risk and those from diverse cultural, social, and educational backgrounds.

A Day in the Life—Duties and Responsibilities

Rehabilitation counselors help people with physical, mental, developmental, or emotional disabilities live independently. They work with clients to overcome or manage the personal, social, or psychological effects of disabilities on employment or independent living. A rehabilitation counselor's daily duties and responsibilities are determined by the individual's area of job specialization and work environment. Rehabilitation counseling specialties include physical rehabilitation, mental health counseling, substance abuse counseling, disability management, corrections, vocational assessment, forensic rehabilitation, pediatric rehabilitation, and geriatric rehabilitation.

Rehabilitation counselors work closely with clients to assess their situations and provide assistance. The rehabilitation counselor's first task is assessment. The rehabilitation counselor may complete client intake interviews for residential rehabilitation or medical facilities. He or she may also undertake client evaluations to assess physical, mental, academic, and vocational aptitude and readiness. The rehabilitation counselor then works with clients to develop counseling goals and objectives, oversees client job search efforts, and assists clients with employment, welfare, childcare, and food stamp applications. Depending on client needs, a rehabilitation counselor may also help clients obtain assistive devices, such as wheelchairs, that enable independence and employment, organize on-site job training for clients, help clients arrange transportation and housing, or lead workshops for clients in residential facilities.

Rehabilitation counselors act as liaisons for their clients. They participate in client team meetings and provide client updates to supervisors and client families. Rehabilitation counselors also develop connections and familiarity with community social service agencies, and refer clients to community services or agencies as needed.

All rehabilitation counselors ensure that rehabilitation programs meet the requirements of the Rehabilitation Act of 1973 and the Americans with Disabilities Act (ADA). In addition, all rehabilitation counselors are responsible for completing client records and required documentation, such as referral forms and insurance forms, on a daily basis.

Duties and Responsibilities

- Provide individual and group counseling to help clients adjust to their disability
- Evaluate clients' abilities, interests, experiences, skills, health, and education
- Develop a treatment plan for clients, in consultation with other professionals, such as doctors, therapists, and psychologists
- Arrange for clients to obtain services, such as medical care or career training
- Help employers understand the needs and abilities of people with disabilities, as well as laws and resources that affect people with disabilities
- Help clients develop their strengths and adjust to their limitations
- Locate resources, such as wheelchairs or computer programs, that help clients live and work more independently
- Maintain client records and monitor clients' progress, adjusting the rehabilitation or treatment plan as necessary
- Advocate for the rights of people with disabilities to live in a community and work in the job of their choice

WORK ENVIRONMENT

Immediate Physical Environment

The immediate physical environment of rehabilitation counselors vary based on their caseload and specialization. Rehabilitation counselors spend their workdays seeing clients in a wide variety of settings, including public or private rehabilitation facilities, mental health facilities, schools and universities, insurance companies, job training and placement programs, prisons and hospitals, and private counseling practices.

Transferable Skills and Abilities

Interpersonal/Social Skills
- Being able to work independently
- Being patient
- Having good judgment
- Motivating others
- Providing support to others

Organization & Management Skills
- Demonstrating leadership
- Making decisions
- Managing time
- Meeting goals and deadlines

Research & Planning Skills
- Predicting

Human Environment

Rehabilitation counselors interact with many people. They should be comfortable meeting with colleagues, staff, client families, incarcerated people, and people living with mental, physical, and emotional disabilities.

Technological Environment

Rehabilitation counselors use computers and a range of telecommunication tools to perform their job. They must be comfortable using computers to access client records. Rehabilitation counselors should also be comfortable traveling for work, as they may be required to frequently visit client homes and facilities.

EDUCATION, TRAINING, AND ADVANCEMENT

High School/Secondary

High school students interested in pursuing a career as a rehabilitation counselor should prepare themselves by developing good study habits. Coursework in foreign languages, public safety, sociology, psychology, and education can provide a strong foundation for college-level work in the rehabilitation counseling field. Due to the diversity of rehabilitation counseling specialties, high school students interested in this career path may benefit from seeking internships or part-time work that expose the students to diverse groups of people and social needs.

Suggested High School Subjects

- Applied Communication
- College Preparatory
- English
- Humanities
- Literature
- Psychology
- Social Studies
- Sociology

Related Career Pathways/Majors

Human Services Cluster

- Counseling & Mental Health Services Pathway
- Family & Community Services Pathway

Postsecondary

Most employers require a master's degree in rehabilitation counseling or a related field. Master's degree programs teach students to evaluate clients' needs, formulate, and implement job placement strategies, and understand the medical and psychological aspects of disabilities. These programs typically include a period of supervised clinical experience, such as an internship.

Although some employers hire workers with a bachelor's degree in rehabilitation and disability studies, these workers typically cannot offer the full range of services that a rehabilitation counselor with a master's degree can provide. Students in bachelor's degree programs learn about issues faced by people with disabilities and about the process of providing rehabilitation services. Some universities offer dual-degree programs in rehabilitation counseling, in which students can earn a bachelor's and master's degree in 5 years. Postsecondary students interested in becoming rehabilitation counselors should work towards an undergraduate degree in counseling or a related field, such as psychology or social work. Coursework in education, public safety, and foreign languages may also prove useful in their future work. Postsecondary students can gain work experience and potential advantage in their future job searches by securing internships or part-time employment in social service agencies or with individuals or groups living with physical, mental, or emotional disabilities.

Interested college students should also research and apply to master's degree programs for rehabilitation counseling. Master's degree programs in rehabilitative counseling typically include such courses as counseling theory, assessment, human development, ethics, evaluation, and case management; a practicum or internship is mandatory for degree completion.

Related College Majors

- Counselor Education/Student Counseling & Guidance Services
- Psychology, General
- Sociology

Adult Job Seekers

Adults seeking employment as rehabilitation counselors should have obtained a master's degree in rehabilitation counseling or a similar field, such as social work, psychology, or sociology, and earned national certification. Adult job seekers should educate themselves about the educational and professional license requirements of their home states and the organizations where they seek employment.

Adult job seekers may benefit from joining professional associations to help with networking and job searching. Professional rehabilitation counseling associations, such as the Commission on Rehabilitation Counselor Certification (CRCC), generally offer career workshops and maintain lists and forums of available jobs.

Professional Certification and Licensure

Licensing requirements for rehabilitation counselors differ by state and by type of services provided. Rehabilitation counselors who provide counseling services to clients and patients must attain a counselor license through their state licensing board. Rehabilitation counselors who provide other services, however, may be exempt from state licensing requirements. For example, rehabilitation counselors who provide only vocational rehabilitation services or job placement assistance may not need a license.

Licensure typically requires a master's degree and 2,000 to 4,000 hours of supervised clinical experience. In addition, counselors must pass a state-recognized exam. To maintain their license, counselors must complete annual continuing education credits.

Applicants should contact their state licensing board for information on which services or counseling positions require licensure. Contact information for these state licensing boards can be found through the Commission on Rehabilitation Counselor Certification.

Some employers prefer or require rehabilitation counselors to be certified. The Commission on Rehabilitation Counselor Certification offers the Certified Rehabilitation Counselor (CRC) certification. Applicants must meet advanced education, work experience, and clinical supervision requirements and pass a test. Certification must be renewed every 5 years. Counselors must complete continuing education requirements or pass a reexamination to renew their certification.

Additional Requirements

Individuals who find satisfaction, success, and job security as rehabilitation counselors will be knowledgeable about the profession's requirements, responsibilities, and opportunities. Successful rehabilitation counselors engage in ongoing professional development. Rehabilitation counselors must have high levels of integrity and ethics as they interact with at-risk people and groups and have access to personal information. Membership in professional counseling associations is encouraged among all rehabilitation counselors as a means of building status in a professional community and networking.

Fun Fact

About 74.6 million Americans have some type of physical disability, making them the largest minority group in the country.

Source: dosomething.org

EARNINGS AND ADVANCEMENT

Rehabilitation counselors may advance with additional education. Those persons with a master's degree will have higher earnings.

The median annual wage for rehabilitation counselors was $34,860 in May 2017. The lowest 10 percent earned less than $22,040, and the highest 10 percent earned more than $62,780.

In May 2017, the median annual wages for rehabilitation counselors in the top industries in which they worked were as follows:

State government, excluding education and hospitals	$48,380
Individual and family services	33,510
Nursing and residential care facilities	30,800
Community and vocational rehabilitation services	30,350

Rehabilitation counselors may receive paid vacations, holidays, and sick days; life and health insurance; and retirement benefits. These are usually paid by the employer.

Depending on where they work, some rehabilitation counselors may work evenings or weekends.

Median annual wages, May 2017

Counselors, social workers, and other community and social service specialists: $43,860

Total, all occupations: $37,690

Rehabilitation counselors: $34,860

Note: All Occupations includes all occupations in the U.S. Economy. Source: U.S. Bureau of Labor Statistics, Occupational Employment Statistics

EMPLOYMENT AND OUTLOOK

Rehabilitation counselors held about 119,300 jobs nationally in 2016. Job prospects are expected to be good because of job growth and the need to replace workers.

Employment of rehabilitation counselors is projected to grow 13 percent from 2016 to 2026, faster than the average for all occupations. Demand for rehabilitation counselors is expected to grow with the increase in the elderly population and with the continued rehabilitation needs of other groups, such as veterans and people with disabilities.

Older adults are more likely than other age groups to become disabled or injured. Rehabilitation counselors will be needed to help the elderly learn to adapt to any new limitations and learn strategies to live independently.

In addition, there will be a continued need for rehabilitation counselors to work with veterans who were disabled during their military service. They will also be needed to work with other groups, such as people who have learning disabilities, autism spectrum disorders, or substance abuse problems.

Percent change in employment, Projected 2016-26

Counselors, social workers, and other community and social service specialists: 16%

Rehabilitation counselors: 13%

Total, all occupations: 7%

Note: All Occupations includes all occupations in the U.S. Economy. Source: U.S. Bureau of Labor Statistics, Employment Projections program

Related Occupations

- Educational Counselor
- Employment Specialist
- Marriage Counselor
- Medical Social Worker
- Occupational Therapist
- Psychologist
- Social Worker
- Vocational Rehabilitation Counselor

Conversation With . . .
JOHN MOLLAHAN

Vocational Rehabilitation Counselor
Oregon Vocational Rehabilitation Services
Portland, OR
Rehabilitation Counselor, 15 years

1. What was your individual career path in terms of education/training, entry-level job, or other significant opportunity?

Originally, I wanted to be a firefighter, so I did a lot of volunteer firefighting and earned an associate degree in fire science technology. The competition was pretty stiff, so I went back to school, got a bachelor's in sociology at Portland State University, and worked for 10 years as a residential life counselor at the Washington State School for the Blind.

While I was there, I returned to Portland State and earned a master's degree in counseling, education, and rehabilitation. I originally applied to become a community counselor, but a professor who was basically the father of vocational rehabilitation told me that with my background, I should think about rehab. I asked: "What's rehab?" We talked, I realized I had already been doing the work, and that's what prompted me to go into this field.

We assist people who have disabilities—sometimes acquired through a sports injury, although it could be anything—and help them get back to work. We break down the barriers to work, and seek accommodations. Every individual has unique needs. A good case in point is a client who came in with multiple concussions, all related to sports injuries. This guy was fairly well-educated. He was having memory problems and mental health issues such as depression. He was working in the sports industry, but couldn't continue because of the memory issues and fatigue. We tried to fully understand his condition, gathering medical records and determining his eligibility for services.

We sent him to get enhanced rehab at a specialized brain injury clinic to help him with organization, and maybe get adaptive equipment to help him remember things. He was also meeting other people adapting to their disabilities. A lot of rehab is grief over the loss of ability to perform at the level you're used to. This gentleman no doubt benefited from meeting others in a similar situation.

We're not therapists, although I do have a private practice for mental health therapy. We do counseling and guidance. We do a lot of referrals, including for physical capacity exams. We keep people employed, help them access employment, and advocate for them on the job. Maybe they need a special chair, or desk.

2. What are the most important skills and/or qualities for someone in your profession?

Interpersonal skills such as empathy—the ability to enter a person's world and walk with them. People in this position need a master's degree—usually a counseling background. It's also helpful if a vocational rehabilitation counselor has done a variety of jobs, whether it's working at Taco Bell or working as a laborer, so that you have a varied background to help a person enter a field.

3. What do you wish you had known going into this profession?

Rehab counselors do a lot of procurement of services. I wish I'd had more training on how to handle a budget. In my master's degree studies, we didn't talk a lot about allocating and spending money.

4. Are there many job opportunities in your profession? In what specific areas?

There are a number of jobs in the field. Vocational rehabilitation counseling is a relatively small field, but there are jobs in state and federal programs, including working with veterans, and jobs with insurance companies. Some insurance companies contract out their vocational rehab work to private counselors.

5. How do you see your profession changing in the next five years as it relates to fitness and/or sports injuries? What role will technology play, and what skills will be required?

We use case management software systems that are always being improved. What we struggle with is making sure our services are seamless, so we've moved toward online applications. Technology will continue to help people access our services, but you will always need some interpersonal interaction.

6. What do you enjoy most about your job? What do you enjoy least about your job?

I really enjoy helping people reach their job goals and overcome their disabilities. I least enjoy the bureaucracy involved in serving our clients.

7. Can you suggest a valuable "try this" for students considering a career in your profession?

Job shadow, do informational interviews, and volunteer to work for a social service agency. Become a camp counselor, work at the teen center, work at a Boys & Girls Club. See if working with people gives you pleasure.

MORE INFORMATION

American Case Management Association
11707 W. 36th Street
Little Rock, AR 72211
501.907.2262
www.acmaweb.org

American Counseling Association
5999 Stevenson Avenue
Alexandria, VA 22304
800.347.6647
www.counseling.org

Association for Education and Rehabilitation of the Blind and Visually Impaired
1703 N. Beauregard St., Suite 440
Alexandria, VA 22311
703.671.4500
markr@aerbvi.org
www.aerbvi.org

Commission on Rehabilitation Counselor Certification
1699 E. Woodfield Road, Suite 300
Schaumburg, IL 60173
847.944.1325
info@crccertification.com
www.crccertification.com

National Board for Certified Counselors
3 Terrace Way, Suite D
Greensboro, NC 27403-3660
336.547.0607
nbcc@nbcc.org
www.nbcc.org

National Clearinghouse for Professions in Special Education
2900 Crystal Drive, Suite 1000
Arlington, VA 22202-3557
888.232.7733
ncpse@cec.sped.org
www.special-ed-careers.org

National Clearinghouse of Rehabilitation Training Materials
Utah State University
6524 Old Main Hill
Logan, UT 84322-6524
866.821.5355
ncrtm@usu.edu
ncrtm.org/moodle

National Organization for Human Services
5341 Old Highway 5, Suite 206, #214
Woodstock, GA 30188
770.924.8899
www.nationalhumanservices.org
NOHS Awards, Scholarships, and Grants:
www.nationalhumanservices.org/index.php?option=com_content&view=article&id=24&Itemid=111

Sport Psychologist

Snapshot

Career Cluster(s): Business, Management & Administration, Education & Training, Health Science, Human Services
Interests: Mental health, human behavior, emotional issues, psychological counseling, behavior modification
Earnings (median in 2017): $77,030 per year; $37.03 per hour
Employment & Outlook through 2026: 14% (Faster than average growth expected)

OVERVIEW

Sphere of Work

Psychologists study the human mind, and try to understand human behavior. Many people think of psychologists as people who provide counseling services to help people cope with issues in their lives, but that is only one area of specialization in this broad field. Psychologists may work directly with clients in an office, a hospital, or in a school; they may work for companies or organizations, figuring out how best to accomplish tasks or convey messages; or they may work at a university or research institution, conducting psychological research or teaching psychology to others. These various areas of specialization

are denoted by terms such as clinical psychology, school psychology, industrial/organizational psychology, developmental psychology, social psychology, research psychology, and others.

Work Environment

Psychologists are often self-employed, working as private practitioners or independent consultants. They may work from home or in private offices, where they set their own hours, sometimes working evenings and weekends to accommodate working clients. Others work in institutional team environments, such as in schools or with corporations, and provide their services during regular business hours. Research psychologists may work in labs carrying out various kinds of experiments and evaluating research results. Psychologists also work at hospitals, nonprofit organizations, and government agencies.

Profile

Interests: Data, People
Working Conditions: Work Inside
Physical Strength: Light Work
Education Needs: Master's Degree, Doctoral Degree
Licensure/Certification: Required
Physical Abilities Not Required: Not Climb, Not Handle, Not Kneel
Opportunities for Experience: Military Service, Volunteer Work
Holland Interest Score*: SIA

* See Appendix A

Occupation Interest

Psychology is an appropriate career pursuit for people who are interested in how the human mind works, and in how this knowledge can be used to improve people's lives. To varying degrees, depending on their area of specialization, psychologists should have good people skills (for one-on-one work with patients or other members of a team) as well as strong analytical skills (for conducting research or evaluating patients' needs). Psychologists usually have graduate degrees, and most commonly, a doctorate.

A Day in the Life—Duties and Responsibilities

Again, the typical day for a psychologist depends on his or her specialty. Clinical or counseling psychologists may spend their days helping clients cope with mental illness or simply managing the issues in their life—family or marital distress, bereavement, substance abuse, or problems at work or school. They may also work with medical patients trying to cope with illness or injury.

In the process of helping clients, psychologists conduct diagnostic testing and interviews that can help them pinpoint central issues and behavioral triggers. They provide various kinds of psychotherapy, or psychological counseling, sometimes over just a few sessions and sometimes on a longer-term basis. They may help clients develop behavior modification programs or other strategies to help achieve wellness. In most cases, psychologists are not qualified to prescribe medication, and may recommend other medical providers to patients who could benefit from medication.

Research psychologists and industrial/organizational psychologists do not typically provide services directly to individuals. Rather, they work for organizations or institutions, perhaps expanding knowledge and understanding through large research experiments, or helping develop work processes and approaches that help fulfill business-related needs, such as greater employee productivity or more effective product marketing. Research psychologists may conduct experiments on people or animals; they may administer surveys or conduct ongoing interviews with human volunteers; or they may study how animals react to various stimuli in order to learn more about very basic mental processes. Industrial/organizational psychologists may help companies develop more effective communication strategies between managers and employees, or assess other aspects of work life and generate recommendations for improvement.

Duties and Responsibilities

- **Diagnosing and treating psychological problems**
- **Collecting data by using interviews, case histories, observational techniques and other methods**
- **Administering and interpreting psychological tests**
- **Counseling people individually and in groups**
- **Conferring with parents, counselors, administrators and others**

OCCUPATION SPECIALTIES

Clinical Psychologists

Clinical psychologists constitute the largest specialty; they help mentally and emotionally disturbed people adjust to life.

Counseling Psychologists

Counseling psychologists use such techniques as interviewing and testing to advise people on how to deal with problems of everyday living—personal, educational, vocational and social.

Educational Psychologists

Educational psychologists design, develop and evaluate psychological programs that are applicable to educational problems.

School Psychologists

School psychologists evaluate children within an educational system and plan and implement corrective programs. They work with teachers, parents, and administrators to resolve students' learning and behavioral problems.

Psychometrists

Psychometrists administer, score, and interpret intelligence, aptitude, achievement and other psychological tests.

Experimental Psychologists

Experimental psychologists conduct experiments with human beings and animals, such as rats, monkeys and pigeons, in the prominent areas of experimental research that includes motivation, thinking, learning and retention, sensory and perceptual processes and genetic and neurological factors in behavior.

Industrial Organizational Psychologists

Industrial organizational psychologists develop and apply psychological techniques to administration, management, and marketing problems. They are involved in policy planning, applicant screening, training and development, psychological test research, counseling and organizational development.

Engineering Psychologists

Engineering Psychologists conduct research, development, application, and evaluation of psychological principles relating human behavior to characteristics, design, and the use of environments and systems within which human beings work and live.

Social Psychologists

Social psychologists investigate the psychological aspects of human interrelationships to gain understanding of individual and group thought, feeling and behavior, using observation, experimentation, and survey techniques.

WORK ENVIRONMENT

Immediate Physical Environment

Psychologists usually see clients in comfortable and quiet office or home settings where there are few distractions. Research and organizational psychologists can be found in labs and office buildings, and other psychologists can be found in their respective places of specialization, such as schools, hospitals, and places of business.

Human Environment

Clinical and counseling psychologists work with clients who may be in various states of distress, and they also frequently collaborate with other psychologists, social workers, psychiatrists, and other

Transferable Skills and Abilities

Communication Skills
- Expressing thoughts and ideas
- Speaking effectively
- Writing concisely

Interpersonal/Social Skills
- Cooperating with others
- Working as a member of a team

Organization & Management Skills
- Managing time
- Meeting goals and deadlines
- Performing duties which change frequently

Research & Planning Skills
- Analyzing information
- Developing evaluation strategies
- Using logical reasoning

Technical Skills
- Performing scientific, mathematical and technical work

kinds of social service and health care providers. Research psychologists work with colleagues and other professionals, and teaching psychologists work with undergraduate and graduate students.

Technological Environment

Unless working in a research laboratory with humans, animals, and scientific equipment, psychologists mostly listen, ask questions, take notes, and often they use computers to keep records of their clients' status and progress.

EDUCATION, TRAINING, AND ADVANCEMENT

High School/Secondary

High school students can best prepare for a career in psychology by focusing on science, English, and math. Some high schools may offer advanced placement psychology as an elective. Otherwise, students should generally cultivate their skills in writing, speech, critical thinking, and scientific research. Biology is the science that is most relevant to psychology, and it is also useful to take classes in the social sciences.

High school guidance counselors can help students learn more about career and university offerings.

Suggested High School Subjects

- Algebra
- Child Growth & Development
- College Preparatory
- Composition
- English
- Psychology
- Social Studies
- Sociology
- Statistics

Related Career Pathways/Majors

Business, Management & Administration Cluster

- Human Resources Pathway

Education & Training Cluster

- Professional Support Services Pathway

Health Science Cluster

- Therapeutic Services Pathway

Human Services Cluster

- Counseling & Mental Health Services Pathway

Famous First

In England, early psychology involved phrenology and the response to social problems including alcoholism, violence, and the country's well-populated mental asylums. Phrenology is a process that involves observing and/or feeling the skull to determine an individual's psychological attributes. Phrenologists would run their fingertips and palms over the skulls of their patients to feel for enlargements or indentations and often took measurements with a tape measure or a *craniometer*, a special version of a caliper.

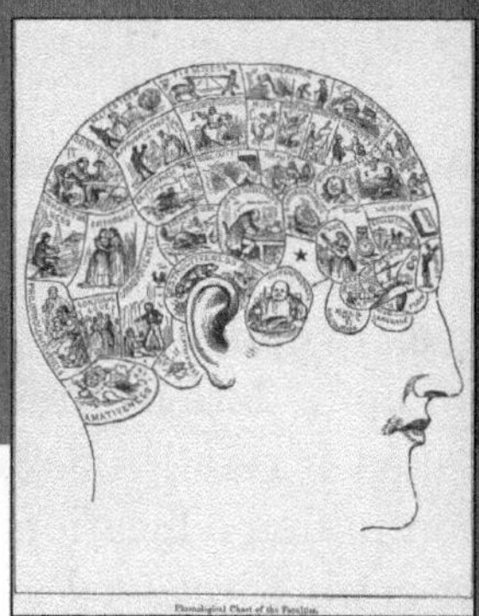

Postsecondary

In order to practice psychology, students need a master's or doctoral degree in the field. Since competition in this occupation is stiff, it is best to earn a doctoral degree covering counseling, teaching, and/or research. Those with just an undergraduate degree will find it very difficult to qualify for a psychologist position.

Universities all over the United States encourage psychology students to understand and conduct varying levels of analysis of written documents and the interpretation of scientific cases. Coursework includes topics such as critical thinking, psychopathology, the biological bases of behavior, psychological assessment, interpersonal behavior, psychophysiology, psychosocial adjustment, and research design and methodology.

The largest professional organization of U.S. psychologists, the American Psychological Association, normally requires a doctoral degree for full membership, and a master's degree for associate membership. Doctoral degrees available in psychology include: a regular doctorate, or PhD, the most wide-ranging option; a doctorate of psychology (PsyD), which is geared more toward clinical practice than research; and a doctorate of education (EdD) focused on psychology, usually counseling, developmental, or educational psychology.

Related College Majors

- Clinical Psychology
- Criminology
- Gerontology
- Psychology, General

Adult Job Seekers

For those adults with the appropriate education and training, who seek to update their professional credentials, it is important to have an up-to-date resume, and determine which courses may need to be taken or retaken. Other ways to enhance credentials include taking continuing education courses, applying for scholarships or grants, or getting involved in work with professional associations to make contacts for future employment opportunities.

Professional Certification and Licensure

Those psychologists who have their own practice need a license from the state in which they work. Getting a license requires education, work experience, and passing a qualifying test.

Additional Requirements

Psychologists are often empathetic and compassionate people, interested in the complexities of the mind and the individual's ability to navigate an increasingly complex world. Successful psychologists are discrete and patient, understanding that patient treatment is a complex process with both successes and failures. An ability to motivate others to continue to work towards long-term mental health is critical.

Fun Fact

A former addict who found meditation through AA has helped NBA giants Michael Jordan, Shaquille O'Neal, and Kobe Bryant with their game. Sport psychologist George Mumford teaches mindfulness meditation so athletes can be "warriors" and stay "in the zone."

Source: ABC News

EARNINGS AND ADVANCEMENT

The median annual wage for psychologists was $77,030 in May 2017. The lowest 10 percent earned less than $42,330, and the highest 10 percent earned more than $124,520.

Median annual wages for psychologists in May 2017 were as follows:

Psychologists, all other	$97,740
Industrial-organizational psychologists	87,100
Clinical, counseling, and school psychologists	75,090

In May 2017, the median annual wages for psychologists in the top industries in which they worked were as follows:

Government	$94,910
Hospitals; state, local, and private	83,910
Ambulatory healthcare services	77,030
Elementary and secondary schools; state, local, and private	74,470

Psychologists in private practice often set their own hours, and many work part time as independent consultants. They may work evenings or weekends to accommodate clients. Those employed in hospitals or other healthcare facilities also may have evening or weekend shifts. Most psychologists in clinics, government, industry, or schools work full-time schedules during regular business hours.

Median annual wages, May 2017

Psychologists, all other: $97,740

Industrial-organizational psychologists: $87,100

Social scientists and related workers: $76,970

Clinical, counseling, and school psychologists: $75,090

Total, all occupations: $37,690

Note: All Occupations includes all occupations in the U.S. Economy. Source: U.S. Bureau of Labor Statistics, Occupational Employment Statistics

EMPLOYMENT AND OUTLOOK

Employment of clinical, counseling, and school psychologists is projected to grow 14 percent from 2016 to 2026, faster than the average for all occupations. Greater demand for psychological services in schools, hospitals, mental health centers, and social service agencies should drive employment growth.

Demand for clinical and counseling psychologists will increase as people continue to turn to psychologists for help with their problems. Psychologists also will be needed to provide services to an aging population, helping people deal with the mental and physical changes that happen as they grow older. Psychological services will also be needed for veterans suffering from war trauma, for survivors of other trauma, and for individuals with autism.

Employment of school psychologists will continue to grow because of the raised awareness of the connection between mental health and learning and because of the increasing need for mental health services in schools. School psychologists will be needed to work with students, particularly those with special needs, learning disabilities, and behavioral issues. Schools rely on school psychologists to assess and counsel students. In addition, school psychologists will be needed to study how factors both in school and outside of school affect learning. Once aware of those factors, teachers and administrators can use them to improve education. Job opportunities may be limited, however, because employment of school psychologists in public schools and universities is contingent on state and local budgets.

Employment of industrial–organizational psychologists is projected to grow 8 percent from 2016 to 2026, about as fast as the average for all occupations. Organizations will continue to use industrial–organizational psychologists to help select and retain employees, increase organizational productivity and efficiency, and improve office morale.

Competition for jobs for psychologists will vary by specialty and level of education obtained.

Industrial–organizational psychologists are expected to face competition for positions because of the large number of qualified applicants. Industrial–organizational psychologists with extensive training in quantitative research methods may have a competitive edge.

Candidates with a doctoral or education specialist degree and postdoctoral work experience will have the best job opportunities in clinical, counseling, or school psychology positions.

There are expected to be better opportunities for psychologists who specialize in working with the elderly and in rehabilitation psychology.

Percent change in employment, Projected 2016-26

Clinical, counseling, and school psychologists: 14%

Social scientists and related workers: 11%

Psychologists, all other: 11%

Industrial-organizational psychologists: 8%

Total, all occupations: 7%

Note: All Occupations includes all occupations in the U.S. Economy. Source: U.S. Bureau of Labor Statistics, Employment Projections program

Related Occupations

- Educational Counselor
- Human Resources Specialist/ Manager
- Marriage Counselor
- Medical Social Worker
- Neuropsychologist
- Psychiatrist
- Rehabilitation Counselor
- Social Worker
- Substance Abuse Counselor

Related Military Occupations

- Psychologist

Conversation With . . .
ABBY KEENAN, MS, CMPC

Certified Mental Performance Consultant
Intrepid Performance Consulting
www.intrepidperformance.com
Auburn, GA
Sport Psychology field, 6 years

1. What was your individual career path in terms of education/training, entry-level job, or other significant opportunity?

I completed a Bachelor of Science in psychology at the University of Georgia, then went on to Florida State University to obtain a master's in educational psychology/ sport psychology. In graduate school, I interned with various middle, high school, and college sports teams under the mentorship of a professor. I learned how to teach athletes to set effective goals, have effective thoughts, build confidence, manage their energy, focus on the right thing at the right time, and visualize success, among other mental skills. At the end of my graduate degree, I worked at a sports academy that groomed athletes, mostly baseball players, to play at a higher level. My job was to develop a mental skills training program.

I also worked as a military contractor at Fort Bragg, training Special Operations soldiers to use mental skills to improve performance in the classroom and during field exercises. This experience, combined with interning, gave me enough mentored hours to apply for the Certified Mental Performance Consultant (CMPC) credential from the Association for Applied Sport Psychology. Because I don't have a doctorate degree, I cannot legally call myself a sport psychologist.

I also trained as a challenge course facilitator at Florida State and spent years as a summer camp staff member, which taught me how to facilitate team-building activities, work effectively with groups, and lead meaningful reflection.

2. What are the most important skills and/or qualities for someone in your profession?

Active listening, relationship-building, sports knowledge, clear communication, effective questioning, the ability to connect theory and research to practice, and ethical behavior are all key.

In addition, it's important to be skilled at being organized, flexible, creative, and observant. Time management and customer service matter.

From a personal standpoint, you also need to lead a healthy lifestyle, practice mental performance skills, and have competitive athletic experience.

3. What do you wish you had known going into this profession?

I wish I'd known that there aren't many jobs for master's-level practitioners. Even if your graduate degree and training are in sport psychology, you cannot use that title because "psychology" is legally protected in most states. You have to obtain a PhD or PsyD in counseling or clinical psychology and sit for licensure before calling yourself a "sport psychology consultant" or "sport psychologist."

Currently, there's no accreditation of graduate programs in the mental performance training field, meaning there are no standards that schools must meet to ensure graduates are prepared to enter the workforce and/or apply for the CMPC credential. There's no recourse when practitioners claim to offer services without proper training. Anyone can call themselves a "performance coach," "life coach," "sport performance expert," "mental coach," and the like. That makes it difficult for those of us who have spent years training.

4. Are there many job opportunities in your profession? In what specific areas?

Job opportunities for master's-level practitioners are scarce. The U.S. Army Ready and Resilient (R2) program is one of the largest employers of master's-level sport psychology graduates in the country. IMG Academy and professional organizations like Major League Baseball employ others, but those opportunities are extremely competitive. Many master's-level practitioners start their own business.

More opportunities are available with a doctorate in counseling or clinical psychology, particularly if you also earn the CMPC credential. You could be a professor, researcher, or consultant. Consultants work in public or private settings, for colleges and universities, in medical settings, or for professional sports organizations. Many employers believe consultants can and should support athletes with mental skills training that is, performance-based skills to help on the field or court—and mental health interventions that are counseling/clinical-based to deal with other issues. Often, consultants aren't trained to do both and shouldn't, due to ethical considerations.

5. How do you see your profession changing in the next five years as it relates to fitness and/or sports injuries? What role will technology play, and what skills will be required?

Sports injuries, particularly concussions, are becoming more common. In the next five years, I believe there will be a heightened focus on these injuries, particularly on how they impact an athlete's sport experience as well as school and work. Professionals will be trained to intervene from a physical and mental perspective for the best return-to-sport results. Technology already plays a large role. Many consultants use videoconferencing to meet with athletes virtually. Often, we encourage athletes to practice mental skills using apps, voice recordings, and shared interfaces like Google Docs. Additionally, many practitioners use biofeedback and neurofeedback.

6. **What do you enjoy most about your job? What do you enjoy least about your job?**

   My favorite moment is when athletes "get it"—when they understand that they are in control of their attitude, effort, and behavior in and out of their sport. When they take the initiative to apply mental skills to new situations and create their own versions of success. When they don't need me anymore.

   What I enjoy least is the marketing and sales side of the job. It can be difficult to gain entry with athletes, coaches, and parents due to budget restrictions and a misunderstanding of what sport psychology is and the benefits that mental skills training can provide.

7. **Can you suggest a valuable "try this" for students considering a career in your profession?**

   Engage in multiple sports and become competitive in at least one. This will allow you to experience what it's like to train hard for something, be a part of a team, interact with coaches, and manage the mental side of sport—dealing with pressure, inflated or deflated confidence, and success and failure.

MORE INFORMATION

American Psychological Association
Education Directorate
750 First Street, NE
Washington, DC 20002-4242
800.374.2721
www.apa.org

Association for Psychological Science
1133 15th Street NW, Suite 1000
Washington, DC 20005
202.293.9300
www.psychologicalscience.org

Mental Health America
2000 N. Beauregard Street, 6th Floor
Alexandria, VA 22311
800.969.6642
infoctr@mentalhealthamerica.net
www.nmha.org

National Alliance on Mental Illness
3803 N. Fairfax Drive, Suite 100
Arlington, VA 22203
800.950.6264
www.nami.org

National Association of School Psychologists
4340 East West Highway, Suite 402
Bethesda, MD 20814
301.657.0270
center@naspweb.org
www.nasponline.org

National Institute of Mental Health
6001 Executive Boulevard
Room 8184, MSC 9663
Bethesda, MD 20892-9663
866.615.6464
nimhinfo@nih.gov
www.nimh.nih.gov

Susan Williams/Editor

Sports Instructor/Coach

Snapshot

Career Cluster(s): Education & Training
Interests: Physical education, kinesiology, physiology, game preparation, psychology, anatomy
Earnings (median in 2017): $32,270 per year
Employment & Outlook through 2026: 13% (Faster than average growth expected)

OVERVIEW

Sphere of Work

Sports instructors and coaches work to develop the athletic skills of young people and teach them to function in a team setting. They instruct individuals or teams in the rules, techniques, and strategies of a particular sport, and help them train in order to achieve success.

Work Environment

Sports instructors and coaches work with young athletes in a wide range of environments, including athletic fields, gymnasiums, and classrooms. Those who work outdoors will have to factor in the risks or limitations posed by different types of weather.

Depending on their level of active participation, instructors and coaches may be at risk for sports-related injuries.

Profile

Interests: People
Working Conditions: Work Both Inside and Outside
Physical Strength: Light Work, Medium Work
Education Needs: Bachelor's Degree
Licensure/Certification: Usually Not Required
Physical Abilities Not Required: Not Climb
Opportunities for Experience: Internship, Volunteer Work, Part Time Work
Holland Interest Score*: ESR

* See Appendix A

Occupation Interest

A sports instructor or coach should possess a strong background in, and knowledge of, the various sports for which he or she will be responsible. This includes not only an understanding of the basic physical skills needed to participate in these sports, but also how to teach people to work in a group and develop team goals.

A Day in the Life—Duties and Responsibilities

Sports instructors and coaching professionals work in a setting that requires tremendous social communication skills, as well as knowledge of motivational and educational techniques. They impart the knowledge and understanding required to effectively participate in an individual or team sport, while teaching young athletes the benefits of working in a group setting toward a common goal. The instructor or coach implements a learning progression, using a variety of repetitive physical drills that allows the athlete to build confidence by properly executing the skills required to compete in the sport being practiced. This is done in team practice sessions, which work progressively from an individual skill development period to a group development period, ending with an exercise in which both individual and group development learning and repetitive drill work are incorporated into the complete team setting. This is essential preparation for athletic contests.

Duties and Responsibilities

- Organizing and running practice sessions
- Developing an individual's athletic talent
- Directing and orchestrating workouts
- Creating and executing game strategy

OCCUPATION SPECIALTIES

Head Coaches

Head Coaches work with groups of athletes through subordinate assistant coaches.

Coaches of Professional Athletes

Coaches of Professional Athletes work with groups of paid professional athletes and paid assistant coaches. Their duties often include not only game preparation and game coaching, but recruiting, assessing and selecting new professional talent.

Physical Instructors

Physical Instructors work with individuals and small groups in beginning or advanced exercises for reducing weight or improving health.

WORK ENVIRONMENT

Transferable Skills and Abilities

Communication Skills

- Speaking effectively
- Writing concisely

Interpersonal/Social Skills

- Being patient
- Cooperating with others
- Motivating others
- Providing support to others
- Teaching others
- Working as a member of a team

Organization & Management Skills

- Coordinating tasks
- Managing people/groups
- Managing time
- Organizing information or materials

Immediate Physical Environment

Sports instructors and coaches work in athletic fields, gymnasiums, weight rooms, pools, classrooms, and offices. In certain sports, athletes are introduced to the individual and comprehensive team concepts via classroom instruction.

Human Environment

Sports instructors and coaches work with athletes of varying ages and skill levels. They may also work with other coaching professionals, office and teaching personnel, the media, and the community at large.

Technological Environment

Sports instructors and coaches use a variety of tools, including sports-related physical equipment and audiovisual devices. The physical equipment is designed to improve individual kinetic skills and techniques, which in turn improves the athlete's ability to compete. Audiovisual equipment allows athletes to observe their drill work and exercises, so that they can properly gauge what they need to improve to be competitive.

EDUCATION, TRAINING, AND ADVANCEMENT

High School/Secondary

High school students should study biology, physical education, and computers. English, psychology, and speech communication courses are also helpful, as is participation in whichever sport(s) the student wants to teach. During the summer, students should consider attending athletic camps for further development of individual skills.

Suggested High School Subjects

- English
- First Aid Training
- Health Science Technology
- Physical Education
- Psychology
- Social Studies

Related Career Pathways/Majors

Education & Training Cluster

- Teaching/Training Pathway

Famous First

The term *coach* refers to a horse-drawn carriage. Students at the University of Oxford in the early nineteenth century used the term as a slang word to refer to a private tutor who could "drive" a student through his examinations. In fact, Britain took the lead in upgrading the status of sports in the 19th century, with the result that the coach became considered a professional in the Victorian era. During the First World War, coaches supervised physical conditioning and morale-building for British military units.

Postsecondary

Over the years, the job of sports instruction has come to place more of an emphasis on the development of professional standards for those who enter the field. Sports instructors and coaches in schools usually have at least a bachelor's degree, and are often also teachers or other education professionals. Colleges and universities in the United States offer a variety of coaching degree programs, which include courses in subjects such as human kinesiology, biology, physiology, nutrition, sports science and medicine, and professional standards. University programs may also offer internships for interested students, which allow them to observe professionals at work in their chosen sports and develop professional contacts for the future.

Related College Majors

- Physical Education Teaching & Coaching

Adult Job Seekers

Sports instructors and coaching professionals are generally also educators seeking employment in local school districts. Depending on the economic conditions and availability of qualified teachers, college graduates may be required to work as substitute teachers until a full-time opportunity presents itself. Substitute teacher work does not preclude an individual from working as a sports coach in a school district at the same time, and doing so can afford a recent college graduate the opportunity to further develop his or her individual skills and knowledge, while also becoming familiar with the school district personnel and administration. This can be beneficial in the highly competitive job market, as can being certified to teach multiple disciplines.

Participation in professional associations can also provide good opportunities for employment and personal development of one's professional skills. Each state has an official organization for high school sports, coordinated through the National Federation of State High School Associations (NFHS). Other national organizations, such as the Amateur Athletic Union, may also be helpful.

Professional Certification and Licensure

At the high school level, various states have different requirements for professional certification or endorsements in coaching. Some states may require teaching certification. Students interested in pursuing this profession should investigate the requirements of the state and school district in which they wish to work.

Additional Requirements

As in education, a sports instructor or coaching professional's strong commitment to continued learning and training is important for his or her own professional development, as well as for the safety and instruction of the athletes being coached.

EARNINGS AND ADVANCEMENT

Earnings in this field span the range from zero to many hundreds of thousands of dollars. Most sports instructors and coaches earn very modest amounts of money and usually must supplement their incomes from other sources. Advancement is based on ability and experience.

The median annual wage for coaches and scouts was $32,270 in May 2017. The lowest 10 percent earned less than $18,670, and the highest 10 percent earned more than $75,400.

In May 2017, the median annual wages for coaches and scouts in the top industries in which they worked were as follows:

Colleges, universities, and professional schools; state, local, and private	$44,340
Arts, entertainment, and recreation	35,480
Elementary and secondary schools; state, local, and private	26,880

Only successful professional coaches in established professional organizations or schools can usually expect any fringe benefits. These usually include paid vacations, holidays, and sick days; life and health insurance; and retirement benefits.

Coaches and scouts often work irregular hours, including evenings, weekends, and holidays. Professional or college coaches usually work more than 40 hours a week for several months during the sport's season, if not most of the year. Many high school coaches work part time and may have other jobs aside from coaching.

Median annual wages, May 2017

Entertainers and performers, sports and related workers: $42,010

Total, all occupations: $37,690

Coaches and scouts: $32,270

Note: All Occupations includes all occupations in the U.S. Economy. Source: U.S. Bureau of Labor Statistics, Occupational Employment Statistics

EMPLOYMENT AND OUTLOOK

There were about 276,100 sports instructors and coaches employed nationally in 2016. About half of all sports instructors and coaches worked part-time, and about one-fourth were self-employed, earning fees for lessons.

Employment of coaches and scouts is projected to grow 13 percent from 2016 to 2026, faster than the average for all occupations. Rising participation in high school and college sports should increase demand for coaches and scouts.

High school enrollment is projected to increase over the next decade, resulting in a rise in the number of student athletes. As schools offer more athletic programs and as more students participate in sports, the demand for coaches may increase.

Participation in college sports also is projected to increase over the next decade, particularly at smaller colleges and in women's sports. Many small, Division III colleges are expanding their sports programs and adding new teams as a way to help promote the school and recruit potential students. However, new rules allowing an increase in scholarship payments to student athletes may result in funding cuts to smaller collegiate sports programs and the accompanying coaching staffs.

The growing interest in college and professional sports also will increase demand for scouts. Colleges must attract the best athletes to remain competitive. Successful teams help colleges enhance their reputation, recruit future students, and raise donations from alumni. Colleges, therefore, will increasingly rely on scouts to recruit the best possible high school athletes. In addition, as college tuition increases and scholarships become more competitive, high school athletes will hire scouts directly, in an effort to increase the athletes' chances of receiving a college scholarship.

However, funding for athletic programs at schools often is cut first when budgets become tight. For example, some high schools within the same school district may combine their sports programs in an effort to cut costs. Still, the popularity of team sports often enables shortfalls to be offset with help from fundraisers, booster clubs, and parents.

Strong competition is expected for higher paying jobs at the college level, and competition will be even greater for jobs in professional sports. Job prospects at the high school level should be good, but coaching jobs typically go to those teaching in the school. Candidates who have a degree or are state certified to teach academic subjects, therefore, should have the best prospects for getting coaching jobs at high schools. The need to replace the number of high school coaches who change occupations or leave the labor force also will provide some jobs.

Coaches in girls' and women's sports may have better job opportunities because of a growing number of participants and leagues.

Competition is also likely to be strong for jobs as scouts, particularly for professional teams.

Persons who are certified to teach academic subjects in addition to physical education will have the best chances of finding sports instructor and coach jobs.

Conversation With . . .
CHUCK KYLE

Head Football Coach & Head Track Coach
Saint Ignatius High School
Cleveland, OH
Coaching and Teaching, 44 years

1. What was your individual career path in terms of education/training, entry-level job, or other significant opportunity?

I majored in English and wanted to either go to law school or become a teacher. During sophomore year, I took the introductory education course and realized that was the path I wanted to take. I was playing football at John Carroll University here in Ohio and hurt my shoulder early my junior year. After that season, I had a conversation with the St. Ignatius head coach about helping him coach. It sounded like a great idea. I didn't think my shoulder was ever going to come back. So when I was a college senior, I scheduled my classes early in the day and drove down to St. Ignatius to work as an assistant coach. Fortunately, there was an opening the following April and I was hired to teach English. I've been here ever since.

The National Federation of State High School Associations inducted me into its 2016 Hall of Fame, which is humbling because it's not just the football hall of fame. It encompasses all of athletics as well as teachers of art and music. Since last year, I've been a youth football advisor for the Cleveland Browns. The Haslams (the team owners) firmly believe if a kid is involved in athletics, he or she will also do well in school. They want to be the model NFL team that works with youth. So far it's been wonderful.

2. What are the most important skills and/or qualities for someone in your profession?

If someone thinks he wants to get into this vocation—and I call it a vocation—it shouldn't be because he or she is an expert in strategy. It's really not that. It's the enjoyment of working with people. If you show you care about kids, they'll care about you, they'll care about the program. I find sports an excellent teaching tool. Teaching English is very interesting, but where does a young person learn how to work with other people? Where do they learn the idea of commitment? You learn it vividly on a practice field or in a gym. It's difficult to find a poem or a novel that clearly teaches that.

3. What do you wish you had known going into this profession?

As a young person, I don't think you realize the time commitment that it takes to do coaching right. That's an issue; it does take time. There's no shortcut.

4. Are there many job opportunities in your profession? In what specific areas?

Overall, there are. I'm an anomaly because I've been a head coach here for so many years. Usually, a person's coaching for 6, 7, 8 years at a place. Most coaches are also teachers. It really helps to be a teacher and a coach. It's important that you have as many coaches as you can in the school building, because things come up during the day, from other teachers or from the kids themselves.

5. How do you see your profession changing in the next five years? What role will technology play in those changes, and what skills will be required?

High school sports are struggling financially, because schools are struggling. It's a shame because they're a very important part of education. In Europe, all the sports are club sports. School ends and they shut the doors and the kids go to club sports. There's no connection to school spirit.

There are definitely good things about technology. Years ago, I would mail DVDs all over America, and an assistant coach at some college would have 500 of them stacked up. Nowadays, I push a button and highlight films are on the college coach's computer. He's at the airport and can analyze 10 kids as he waits for his plane. Also, you can film the game on an iPad so that when the defense comes off the field, you can say, "Hey fellas, this happened the last couple of plays, look at this."

6. What do you enjoy most about your job? What do you enjoy least about your job?

Working with young people keeps me young. When the day comes that I don't have that kind of energy, it'll be time to stop.

One thing I don't enjoy is the idea of the win. You build up that pressure and most of the time it's self-inflicted. You have to say, "Come on, the world's a big place, I'm not going to really worry about this football game we're having."

7. Can you suggest a valuable "try this" for students considering a career in your profession?

Help out with youth leagues or rec leagues. Starting with a younger, simpler age is a good idea. Just because a person is a great player doesn't mean he'll make a good coach. A lot of times, a second team player goes on to be a great coach because he or she had to know the technique well because he or she didn't have the speed or the size.

[Note: This interview was conducted in 2016.]

MORE INFORMATION

Amateur Athletic Union
P.O. Box 22409
Lake Buena Vista, FL 32830
407.934.7200
www.aausports.org

American Federation of Teachers
555 New Jersey Avenue NW
Washington, DC 20001
202.879.4400
www.aft.org

National Collegiate Athletic Association
700 West Washington Street
P.O. Box 6222
Indianapolis, IN 46206
317.917.6222
www.ncaa.org

National Federation of State High School Associations
P.O. Box 690
Indianapolis, IN 46206
317.972.6900
www.nfhs.org

National High School Athletic Coaches Association
P.O. Box 3181
Clearwater, FL 33767
407.592.9212
www.nhsaca.org

National Junior College Athletic Association
1631 Mesa Avenue, Suite B
Colorado Springs, CO 80906
719.590.9788
www.njcaa.org

Positive Coaching Alliance
1001 North Rengstorff Avenue
Suite 100
Mountain View, CA 94043
866.725.0024
pca@positivecoach.org
www.positivecoach.org

Chuck Goodwin/Editor

Surgeon

Snapshot

Career Cluster(s): Health Science
Interests: Medicine, science, solving problems, analyzing information, detailed work, communicating with others
Earnings (median in 2017): equal to or greater than $208,000 per year or $100.00 per hour
Employment & Outlook through 2026: 13% (Faster than average growth expected)

OVERVIEW

Sphere of Work

Surgeons treat a variety of ailments, including injuries, cancerous tumors, and diseases, using invasive methods. They operate on patients using an assortment of surgical instruments and methods. Most surgeons specialize in a specific field, such as brain surgery, pediatric surgery, or cosmetic surgery. Like others in the medical profession, surgeons examine patients, perform specific tests, and counsel patients on medical issues. They look at patients' medical histories and test results to determine the best surgical procedures to use.

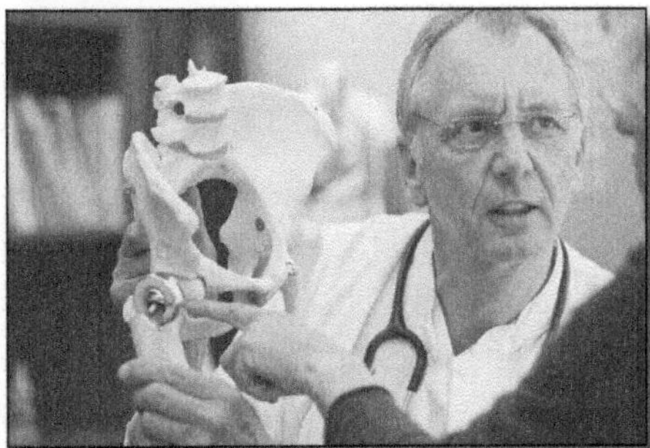

Work Environment

Most surgeons work out of medical facilities, especially hospitals, where they are assisted by nurses and other personnel. The work environment is usually well lit and sterile. While performing an operation, a surgeon typically stands for a long period of time. Many surgeons work irregular hours and often work more than forty hours per week. Travel is a frequent part of a surgeon's career as well, and most spend several hours each week moving between offices and hospitals. Surgeons at times work on call and must be able to travel quickly to a hospital if there is an emergency.

Profile

Interests: People, Things
Working Conditions: Work Inside
Physical Strength: Light Work
Education Needs: Doctoral Degree
Licensure/Certification: Required
Physical Abilities Not Required: Not Climb, Not Kneel
Opportunities for Experience: Military Service, Volunteer Work
Holland Interest Score*: IRA

* See Appendix A

Occupation Interest

Like most medical professionals, surgeons must undergo extensive education and training. They are empathetic and believe in making a difference in the lives of others. Surgeons must be very understanding of their patients' needs and strive to educate them as best they can. Since a surgeon's work requires precision and accuracy, the profession calls for great attention to detail.

A Day in the Life—Duties and Responsibilities

The primary duty of a surgeon is to perform operations on patients. In addition to the actual act of surgery, surgeons also examine patients and their medical histories, make diagnoses, and perform specialized tests. Depending on the specialization of the surgeon, the day-to-day activities can vary.

When a surgeon first meets a patient, he or she will analyze the patient's medical history, physical condition, allergies, and other physical aspects. Based on the examination and the patient's symptoms, the surgeon may call for further tests to be administered. Once the surgeon has determined the best surgical method to use, he or she will thoroughly explain what the procedure entails, its risks, and what the recovery will be like. Making the patient feel comfortable is an important aspect of the surgeon's job.

During the operation, nurses, anesthesiologists, residents, and other specialists aid the surgeon, who directs and manages those assisting. Surgical instruments and tools must be checked for sterility. In addition to a variety of small surgical instruments, modern surgeons use miniature cameras and powered tools.

Surgeons also conduct research concerning surgical techniques and instruments that can help improve operating procedures and results. Many surgeons publish their research findings in medical journals and attend related conferences.

Duties and Responsibilities

- **Conducting personal and medical interviews**
- **Evaluating medical test results and x-rays**
- **Examining surgical equipment to insure a sterile and safe environment**
- **Overseeing the work of numerous assistants and medical technicians**
- **Prescribing medication**

WORK ENVIRONMENT

Transferable Skills and Abilities

Communication Skills
- Speaking effectively
- Writing concisely

Interpersonal/Social Skills
- Being able to remain calm
- Being patient
- Working as a member of a team

Organization & Management Skills
- Following instructions
- Handling challenging situations
- Making decisions
- Managing people/groups
- Managing time
- Organizing information or materials
- Paying attention to and handling details

Research & Planning Skills
- Using logical reasoning

Technical Skills
- Performing scientific, mathematical and technical work
- Working with your hands

Work Environment Skills
- Working in a medical setting

Immediate Physical Environment

Surgeons work in various medical facilities, such as hospitals and surgical outpatient centers, as well as their own offices. Travel between hospitals and offices is common as well.

Human Environment

Surgeons work alongside a variety of other individuals in the medical profession, including physicians, nurses, and specialists. They work closely with their patients as well as with patients' families, and the nature of their work requires them to make frequent physical contact with patients.

Technological Environment

Surgeons use a wide range of specially designed instruments and tools, including scalpels, retractors that open tissue, clamps for blood vessels, tubes and needles for injecting fluids, fiber optic endoscopes, and different measuring devices. They may also use tools such as drills and dermatomes.

EDUCATION, TRAINING, AND ADVANCEMENT

High School/Secondary

The education and training requirements for surgeons are highly demanding. A high school diploma is required in order to move on to the postsecondary education and training required of surgeons. High schools offer an assortment of basic and advanced courses that would be beneficial to a student interested in becoming a surgeon. These courses include anatomy, biology, and chemistry.

Suggested High School Subjects

- Biology
- Chemistry
- College Preparatory
- Computer Science
- English
- Health Science Technology
- Physics
- Physiology
- Science

Related Career Pathways/Majors

Health Science Cluster

- Therapeutic Services Pathway

Famous First

The oldest operation for which evidence exists is trepanation; a hole is drilled or scraped into the skull to expose the *dura mater* to treat health problems, investigate and diagnose head wounds and remove bone splinters. Evidence comes from human remains dated to Proto-Neolithic and Neolithic times and in cave paintings and was also recorded by ancient Greek writers. Out of 120 prehistoric skulls in France dated to 6500 BCE, 40 had trepanation holes. A Swedish doctor asserts that excavations at the Dnieper River demonstrate the existence of trepanation as cure for epileptic seizures, migraines, and certain mental disorders as early as 12000 BCE. Evidence that the skull bones healed suggest that many survived their operation.

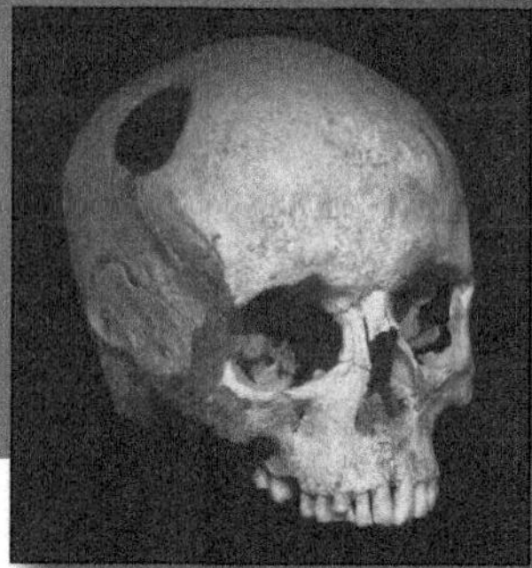

Postsecondary

Eight years of formal education is required for surgeons to complete their schooling. This typically includes four years of undergraduate studies and four years of medical school. Further education may be necessary depending on the surgeon's specialty. An undergraduate studying to be a surgeon should complete courses in biology, physics, chemistry, and mathematics. Learning to communicate well with others both orally and in written form is crucial, so students should also take English and humanities courses. Students can volunteer at hospitals or outpatient clinics in order to gain experience and work alongside professionals.

To continue on to medical school, a student must typically hold a bachelor's or more advanced degree. Applicants must submit transcripts, letters of recommendation, and sometimes essays detailing why they believe they should be selected. An interview with an admissions board is often required. Students must also successfully complete the Medical College Admission Test (MCAT). Medical schools are very competitive, so students should be sure to excel in their undergraduate studies and MCAT. Some medical schools offer combined undergraduate and medical school programs that can last six to seven years.

The first two years of medical school are typically spent in a formal classroom and laboratory where students are instructed in anatomy, biochemistry, pathology, medical ethics, and a variety of related topics. Students acquire practical knowledge and skills, such as how to record a patient's medical history, examine patients, and make diagnoses. The last two years are spent working with patients in hospitals or clinics, where students learn about the procedures and techniques involved in surgery under the guidance of experienced professionals. After medical school, surgeons enter a rotating residency in which they acquire hands-on training in a hospital. Residencies can last anywhere from two to eight years.

Related College Majors

- Anatomy
- Human & Animal Physiology
- Medicine (M.D.)
- Osteopathic Medicine
- Pre-Medicine Studies

Adult Job Seekers

An adult job seeker interested in becoming a surgeon should consider the amount of education and training needed. Factors that should also be considered include the irregular hours required of many surgeons and the cost of medical school. Due to the amount of time spent training and the irregular hours, surgeons may spend long periods of time away from their families.

Professional Certification and Licensure

A surgeon must be licensed by his or her state of residence in order to practice. In order to be licensed, a surgeon must graduate from an accredited medical school, pass an examination, and complete one to seven years of graduate medical education. Some states allow license reciprocity.

Additional Requirements

Surgeons must be detail oriented, persistent, and passionate about helping other people. They need to be physically able to work long, irregular hours and should be able to make decisions quickly during emergencies. The nature of the work requires surgeons to follow strict safety procedures.

EARNINGS AND ADVANCEMENT

Wages for physicians and surgeons are among the highest of all occupations, with a median wage equal to or greater than $208,000 per year. Median wages showing the differences in pay between types of physicians and surgeons are not available, but mean (average) annual wages for physicians and surgeons in May 2017 were as follows:

Anesthesiologists	$265,990
Surgeons	251,890
Obstetricians and gynecologists	235,240
Psychiatrists	216,090
Physicians and surgeons, all other	211,390
Family and general practitioners	208,560
Internists, general	198,370
Pediatricians, general	187,540

Many physicians and surgeons work long, irregular, and overnight hours. Physicians and surgeons may travel between their offices and hospitals to care for their patients. While on call, a physician may need to address a patient's concerns over the phone or make an emergency visit to a hospital or nursing home.

Neurologists may receive paid vacations, holidays, and sick days; life and health insurance; and retirement benefits. Self-employed neurologists must arrange for their own health insurance and retirement programs. Some employers provide for paid educational leave.

Median annual wages, May 2017

Physicians and surgeons: This wage is equal to or greater than $208,000 per year.

Health diagnosing and treating practitioners: $79,480

Total, all occupations: $37,690

Note: All Occupations includes all occupations in the U.S. Economy. Source: U.S. Bureau of Labor Statistics, Occupational Employment Statistics

EMPLOYMENT AND OUTLOOK

Overall employment of physicians and surgeons is projected to grow 13 percent from 2016 to 2026, faster than the average for all occupations.

The growing and aging population is expected to drive overall growth in the demand for physician services. As the older population grows and rates of chronic illnesses increase, consumers will seek high levels of care that use the latest technologies, diagnostic tests, and therapies.

Demand for physicians and surgeons is expected to increase despite factors that can temper growth. New technologies, such as improved information technologies or remote monitoring, are expected to allow physicians to treat more patients in the same amount of time. If adopted, new technologies can reduce the number of physicians who would be needed to complete the same tasks. In addition, physician assistants and nurse practitioner can do many of the routine duties of physicians and may be used to reduce costs at hospitals and doctor's offices.

Demand for physicians' services is sensitive to changes in healthcare reimbursement policies. Consumers may seek fewer physician services if changes to health coverage result in higher out-of-pocket costs for them.

Job prospects are expected to be very good because almost all graduates of domestic medical schools are matched to residencies (their first jobs as physicians) immediately after graduating.

Prospects should be especially good for physicians who are willing to practice in rural and low-income areas, because these areas tend to have difficulty attracting physicians. Job prospects also should be good for physicians in specialties dealing with health issues that mainly affect aging baby boomers. For example, physicians specializing in cardiology and radiology will be needed because the risks for heart disease and cancer increase as people age.

Percent change in employment, Projected 2016-26

Health diagnosing and treating practitioners: 16%

Physicians and surgeons: 13%

Total, all occupations: 7%

Note: All Occupations includes all occupations in the U.S. Economy. Source: U.S. Bureau of Labor Statistics, Employment Projections program

Related Occupations

- Allergist & Immunologist
- Anesthesiologist
- Cardiologist
- Dentist
- Medical Scientist
- Neurologist
- Ophthalmologist
- Pediatrician
- Physician
- Podiatrist
- Radiologist

Related Military Occupations

- Physician & Surgeon

Conversation With . . .

DR. ELIZABETH MATZKIN

Chief of Women's Sports Medicine
Brigham and Women's Hospital
Boston, MA
Orthopedic Surgeon, 14 years

1. What was your individual career path in terms of education/training, entry-level job, or other significant opportunity?

As a kid, I always wanted to be a physician or surgeon. I earned my bachelor of science in biology. To support myself while getting my master's degree in applied physiology from Chicago Medical School, I spent two years bartending at Murphy's, across from the bleachers at Wrigley Field. When I went to medical school, I was pretty sure I wanted to be an orthopedic surgeon. Although many people thought I was "too small" to be an orthopedic surgeon, a little grit can take you pretty far in life. I did four years of medical school at Tulane University School of Medicine in New Orleans, followed by five years in an orthopedic residency in Hawaii and a one-year fellowship in orthopedic shoulder and sports medicine at Duke University in North Carolina.

I was in private practice for three years, then spent four years at Tufts Medical Center in Boston. For the past seven years, I've been an assistant professor at Harvard Medical School, in addition to practicing at Brigham & Women's Hospital in Boston.

I'm a team physician for the U.S. Women's National Soccer Team, U.S. Paralympics Soccer Team, and the U.S. Women's National Hockey Team. I'm also the head team physician at Stonehill College in Massachusetts. At Duke, I served as a team physician for the men's football team and the men's and women's basketball teams.

My advice to aspiring orthopedic surgeons is to be passionate about what you are doing and persevere. I love what I do!

2. What are the most important skills and/or qualities for someone in your profession?

You must be passionate about wanting to be an orthopedic sports medicine surgeon. It's extremely rewarding when you love what you do, especially because it has taken a lot of training and time. You must be committed, hard-working, and compassionate. You need some strength to be an orthopedic surgeon.

3. **What do you wish you had known going into this profession?**

   I wish I had known to be more confident and assertive to promote my career—especially as a female. Women currently account for only about 6 percent of orthopedic surgeons.

4. **Are there many job opportunities in your profession? In what specific areas?**

   There are amazing opportunities within orthopedic surgery! You can choose to subspecialize in areas such as sports medicine, shoulder, total joints, foot and ankle, hand, spine, trauma and orthopedic oncology. You can also choose what type of practice you want to work in—private or academic. Or you could choose to work with high school, college, or professional sports teams.

5. **How do you see your profession changing in the next five years as it relates to fitness and/or sports injuries, how will technology impact that change, and what skills will be required?**

   As a sports medicine surgeon, there are always patients to take care of. Youth sports injuries have been on the rise—every year more than 3.5 million children are treated for a sports-related injury. Fifty percent of the injuries in middle and high school students are overuse injuries and potentially preventable. As research and our understanding of injuries continue to evolve, there will be new ways to prevent injuries and new ways to manage them surgically. One of the most exciting things about orthopedic surgery is that it's always evolving. Techniques are changing, the instruments we use are changing, and biologics/stem cell treatments are also progressing. But even as technology continues to advance, orthopedic surgeons will still need to be able to diagnose and treat patients.

6. **What do you enjoy most about your job? What do you enjoy least about your job?**

   What I like most about my job is being able to meet so many different people and help them stay active in their lives. What I like least about my job is sometimes being on-call, which may take me away from family.

7. **Can you suggest a valuable "try this" for students considering a career in your profession?**

   If you like building things or trying to put things back together, then you may have a future in orthopedics. If you enjoy carpentry, woodwork, and hands-on problem solving, you may want to consider getting exposure to orthopedics. If you love medicine and love working with athletes, then specializing in orthopedic sports medicine could be a rewarding future for you. There are opportunities for students to gain exposure to sports medicine in athletic training rooms. And some medical schools, hospitals, and private practices run summer programs that allow students to shadow orthopedic surgeons. If you can't find a formal program, most orthopedic surgeons are happy to mentor the younger generation and teach you about what we do, so reach out!

MORE INFORMATION

American College of Surgeons
633 N Saint Clair Street
Chicago, IL 60611
312.202.5000
postmaster@facs.org
www.facs.org

American Medical Association
Attn: Undergraduate Medical Education
515 N. State Street
Chicago, IL 60610
800.621.8335
www.ama-assn.org

American Medical Women's Association
Attn: Career Information
100 North 20th Street, 4th Floor
Philadelphia, PA 19103
215.320.3716
info@amwa-doc.org
www.amwa-doc.org

American Osteopathic Association
Public Relations Department
142 East Ontario Street
Chicago, IL 60611
800.621.1773
www.aoa-net.org

American Surgical Association
500 Cummings Center, Suite 4550
Beverly, MA 01915
978.927.8330
www.americansurgical.info

Association of American Medical Colleges
2450 N Street, NW
Washington, DC 20037-1126
202.828.0400
amcas@aamc.org
www.aamc.org

Patrick Cooper/Editor

Yoga Instructor

Snapshot

Career Cluster(s): Education & Training, Hospitality & Tourism, Human Services
Interests: Exercise, being active, motivating others
Earnings (median in 2017): $39,210 per year; $18.85 per hour
Employment & Outlook through 2026: 10% (Faster than average growth expected)

OVERVIEW

Sphere of Work

Yoga is a system of physical and mental wellness that was developed more than 5,000 years ago in India. There are many variations of yoga practiced around the world, including hatha yoga, which is the variation most commonly practiced in the United States, as well as ananda, bikram, chair yoga, hot yoga, integral, kripalu, kundalini, power, prana, vinyasa, and others.

Yoga instructors help practitioners learn and master the techniques of yoga, including breathing, meditation, and exercise.

Yoga instructors are typically skilled practitioners of a yoga variant. They may receive their training through a school or under the guidance of a mentor whose philosophy they find appealing. There is more to teaching yoga than being a skilled practitioner, however, and prospective instructors must also learn how to lead a class and guide students.

Work Environment

Yoga instructors work in a variety of settings, from health clubs and exercise studios to resorts and universities. Some travel to clients' homes to provide regular instruction, while others organize fitness programs for large businesses. The majority of yoga instructors work indoors in cool climates; however, some offer instruction in pleasant outdoor environments. They often work early in the morning, at night, on weekends, and during holidays. Yoga instructors spend most of their time standing, walking, and participating in physical activities.

Profile

Interests: People, Things
Working Conditions: Work Inside, Work Outside, Work Both Inside and Outside
Physical Strength: Medium Work
Education Needs: Bachelor's Degree
Licensure/Certification: Recommended
Physical Abilities Not Required: Not Climb
Opportunities for Experience: Internship, Volunteer Work
Holland Interest Score*: ESR

* See Appendix A

Occupation Interest

Although a love of yoga and experience in the discipline is an excellent, first step to becoming a an instructor who specializes in yoga, your main goal should be to complete an educational program that will provide you with a solid foundation in the science of body movement and how the body responds to physical exercise.

A Day in the Life—Duties and Responsibilities

Yoga instructors who gain experience and build a strong reputation in their community can attract more clients and charge higher rates for their services. Some instructors are eventually able to open their own yoga studios and may even train new instructors.

Many instructors find it difficult to live only on the wages earned from teaching, and may supplement their income in other ways.

Many yoga instructors are self-employed and either have their own studios or contract with existing studios. Contact health clubs, spas, bodywork studios, complementary medicine practices, religious institutions, and community organizations to offer your services as a yoga instructor. Nursing homes, hospitals, schools, and businesses may also be interested in offering yoga instruction to their residents, patients, students, and employees.

Teaching in Fitness Centers

A broad knowledge of many yoga styles is ideal. Most fitness centers cater to a diverse audience and focus on the physical aspects of yoga rather than the philosophical or spiritual teachings. Small family gyms may pay yoga instructors as little as $12 per class, while high-end gyms may pay as much as $1 a minute or $75 for 75-minute class. In a mid-range health club, $35 to $45 per class is typical.

Giving Private Yoga Lessons

One-on-one instruction is one of the most profitable career paths. You can offer private yoga lessons in your home, in client homes, or in another location. The challenge is getting regular clientele. You may need to teach in other settings to build up your reputation before people are willing to pay top dollar for your undivided attention. Private yoga lessons typically start around $50 to 75 for new teachers and go as high as $250 an hour for in-demand celebrity yoga teachers.

Group Yoga Lessons

Some corporations may offer yoga classes to employees to reduce stress, lower insurance costs or enhance productivity. Students of all ages—from elementary schools to universities—are being encouraged to practice yoga to improve their health and prepare them for more effective learning. Group yoga classes in all these settings are typically provided on a freelance basis, giving you the flexibility to negotiate your rates with employers.

Resort Yoga

Yoga classes have become part of the resort experience and are often included in package rates. Yoga students take "yoga retreats" to resorts to deepen their practice with daily classes and private instruction. You may be able to get a part-time or full-time job as a yoga instructor working for a resort. If you have enough experience, you may decide to start your own business leading yoga retreats.

Famous First

Hatha literally means "force" and thus alludes to a system of physical techniques. Hatha yoga is associated with the 'Yogis' of the Natha Sampradaya. The mythical founder of hatha yoga, Matsyendranath, is celebrated as a saint in both Buddhist and Hindu tantric and hatha yoga schools. The oldest dated text to describe hatha yoga, the *Amṛtasiddhi*, comes from a tantric Buddhist tradition, while the oldest texts to use the actual term hatha are Vajrayana Buddhist. In the 20th century, hatha yoga, particularly *asanas* (the physical postures), became popular throughout the world as a form of physical exercise, often referred to simply as "yoga."

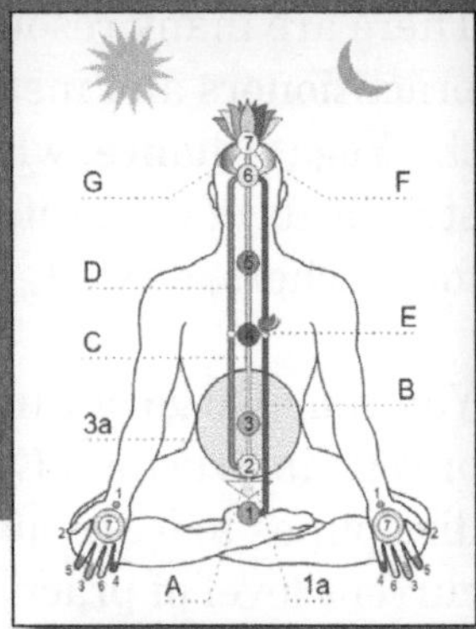

EDUCATION, TRAINING, AND ADVANCEMENT

College/Post Secondary

One of the best, first steps should be to complete an associate or bachelor degree program in personal training or a related field, such as:

- Exercise science
- Physical education
- Exercise physiology
- Sports medicine

These types of degree programs are designed to provide you with a scientific base of knowledge through coursework in anatomy and physiology, biology, human anatomy, and kinesiology, but also through coursework directly related to fitness and exercise prescription, such as:

- Foundation of physical conditioning
- Exercise physiology: foundation and theory

- Strength and conditioning
- Exercise testing: foundation and theory
- Biomechanics
- Exercise prescription

Adult Job Seekers

There are many resources, both online and in print, for yoga practitioners and instructors. You can start your investigation with the Yoga Alliance, which is an organization committed to raising the standards of the profession. The Yoga Journal offers many resources for teachers, as well.

You can also go out in your community and talk to different kinds of yoga instructors. Contact teachers who practice different yoga disciplines to learn about the training they've completed to reach their current level of practice.

Professional Certification and Licensure

It can take anywhere from several weeks to several months to complete an instructor training program, but instructors may spend months or years as a yoga student before they are ready to learn how to teach.

There are many schools across the country that offer training programs to those who want to become instructors. These programs can cost anywhere from $1,500 to $3,000 and can last several weeks or several months.

Part of an instructor's training focuses on helping students avoid injuries. Instructors learn about human anatomy and physiology and proper alignment for each yoga pose. They also learn how to read their students' bodies and to use touch to guide them into proper position.

Students who are training to become instructors also learn how to lead a class. Instructors must know how to design a sequence of poses, how to use their voice effectively, and how to build a teacher-student relationship, for example.

Some training programs also focus on business and marketing skills, as instructors are often self-employed, either freelancing with existing studios or opening their own.

State governments do not require yoga instructors to obtain a license to teach students, but instructors can pursue voluntary certifications and designations. There are many different types of yoga practice and philosophy, and schools that train instructors in a certain philosophy may offer a certification to those who complete their program. These certifications can be attractive to potential employers and clients who are looking for an instructor who has been trained in a specific type of yoga practice. Some organizations, like the Yoga Alliance, do not offer certifications, but register yoga instructors who have gained a certain amount of training and teaching experience.

Many states are moving toward requiring yoga schools who train instructors to become licensed. Yoga instructors who open their own schools and train new instructors will have to meet these requirements, which include paying a fee and passing a site inspection, when the time comes.

Fun Fact

Sun salutations are awesome! Regularly practiced, they may increase lung capacity, stamina, and cardiac development; strengthen and flex muscles around the neck, shoulder, arms, wrists, thighs, calves, and ankles; may help control diseases such as hypertension, palpitation; and even ease constipation or insomnia.

Source: organicfacts.net

EARNINGS AND ADVANCEMENT

The US Bureau of Labor Statistics groups yoga instructors with other fitness trainers and instructors. Their data show that the median yearly pay for fitness trainers in the United States in 2017 was $39,210 per year or $18.85 per hour.

Individuals can advance by locating jobs in more prestigious settings and by obtaining jobs with more responsibilities. Those who continually improve their skills by attending workshops, seminars, training sessions and classes will advance more quickly.

Median annual wages, May 2017

Fitness trainers and aerobics instructors: $39,210

Total, all occupations: $37,690

Other personal care and service workers: $23,480

Note: All Occupations includes all occupations in the U.S. Economy. Source: U.S. Bureau of Labor Statistics, Occupational Employment Statistics

The median annual wage for fitness trainers and instructors was $39,210 in May 2017. The lowest 10 percent earned less than $19,640, and the highest 10 percent earned more than $74,520.

In May 2017, the median annual wages for fitness trainers and instructors in the top industries in which they worked were as follows:

Fitness and recreational sports centers	$41,480
Educational services; state, local, and private	38,010
Government	34,640
Civic and social organizations	32,390

Fitness trainers and instructors may work nights, weekends, or holidays. Some travel to different gyms or to clients' homes to teach classes or conduct personal training sessions. Some group fitness instructors and personal fitness trainers work other full-time jobs and teach fitness classes or conduct personal training sessions part time during evenings or weekends.

Fitness trainers and instructors may receive paid vacations, holidays, and sick days; life and health insurance; and retirement benefits. These are usually paid by the employer.

EMPLOYMENT AND OUTLOOK

Fitness trainers and instructors held about 299,200 jobs nationally in 2016. About ten percent were self-employed, mostly as personal trainers. As businesses, government, and insurance organizations continue to recognize the benefits of health and fitness programs for their employees, incentives to join gyms or other types of health clubs are expected to increase the need for fitness trainers and instructors. For example, some organizations may open their own exercise facilities onsite to promote employee wellness.

Other employment growth will come from the continuing emphasis on exercise to combat obesity and encourage healthier lifestyles for people of all ages. In particular, the baby-boom generation should continue to remain active to help prevent injuries and illnesses associated with aging.

Participation in yoga and Pilates is expected to continue to increase, driven partly by older adults who want low-impact forms of exercise and relief from arthritis and other ailments.

Job prospects should be best for workers with professional certification or increased levels of formal education in health or fitness. Overall opportunities are expected to be good because of the need to replace workers who leave the occupation.

Percent change in employment, Projected 2016-26

Other personal care and service workers: 23%

Fitness trainers and aerobics instructors: 10%

Total, all occupations: 7%

Note: All Occupations includes all occupations in the U.S. Economy. Source: U.S. Bureau of Labor Statistics, Employment Projections program

Conversation With . . .
AMY ARCHINAL
RYT-500, E-YT 200

IAYT Certified Yoga Therapist, Yoga Instructor
New Orleans, LA
Yoga Professional, 11 years

1. **What was your individual career path in terms of education/training, entry-level job, or other significant opportunity?**

I became interested in yoga in high school, and found information in books because I didn't have access to teachers. Later, in my 20s, I began studying avidly. I majored in art and English at the University of Richmond, then earned my MFA from the University of New Orleans. As a painter, I've shown in any number of galleries, and, early in my career, was an art teacher at the elementary, high school, and college levels. I went on to work my way up the ladder at Whole Foods for many years, including as a store manager. Training and coaching were a significant part of my job.

Then came Hurricane Katrina. It was a time of crisis, change, and soul-searching for an enormous community. My yoga practice became much more important, and helped me through the crisis and its aftermath. During this time, I became interested in teaching yoga and decided to make a life transition.

I'd been introduced to Phoenix Rising Yoga Therapy, and decided to earn my certification in their program. I've continued to work as a program mentor for new students, and see a number of clients.

Then I did my yoga teacher training at the Shambhava School—also called Shoshoni Yoga Retreat—in Nederland, Colorado. A lot of people get their training by doing a weekend a month over a year, but this was an intensive, month-long retreat style of yoga training.

After I started teaching at a studio, I found that as a teacher, I preferred a slower, gentler approach to yoga, and began to see a great need in the aging population of baby boomers. I also became interested in working with veterans—many of whom are seniors—because yoga helps people with trauma. Many veterans have had multiple surgeries or physical injuries.

I still teach clients in the general population but have found I have a special knack for working with seniors. Looking back, I can see that my earlier experience as an art teacher, and training and coaching people at Whole Foods, gave me more confidence in front of a group. It also gave me the ability to speak clearly and give direction. All of that is beneficial to a yoga teacher.

2. **What are the most important skills and/or qualities for someone in your profession?**

   You need the ability to be fully present with people when you are with them. That means you're tuned in and interacting in a genuine way and can listen and respond to their specific needs.

   You also need a keen eye for safety so people have a positive experience and don't get hurt.

3. **What do you wish you had known going into this profession?**

   How much time I'd spend in a car traveling from class to class at different sites, and how erratic a schedule I would have teaching 12 to 16 classes each week, plus meeting with my private clients.

4. **Are there many job opportunities in your profession? In what specific areas?**

   Yes and no. There are a ton of yoga teachers out there and more constantly in training, but more and more people are practicing yoga, which creates more opportunity. Particularly working with special populations—children, the elderly, people with specific injuries, or athletes who are rehabbing. Sometimes when you're teaching at a facility with a specific population, the base pay is more lucrative than the per-student rate you'll get at a studio.

   It's fair to say it takes time to develop a network, and an investment in teaching free classes in the community is necessary to make yourself known.

5. **How do you see your profession changing in the next five years as it relates to fitness and/or sports injuries? How will technology impact that change, and what skills will be required?**

   Given so many online offerings, you can do yoga anywhere, anytime, streaming with some of the best teachers. But there will always be a need for in-person yoga instruction. There's no doubt the relationships you build by being in contact with people serve you as a student and as a teacher. Yoga's appeal continues to grow, and it is getting more research and validation from the medical community. Teaching seniors is wide-open territory. Many people begin practicing yoga later in life when they start having health issues or give up more active physical fitness regimens.

6. **What do you enjoy most about your job? What do you enjoy least about your job?**

   I most like knowing I'm helping people be more comfortable in their bodies and have a more vibrant life. I least like the necessity of finding my own substitutes when I need to take time off. There's no structure around that, and you can't call in sick.

7. Can you suggest a valuable "try this" for students considering a career in your profession?

Shadow an experienced teacher who is working with a population that interests you, and let that teacher help you hone your skills.

MORE INFORMATION

Just a few of the professional organizations that offer yoga certification include:

American Council on Exercise (ACE)
American Council on Exercise
4851 Paramount Drive
San Diego, California 92123
Phone: 1 (888) 825-3636
https://www.acefitness.org/

National Exercise and Sports Trainers Association (NESTA)
31441 Santa Margarita Pkwy A-365
Rancho Santa Margarita
CA 92688, USA
Phone: 1-877-573-6474
Fax: 949- 589-8216
https://www.nestacertified.com/

National Exercise Trainers Association (NETA)
2800 Industrial Park Blvd Ste 220
Minneapolis MN, 55441–3929
Phone: 800.237.6242
https://www.netafit.org

American Fitness Professional Association (AFPA)
Phone: 800.494.7782
https://www.afpafitness.com/

American Sports and Fitness Association (ASFA)
https://www.americansportandfitness.com/

Health and Fitness Alliance (HFA)
Box 7827 Pine Island
WPB, FL 33411
Tel: 212.808.0765
Fax: 212.988.3130
health-fitness.org

What Are Your Career Interests?

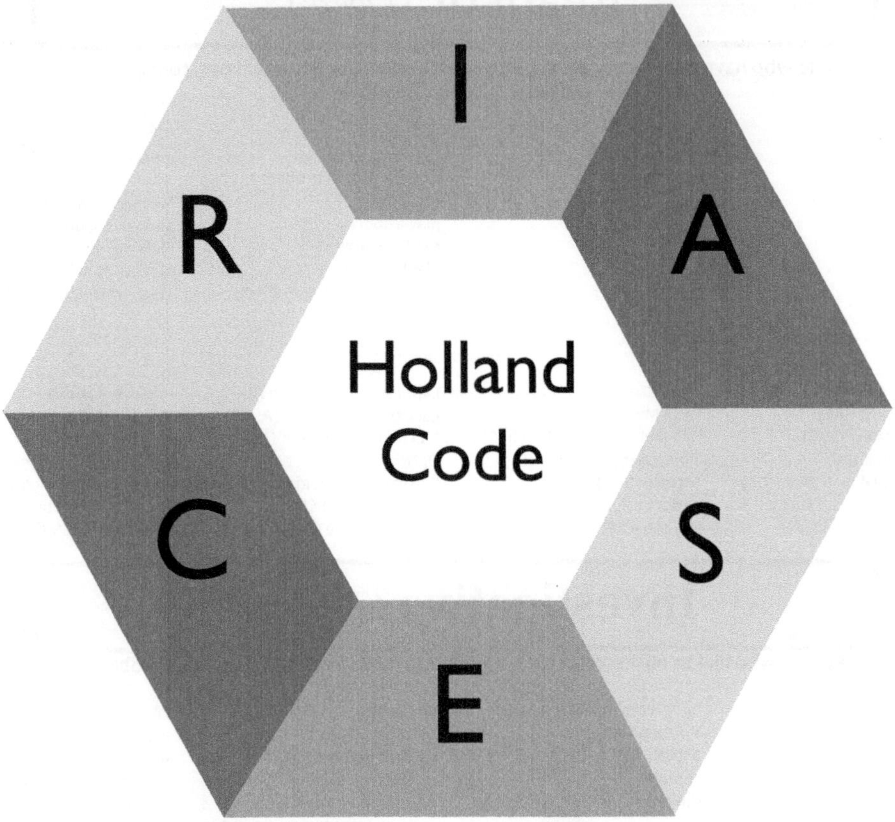

This is based on Dr. John Holland's theory that people and work environments can be loosely classified into six different groups. Each of the letters above corresponds to one of the six groups described in the following pages.

Different people's personalities may find different environments more to their liking. While you may have some interests in and similarities to several of the six groups, you may be attracted primarily to two or three of the areas. These two or three letters are your "Holland Code." For example, with a code of "RES" you would most resemble the Realistic type, somewhat less resemble the Enterprising type, and resemble the Social type even less. The types that are not in your code are the types you resemble least of all.

Most people, and most jobs, are best represented by some combination of two or three of the Holland interest areas. In addition, most people are most satisfied if there is some degree of fit between their personality and their work environment.

The rest of the pages in this booklet further explain each type and provide some examples of career possibilities, areas of study at MU, and co-curricular activities for each code. To take a more in-depth look at your Holland Code, take a self-assessment such as the SDS, Discover, or a card sort at the MU Career Center with a Career Specialist.

Realistic *(Doers)*

People who have athletic ability, prefer to work with objects, machines, tools, plants or animals, or to be outdoors.

Are you?
practical
straightforward/frank
mechanically inclined
stable
concrete
reserved
self-controlled
independent
ambitious
systematic

Can you?
fix electrical things
solve electrical problems
pitch a tent
play a sport
read a blueprint
plant a garden
operate tools and machine

Like to?
tinker with machines/vehicles
work outdoors
be physically active
use your hands
build things
tend/train animals
work on electronic equipment

Career Possibilities (Holland Code):

Air Traffic Controller (SER)
Archaeologist (IRE)
Athletic Trainer (SRE)
Cartographer (IRE)
Commercial Airline Pilot (RIE)
Commercial Drafter (IRE)
Corrections Officer (SER)
Dental Technician (REI)
Farm Manager (ESR)
Fish and Game Warden (RES)
Floral Designer (RAE)
Forester (RIS)
Geodetic Surveyor (IRE)
Industrial Arts Teacher (IER)
Laboratory Technician (RIE)
Landscape Architect (AIR)
Mechanical Engineer (RIS)
Optician (REI)
Petroleum Geologist (RIE)
Police Officer (SER)
Practical Nurse (SER)
Property Manager (ESR)
Recreation Manager (SER)
Service Manager (ERS)
Software Technician (RCI)
Ultrasound Technologist (RSI)
Vocational Rehabilitation Consultant (ESR)

Investigative *(Thinkers)*

People who like to observe, learn, investigate, analyze, evaluate, or solve problems.

Are you?
inquisitive
analytical
scientific
observant/precise
scholarly
cautious
intellectually self-confident
Independent
logical
complex
Curious

Can you?
think abstractly
solve math problems
understand scientific theories
do complex calculations
use a microscope or computer
interpret formulas

Like to?
explore a variety of ideas
work independently
perform lab experiments
deal with abstractions
do research
be challenged

Career Possibilities (Holland Code):

Actuary (ISE)
Agronomist (IRS)
Anesthesiologist (IRS)
Anthropologist (IRE)
Archaeologist (IRE)
Biochemist (IRS)
Biologist (ISR)
Chemical Engineer (IRE)
Chemist (IRE)
Computer Systems Analyst (IER)
Dentist (ISR)
Ecologist (IRE)
Economist (IAS)
Electrical Engineer (IRE)
Geologist (IRE)
Horticulturist (IRS)
Mathematician (IER)
Medical Technologist (ISA)
Meteorologist (IRS)
Nurse Practitioner (ISA)
Pharmacist (IES)
Physician, General Practice (ISE)
Psychologist (IES)
Research Analyst (IRC)
Statistician (IRE)
Surgeon (IRA)
Technical Writer (IRS)
Veterinarian (IRS)

Artistic *(Creators)*

People who have artistic, innovating, or intuitional abilities and like to work in unstructured situations using their imagination and creativity.

Are you?
creative
imaginative
innovative
unconventional
emotional
independent
Expressive
original
introspective
impulsive
sensitive
courageous
complicated
idealistic
nonconforming

Can you?
sketch, draw, paint
play a musical instrument
write stories, poetry, music
sing, act, dance
design fashions or interiors

Like to?
attend concerts, theatre, art exhibits
read fiction, plays, and poetry
work on crafts
take photography
express yourself creatively
deal with ambiguous ideas

Career Possibilities (Holland Code):

Actor (AES)
Advertising Art Director (AES)
Advertising Manager (ASE)
Architect (AIR)
Art Teacher (ASE)
Artist (ASI)
Copy Writer (ASI)
Dance Instructor (AER)
Drama Coach (ASE)
English Teacher (ASE)
Entertainer/Performer (AES)
Fashion Illustrator (ASR)
Interior Designer (AES)
Intelligence Research Specialist (AEI)
Journalist/Reporter (ASE)
Landscape Architect (AIR)
Librarian (SAI)
Medical Illustrator (AIE)
Museum Curator (AES)
Music Teacher (ASI)
Photographer (AES)
Writer (ASI)
Graphic Designer (AES)

Social *(Helpers)*

People who like to work with people to enlighten, inform, help, train, or cure them, or are skilled with words.

Are you?
friendly
helpful
idealistic
insightful
outgoing
understanding
cooperative
generous
responsible
forgiving
patient
kind

Can you?
teach/train others
express yourself clearly
lead a group discussion
mediate disputes
plan and supervise an activity
cooperate well with others

Like to?
work in groups
help people with problems
do volunteer work
work with young people
serve others

Career Possibilities (Holland Code):

City Manager (SEC)
Clinical Dietitian (SIE)
College/University Faculty (SEI)
Community Org. Director (SEA)
Consumer Affairs Director (SER)Counselor/Therapist (SAE)
Historian (SEI)
Hospital Administrator (SER)
Psychologist (SEI)
Insurance Claims Examiner (SIE)
Librarian (SAI)
Medical Assistant (SCR)
Minister/Priest/Rabbi (SAI)
Paralegal (SCE)
Park Naturalist (SEI)
Physical Therapist (SIE)
Police Officer (SER)
Probation and Parole Officer (SEC)
Real Estate Appraiser (SCE)
Recreation Director (SER)
Registered Nurse (SIA)
Teacher (SAE)
Social Worker (SEA)
Speech Pathologist (SAI)
Vocational-Rehab. Counselor (SEC)
Volunteer Services Director (SEC)

Enterprising *(Persuaders)*

People who like to work with people, influencing, persuading, leading or managing for organizational goals or economic gain.

Are you?
self-confident
assertive
persuasive
energetic
adventurous
popular
ambitious
agreeable
talkative
extroverted
spontaneous
optimistic

Can you?
initiate projects
convince people to do things your way
sell things
give talks or speeches
organize activities
lead a group
persuade others

Like to?
make decisions
be elected to office
start your own business
campaign politically
meet important people
have power or status

Career Possibilities (Holland Code):

Advertising Executive (ESA)
Advertising Sales Rep (ESR)
Banker/Financial Planner (ESR)
Branch Manager (ESA)
Business Manager (ESC)
Buyer (ESA)
Chamber of Commerce Exec (ESA)
Credit Analyst (EAS)
Customer Service Manager (ESA)
Education & Training Manager (EIS)
Emergency Medical Technician (ESI)
Entrepreneur (ESA)
Foreign Service Officer (ESA)
Funeral Director (ESR)
Insurance Manager (ESC)
Interpreter (ESA)
Lawyer/Attorney (ESA)
Lobbyist (ESA)
Office Manager (ESR)
Personnel Recruiter (ESR)
Politician (ESA)
Public Relations Rep (EAS)
Retail Store Manager (ESR)
Sales Manager (ESA)
Sales Representative (ERS)
Social Service Director (ESA)
Stockbroker (ESI)
Tax Accountant (ECS)

Conventional *(Organizers)*

People who like to work with data, have clerical or numerical ability, carry out tasks in detail, or follow through on others' instructions.

Are you?
well-organized
accurate
numerically inclined
methodical
conscientious
efficient
conforming
practical
thrifty
systematic
structured
polite
ambitious
obedient
persistent

Can you?
work well within a system
do a lot of paper work in a short time
keep accurate records
use a computer terminal
write effective business letters

Like to?
follow clearly defined procedures
use data processing equipment
work with numbers
type or take shorthand
be responsible for details
collect or organize things

Career Possibilities (Holland Code):

Abstractor (CSI)
Accountant (CSE)
Administrative Assistant (ESC)
Budget Analyst (CER)
Business Manager (ESC)
Business Programmer (CRI)
Business Teacher (CSE)
Catalog Librarian (CSE)
Claims Adjuster (SEC)
Computer Operator (CSR)
Congressional-District Aide (CES)
Cost Accountant (CES)
Court Reporter (CSE)
Credit Manager (ESC)
Customs Inspector (CEI)
Editorial Assistant (CSI)
Elementary School Teacher (SEC)
Financial Analyst (CSI)
Insurance Manager (ESC)
Insurance Underwriter (CSE)
Internal Auditor (ICR)
Kindergarten Teacher (ESC)
Medical Records Technician (CSE)
Museum Registrar (CSE)
Paralegal (SCE)
Safety Inspector (RCS)
Tax Accountant (ECS)
Tax Consultant (CES)
Travel Agent (ECS)

GENERAL BIBLIOGRAPHY

American Council on Exercise. *ACE Personal Trainer Manual*. 2018.

Bell, Samantha. *Athletic Trainer*. 2016.

Bell, Samantha. *Sports Medicine Doctor*. 2016.

Broad, William J . *The Science of Yoga : the Risks and the Rewards*. Simon & Schuster, 2012.

"Career as a Personal Trainer." *Career as a Personal Trainer.*, search.ebscohost.com/login.aspx?direct=true&scope=site&db=nlebk&db=nlabk&AN=293557.

Edelson, Edward. *Sports Medicine*. Chelsea House., 2000.

Farhi, Donna. *Teaching Yoga : Exploring the Teacher-Student Relationship*. Rodmell Press : Distributed by Publishers Group West, 2006.

Ferguson Publishing. "Careers in Focus." *Careers in Focus.*, public.eblib.com/choice/publicfullrecord.aspx?p=3010817.

Heitzmann, William Ray. *Opportunities in Sports and Fitness Careers*. VGM Career Books, 2003.

Kamberg, Mary-Lane. *A Career as an Athletic Trainer*. Rosen Pub., 2013.

Kenworthy, Kate, and Stephen A Rodrigues. "The Everything Guide to Being a Personal Trainer : All You Need to Get Started on a Career in Fitness." *The Everything Guide to Being a Personal Trainer : All You Need to Get Started on a Career in Fitness*, www.myilibrary.com?id=208262.

Kleiner, Doug, and NATA Board of Certification. *Study Guide for the NATA Board of Certification, Inc. Entry-Level Athletic Trainer Certification Examination*. F.A. Davis, 2002.

La, Bella Laura. *Dream Jobs in Sports Fitness and Medicine*. Rosen Pub., 2013.

McCall, Timothy B . *Yoga as Medicine : the Yogic Prescription for Health & Healing : a Yoga Journal Book*. 2007.

National Athletic Trainers Association. *Study Guide for the NATA Board of Certification, Inc. Entry-Level Athletic Trainer Certification Examination.* F.A. Davis, 1993.

Schmidt, Debra. *Careers in Sports and Fitness*. 2016.

Starkey, Lauren B . *Certified Fitness Instructor/ Personal Trainer : Career Starter*. LearningExpress, 2003.

Thompson, Lisa. *Focusing on Fitness : Have You Got What It Takes to Be a Personal Trainer?* Compass Point Books, 2008.

INDEX

A

B

C

D

E

F

N

O

T

U

V

W

Y